$17.50

D1221692

Violence
and
Religious Commitment

Violence
and
Religious Commitment

Implications of Jim Jones's
People's Temple Movement

Edited by
Ken Levi

The Pennsylvania State University Press
University Park and London

Library of Congress Cataloging in Publication Data

Main entry under title:

Violence and religious commitment.

Includes bibliography and index.
1. Peoples Temple—Addresses, essays, lectures.
2. Jones, Jim, 1931-1978—Addresses, essays, lectures.
3. Cults—Addresses, essays, lectures. 4. Violence—
Moral and religious aspects—Addresses, essays,
lectures. I. Levi, Ken, 1946-
BP605.P46V56   289.9   81-83147
ISBN 0-271-00296-4   AACR2

Copyright © 1982 The Pennsylvania State University

Designed by DOLLY CARR

Printed in the United States of America

Contents

Contents

Preface

On February 18, 1980, the nightly news contained a story about Jeannie Mills, her husband Al, and their oldest daughter, all shot to death in their Berkeley, California, home. The killers were said to be members of a People's Temple hit squad. To me this came as incredible news. I had just sent Jeannie Mills a thank-you note for all her help in preparing this volume, including Chapter 11, which she wrote about her six-year nightmare as a follower of Jim Jones. Now, the fact of religious violence had intruded itself into the writing of a book on religious violence, like a character stepping out of a novel to deliver the message that the plot is real.

During the past decade many Americans have been switching their religious preference from Protestant or Catholic to "none." The cultic movements that arose to fill a felt spiritual gap have been extensively studied with emphasis on their positive effects, providing belief and belonging for their members. However, events in People's Temple, the Unification Church, and such quasi-cultic groups as Synanon indicate a darker side to the extreme commitment that these groups extract from their followers. This violent side of religious commitment has not been systematically explored.

The purpose of this volume is not to test one particular theory, or to advance one particular scholarly perspective, but rather to display the issue of modern cult violence and to consider its various facets. The chapters in Part One (Comparative Perspective on Jonestown) provide the reader with a general orientation to the historical and religious context in which the violent cults of the 1970s emerged. Part Two (Concepts Illuminating the People's Temple Movement) focuses on issues of particular concern: How did the 1970s decade create an identity crisis leading some people to seek shelter in religious sects? And what are the techniques that cults use to radically transform people, once they have become members? Part Three (Understanding the Reactions to Jonestown) shifts the focus from "them" to "us." It considers the dangers of public overreaction, such as the political overreaction of the anticult movement, or the popular overreaction to brainwashing in cults. On a deeper level, the chapters by Erde and Hauerwas explore our emotional, philosophical, and moral assessments of Jonestown. Is there in religion a demonic potential that can drive people to such extremes? Finally, Part Four (Report of a Former

Member of People's Temple) offers a case study of Jonestown, presenting an insider's view of life in the violent cult.

Throughout, *Violence and Religious Commitment* aims to present
a balance of perspectives: from general theories to concrete cases; from
psychology to theology to sociology to law to philosophy; from sectarian actions to societal reactions; from anticult theorists to procult
theorists (who view Jonestown as an aberration). This conceptually
comprehensive and integrated analysis will leave the reader not with
any easy answers but with several well-formulated concerns.

The Contributors

Dick Anthony is research director of the Center for the Study of New Religions at the Graduate Theological Union, Berkeley. He is co-editor with Thomas Robbins of *In Gods We Trust*.

Philip Armour is assistant professor of sociology and political economy at the University of Texas at Dallas. His recent works include *The Cycles of Social Reform* and, with C. L. Estes and M. Noble, "Implementing the Older Americans Act."

David Bromley is professor and chairman of the Department of Sociology at the University of Hartford. He is coauthor, along with Anson Shupe, of *The New Vigilantes* and *"Moonies" in America*.

Ed Erde is associate professor in the Department of Medical Humanities at the University of Texas Medical Center at Galveston. His recent works include *Philosophy and Psycholinguistics* and "Founding Morality: 'Hume vs. Plato' or 'Hume and Plato'?"

John R. Hall is professor of sociology at the University of Missouri. His recent works include *The Ways Out* and "Alfred Schutz, His Critics, and Applied Phenomenology."

Stanley Hauerwas is professor of theology at Notre Dame University. His recent works include *The Character of Christian Life* and, with Richard Bondi, *Truthfulness and Tragedy*.

Ken Levi is assistant professor of sociology at the University of Texas at San Antonio. His recent works include "Homicide as Conflict Resolution" and "Becoming a Hit Man."

Edgar Mills is associate professor of sociology at the University of Texas at San Antonio. His recent works include *Ex-Pastors* and "Resource Inequality and Accumulative Advantage," with W. Broughton.

Jeannie Mills is founder of the Berkeley Human Freedom Center and ex-chief of publications for the People's Temple. She has written *Six Years with God* about her experience as a follower of Jim Jones.

Lawrence J. Redlinger is associate professor of sociology and political economy at the University of Texas at Dallas. His recent works include "Invitational Edges of Corruption" and "Environmental Supports, Organizational Change and School Desegregation."

Jim Richardson is professor of sociology at the University of Nevada at Reno. His recent works include *Conversion Careers* and, with M. W. Harder and R. B. Simmonds, *Organized Miracles*.

Thomas Robbins is a post-doctoral fellow in sociology at Yale. His recent works include "Milton Yinger and the Study of Religious Movements" and, with Dick Anthony, *In Gods We Trust*.

Anson Shupe is associate professor of sociology at the University of Texas at Arlington. He is coauthor with David Bromley of *"Moonies" in America* and *The New Vigilantes*.

Louis Zurcher is professor and dean of the School of Social Work at the University of Texas at Austin. His recent works include *The Mutable Self* and *Poverty Warriors*.

A Brief Chronology of Jim Jones and the People's Temple

In the
Beginning   As a young anthropologist working among African tribes, Lynetta Jones had a dream of her dead mother on the far side of a river telling her she would bear a son who would right the wrongs of the world.

1931   Jim Jones was born the first child of Lynetta and her husband, James Thurmond Jones, in Lynn, a town 70 miles east of Indianapolis with a population, ironically, of about 900 people. The boy's father was a poor railroad worker and member of the Ku Klux Klan. Both parents were Methodists and, contrary to what Jim was later to claim, neither parent had any black or native American blood; in accordance with what Jim was later to claim, however, his mother did believe that she had given birth to a messiah.

1949   After graduating Richmond High School, Jim Jones moved to Indianapolis with his wife, Marceline Baldwin Jones, a nurse four years his senior whom he had met while working part time as an orderly in a hospital.

1950-1954   Jones failed to receive his degree in secondary education at Butler University (until 10 years later in 1961) because his family and religion kept him too busy. Jim and Marceline, after giving birth to a child of their own—Stephen—adopted seven others, including two blacks and three Koreans. To support them, Jones, without any formal theological training, became a circuit preacher traveling from church to church in the poor white and black sections of Indianapolis, and also throughout Indiana, Ohio, and Kentucky. It was during this period that he started performing miracles, turning water into wine and later curing cancer. It was also at this time that his vocal support of racial integration led to his departure from the Methodist Church due to the harassment that he received from local Church members.

xii Violence and Religious Commitment

1955-1959   In 1955, Jones raised $55,000, largely by selling monkeys
            door to door at $29 apiece, in order to form his own
            church, the People's Temple of the Disciples of Christ.
            Over the following years, the People's Temple opened
            up a soup kitchen, distributed clothes for the needy,
            found jobs for ex-addicts and felons, started two nursing
            homes, and agitated for the desegregation of several res-
            taurants and a movie theater in Indianapolis. Additional
            ideas for reform came from a trip Jones made to Phila-
            delphia in the late 1950s to visit with Father Divine, a
            black religious leader claiming to be God incarnate,
            who had established communal homes or "heavens" in
            the slums of Philadelphia and Manhattan.

1960-1964   In the public arena, Jones was named Director of the
            Indianapolis Human Rights Commission, at $6000 a
            year. In Church organization, following the example of
            Father Divine, Jones created an inner circle of loyalists,
            his twelve "angels." In his theology, several changes
            occurred. He renounced belief in the Virgin Birth; dur-
            ing services, he began throwing the Bible to the floor,
            declaring, "Too many people are looking at this and
            not at me"; finally, he voiced increasing concern about
            the threat of nuclear war. In fact, after *Esquire* came out
            with an article about the nine safest places on Earth in
            the event of a nuclear attack, Jones and his family
            moved to one of them, Belo Horizonte, an industrial city
            of 2 million people, 250 miles north of Rio de Janeiro,
            Brazil. There, in 1962, he pursued his welfare work,
            acquainted himself with the Brazilian faithhealer David
            Martins de Miranda, and had occasion to make at least
            one side trip to Guyana for reasons unknown. In 1963,
            Jones moved back to Indianapolis but remained only
            long enough to be ordained by the Disciples of Christ.
            He promptly declared that nuclear war would break out
            on June 15, 1967, and that he did not want to be around
            to see it.

1965-1969   On June 16, 1965, Jones, along with 100 of his follow-
            ers, pulled up roots and moved to a second of *Esquire's*
            safest locations in the event of nuclear war, Ukiah, Cali-
            fornia, an agricultural community some 100 miles north
            of San Francisco. This year also brought the death of

Father Divine, whom Jones claimed was subsequently reincarnated in him. After moving to Ukiah, Jones and his flock immediately instituted a variety of social welfare programs and culled favor with the local press. Jones also became a teacher of government and U.S. history at the Ukian adult school and served on the county's Juvenile Justice and Delinquency Prevention Board. In 1967, as a result of the good work performed by himself and his Church, he was named foreman of the Mendocino County Grand Jury.

1970–1974   By 1971, People's Temple membership had risen to an estimated 2000 in Ukiah, and Jones felt it was time to journey on. He purchased a temple in Los Angeles and one in the black district of San Francisco, where he established a free clinic, legal aid office, free dining hall, and drug rehabilitation program. A year later, he established one additional outpost on 824 acres in the jungleland of Guyana, where the government had invited foreign groups to come and settle. However, even this remote settlement might not be safe, Jones felt, from the encroachment of racism, fascism, and nuclear holocaust which he foresaw, and his sermons began to dwell increasingly on a further avenue of escape, mass suicide. It took the defection of eight People's Temple members in 1973, to trigger the first actual suicide drill—with Jones lining up members of the San Francisco congregation to receive cups of "poisoned" wine.

1975–1977   On the political front, the People's Temple had become a force to be reckoned with. In 1975, Jones set 150 of his followers working San Francisco precincts to assure George Moscone's win in a squeaker mayoral election. Moscone returned the favor by offering the People's Temple leader a seat on the city's Human Rights Commission. Jones turned it down. In 1976, however, Jones accepted the chairmanship of the San Francisco City Housing Authority, a position he deemed more worthy of his merit. He also made public appearances with Rosalynn Carter and with vice presidential candidate Walter Mondale in connection with People's Temple support for the Carter campaign. All this resulted in a new prominence for Jones; it attracted the attention of several newspaper reporters, including Marshall Kilduff of the *San Francisco Chronicle*. He and Phil Tracy, a staffer on *New West* magazine, joined up to write an expose of the People's Temple, based on what 10 defectors had to say about beatings and the misuse of funds within the Church. Meantime, an AP photographer by the name of Sam Houston, whose son had died by mysterious circumstances just as he was about to quit his membership in the People's Temple, prevailed upon Congressman Leo Ryan to keep a closer eye on Jim Jones and his Church. Jones, aware of the pressures mounting against him, and unable to halt publication of the Kilduff and Tracy exposé, decided that it was time to move once again. Weeks before a devastating article on the People's Temple appeared in *New West* magazine on August 1, 1977, Jones had already removed himself to his jungle retreat in Guyana, where he was soon to be joined by some 800 of his followers.

1978   Jim Jones's already poor health rapidly deteriorated after the move to Guyana, leaving him with a lung infection, a prostate condition, high blood pressure, and a temperature that hovered between 101 and 105. His lawyer, Charles Garry, said that Jones was "burning his brains" on drugs. At the same time, the Church suffered a mounting problem with defectors, including Debbie Blakey whose story of mass suicide drills particularly caught the attention of Congressman Ryan.

November   On November 1, 1978, Ryan sent a telegram asking permission to visit Jonestown, the settlement in Guyana. Reluctantly, Jones agreed, and on November 14, the Congressman, along with an NBC news crew and members of the press, flew to Georgetown, the Guyanese capital. On the 17th, after overcoming additional resistance, they flew on to Port Kaituma, a fishing village six miles north of Jonestown, where they were met by a camp dump truck and taken to see Jim Jones. The visit, which began pleasantly enough with food and entertainment, gradually soured as new defectors stepped forward to ask Ryan for asylum and as reporters closed in on Jones during a press conference focusing on the hardships at Jonestown. At 3:15, Monday, November 19, when the

Congressman and his party left, some of Jones's loyalists followed them to the airport. Just as the members of Ryan's group were about to board their plane, Jones's men pulled up alongside them in a truck, brought out their rifles, and opened fire. While a few managed to escape, Ryan and most of the people with him were killed. Back at the camp, Jim Jones summoned his membership to the camp pavilion. "Some of those people who left," he said, referring to the gunmen, "had no intention of leaving. They went to kill somebody...." When the truck returned to the camp, two of Jones's lieutenants informed him of what had happened. Jones turned to the microphone again, "The Congressman is dead...and the journalists. The G.D.F. [Guyanese Defense Forces] will be here in 45 minutes...we must die with dignity." His nurses brought out a tub of strawberry-flavored ade, laced with tranquilizers and cyanide. People lined up, babies first, to receive their drink. Any resistance was countered by armed guards standing at the fringes of the congregation. The last to die was the leader himself, felled by a gunshot from an unknown hand. Around him lay the bodies of 911 other People's Temple members.

Part One
Comparative Perspective
on Jonestown

Part One deals with the general concept of sect violence. Is this merely a stereotype that people have about the goings-on in religions deemed bizarre, or is there something to it? Chapter 1 takes the position that Jonestown was not an isolated event but rather an example of extremist cult behavior that emerges in times of great social upheaval. Chapter 2, by Richardson, takes the opposite position. He denies that People's Temple is typical of the new religious groups of the 1970s and maintains that the Jonestown massacre should be viewed as a secular rather than a religious event. In Chapter 3, Hall takes an in-between position by classifying People's Temple both as a special type of religious group, the apocalyptic sect, and as a unique case within that group.

1
Jonestown and Religious Commitment in the 1970s
Ken Levi

The connection between religion and violence is well known. Religious martyrdom, religious sacrifice, religious persecution, religious zealotry: these have all become stock phrases. Historical precedent includes—to name but a few—Christian crusade, Moslem jihad, Spanish Inquisition, Aztec sacrifice, British Reformation, and the virtual extermination of the Huguenots by French Catholics. In the 1960s we witnessed the self-immolation of Buddhist monks in Saigon. Today, there are major wars between Muslims and Hindus, Palestinians and Jews, and Catholic and Protestant Irish.

The subject matter of this chapter will be restricted to violence among religious sects in the 1970s. It did not begin with the spectacle at Jonestown. That death of more than 900 people by suicide or murder is, of course, the most extreme and striking example. But violence has been reported in other large sects, such as the Unification Church of Sun Myung Moon or the political sects of Northern Ireland (*Newsweek* 12/4/78:38–85). It has also occurred in very small groups, such as the Manson family cult or the small Utah cult headed by excommunicated Mormon Immanuel David; seven members of David's family jumped or were pushed from a hotel balcony in August, 1978, marking the first mass suicide of current times (*US News & World Report* 12/4/78:3–29). The size of the sect does not seem to make a difference. Nor does the denomination. In the decade here examined, violence has occurred in Protestant sects such as the People's Temple, in Catholic sects such as the Irish Republican Army (Easthope 1976), in Mohammedan sects such as the Hanafi Muslims (*US News & World Report* 12/4/78:23–29), in Buddhist sects such as the Soka-Gakkai of Japan, and in nondenominational sects such as Synanon, which is attempting to incorporate formally as a religion (*Newsweek* 12/4/78:38–85).

On the other hand, of the estimated 1000 to 3000 sectlike groups in the United States with about 3 million members (Slade 1979:81), most are not notably violent. Religious sects do not necessarily or even usually promote violent behavior. Often they do the reverse:

> Fifty members of a Brooklyn youth gang that may number 5000 say they have defected from a life of violence and criminal behavior to devote themselves to efforts to make the community a safer and better place to live; this breakthrough is the result of the efforts of Pentecostalist minister Nat Townsley Jr. of the Lighthouse Church of Love and Peace, who conducts rock-gospel services; local political, civic, and educational leaders offer full cooperation to the gang to assist conversion efforts and police are optimistic. (*New York Times* 8/1/73:83)

Conversely, most violent behavior is not notably religious. The more profane matters—domestic quarrels, armed robberies, loss of jobs—ordinarily make people homicidal or suicidal. Religion and violence intersect only under a special set of circumstances. This chapter will attempt to isolate some of those circumstances in order to understand what sparked Jonestown and how it could happen again.

Before Jonestown in November 1978, the scholarly literature paid scant attention to violence in modern-day sects. Hence this chapter is necessarily based on a combination of scholarly articles plus exerpts from popular books, magazines, and newspapers.

Violence and Cohesion

Durkheim (1897/1951) and later Henry and Short (1954) saw violence as an effect of extreme social cohesion (either very high or very low). Lately, in the sociology of religion, there has been a surfeit of writings on new religious movements as *extremely cohesive groups* arising out of an *extremely uncohesive social milieu*; it seems to take a "me generation" to produce pockets of selfless community. The dangers of extremism and violence that Durkheim and his followers warned about have been largely overlooked. As a result, we see mainly the *functions* but few of the *dysfunctions* of the new religious movements, of the decade that produced them, and of extreme religious commitment in general.

The new religions are viewed in the literature as a source of strength in a time of uncertainty. For their members they offer

1. community (Levine and Salter 1976; Ahlstrom 1978; Wilson 1977)
2. a general belief system (Beckford 1976; Glenn and Gotard 1977; Levine and Salter 1976; Solomon 1977; Stone 1978)
3. a clear set of behavioral guidelines (Beckford 1976; Wilson 1977)

For their parent societies they provide

4. a role for disaffected groups (Bellah 1976; Glenn and Gotard 1977; Robbins et al. 1976)
5. functional diversification (Wuthnow 1976)

The upsurge of new religious movements has been explained within this general functional context.

On the other hand, R. N. Bellah (1976), in an ethnographic study of nine "alternative" religious groups in the San Francisco Bay area, warned of authoritarian sects arising out of the current social malaise. In a time of ambiguity, people may be drawn by the promise of absolute, objective truth from a totalitarian movement rigidly intolerant of divergence and dissent. "Perhaps the most likely system" for this type of authoritarian sect, Bellah wrote, "would be right-wing Protestant fundamentalism" (1976).

A few other observers of the new religious movements have also noted dangers of extreme cohesion, regarding

1. the susceptibility of youth to total belief systems (Ahlstrom 1978)
2. the breakup of nuclear families (Stoner and Parke, 1977)
3. the use of coercive control—brainwashing (Stoner and Parke 1977)

Ironically, these dangers all result from the very strength of religious community life that the literature extols.

Almost all current scholars, however, have overlooked violence as the most extreme danger of religious commitment in the 1970s. This is a peculiar oversight in the light of the well-known relation between religious orthodoxy and violent attitudes and behaviors (Easthope 1976; Lewis 1975). Perhaps we share a prevailing image of the 1970s as a decade that moved away from war and political confrontation and turned inward. However, at least one author (Blake 1972) foresaw in the Black Panther concept of *revolutionary suicide* how violence can continue even though the target may change over time. He wrote that a person may commit violence against himself, as a sign of his refusal to submit to "reactionary social forces" (Blake 1972:290). Blake's article is prescient: members of the People's Temple had been regularly tutored in revolutionary suicide. It was their major rallying reference during the Jonestown massacre.

Blake indicates that religious extremism may not be a unidimensional phenomenon, arising solely from the strength of a movement's organization. Other factors also need to be considered, such as doctrine, social context, and stage of development.

The mass suicides-homicides of 912 members of the People's Temple at Jonestown, Guyana, have drawn our attention to violence in cultic groups. The news has carried stories of alleged "hit" lists, suicide rehearsals, and suicide attempts at the Unification Church (*New York Times* 9/30/75:41; ABC-TV 1979), of an alleged murder attempt by Synanon (*San Antonio Express-News* 11/24/78:1-B), of an alleged murder by the Children of God (*New York Times* 4/9/73:7), of an alleged murder attempt by Krishna Consciousness (*New York Times* 11/2/77:2), of a murder allegedly involving members of the Divine Light Mission (*New York Times* 1/14/75:23). It is unlikely that the 1970s will continue to be viewed as a decade of benign spiritual innovation. It will be very difficult for students of religion to see only the functional aspects of the new sects and cults. It is more probable that the undercurrents of concern about religious extremism will now begin to coalesce in the social-science literature.

Therefore, this chapter will attempt to reassess the link between cohesion and violence in light of the altruistic sects and cults of the "me generation." A detailed examination of the interconnection among social disintegration, religious cohesion, and violent behavior should extend the tentative current research on the dysfunctions of religious commitment. Based on prior analysis, theoretical approaches that might be explored are offered below, following some preliminary definitions.

Definitions Religious violence: This term is used operationally to refer to intentional homicide or intentional suicide initiated within a religious group.

Sect: "A sect is a religious group that rejects the social environment in which it exists" (Johnson 1972). This definition includes both sects and cults.

Theoretical Approaches 1. Religious violence is most likely to occur in a highly uncohesive societal context. Times of social change aggravate deprivations that undermine the attraction, and therefore the cohesion, of future sect members to their society. The most potentially violent members are those who suffer what Charles Glock refers to as "psychic deprivation" and economic deprivation (1964), because these would involve the most drastic transformation of society to provide relief for group members. The subjective sense of economic and psychic deprivation is aggravated in a time of social change involving extensive structural differentiation, pluralism, and secularization. Such an upheaval occurred in America during the Second Great Awakening of 1820–1860. During the 1960s and 1970s a like upheaval has been occurring in California where poor blacks, runaway youths, and former drug addicts have participated in religious violence.

2. Religious violence is most likely to be committed by members of a highly cohesive sect. The most violence should therefore occur in authoritarian, totalistic sects. These groups enforce a "single orthodox version of what truth and reality are" (Bellah 1976:351), suppress nonconformity, require particularistic loyalty to the group and especially to the group's leader, and exercise total or around-the-clock control over members' behavior. In addition, the violence should be expected to occur during the most cohesive phase of the sect's evolution. This phase would be at the end of the charismatic stage during a period of isolation, after the initial attraction of members through conversion but before cohesion is undermined by conventionalization and routinization.

3. Extreme cohesion leads to violence only when this cohesion gives rise to extremist views. Thus, religious violence is most likely to occur in sects with religious beliefs, rituals, and traditions that explicitly portray homicide or suicide as a means of obtaining sectarian ends. Such sects also may be found to emphasize intense particularistic loyalties to the charismatic leader, extreme hostility to certain outsiders, and, in the case of suicide, positive concepts of an after-life and a concept of death as meaningfully relevant to religious ends.

The theoretical approaches listed above *will not be systematically tested* in this chapter. Instead, examples are presented from the popular and scholarly literature that support, expand, and illustrate some of the major assertions for each level of analysis.

Societal Context

As groups that "reject the social environment," religious sects are places for rootless people who have been severed from their psychic or economic ties to society during times of radical change.

Times of Change Religious sects have arisen in times of radical change, such as the Industrial Revolution, the French Revolution, and the westward movement in the United States (Barnes 1978; *Newsweek* 12/4/78:38–85; Pritchard 1976). The defeat of Japan at the end of World War II and the subsequent secularization and rationalization of Japanese society are associated with a flurry of new sects, including the Soka-Gakkai and the Seventh Day Adventists (Wilson 1977). The end of the war also produced the social and political instability associated with the rise of the Palestine Liberation Organization and the Irish Republican Army. In the United States, most of the current sects began to form in the late 1960s and the early 1970s (Singer 1979). This is often attributed to the increasing differentiation and pluralism of our mass society, in combination with the Vietnam protest, the drug revolution, and the civil-rights movement, giving rise to a variety of "religions for the young" and the disaffiliated (Galanter 1978; Robbins et al. 1976).

Rootless People Conditions of racial change are believed to produce the kinds of people who would be most vulnerable to the appeal of the religious sect. The rootless people described by Marty lack strong ties to family or to close friends or to a system of values. Such people find "the seemingly endless choices afforded in modern life" frustrating or overwhelming (Marty 1977). Margaret Singer provides a description of one former cult member whose state of disorganization, once she left the cult, may indicate her need for the group in the first place.

> I come in and I can't decide whether to clean the place, make the bed, cook, sleep, or what. I just can't decide about anything and I sleep instead. I don't even know what to cook. (Singer 1979)

Sects recruit heavily from people concentrated in urban centers throughout the country (Galanter 1978; Robbins et al. 1976). Part of the reason is that urban centers provide large communication networks for mass proselytization. Islam and Christianity, for example, first appeared along major trade routes (Babbie 1973:247). For modern sectarian groups an additional factor is the choice of tolerant, cosmopolitan urban centers known to have been "the playing fields of the counter-culture." In 1967, A. C. Bhaktivedanta relocated half of his New York temple to San Francisco in order to attract the type of young people he felt would be particularly receptive to Krishna Consciousness (Johnson 1976:33). Earlier, Jim Jones of Indianapolis had also moved to the San Francisco area.

The urban populations targeted for recruitment were largely people experiencing what Glock (1964) has termed "psychic deprivation." Many had moved to the city, abandoning family and friends. Proclaiming that "God is dead," these had dropped out of conventional society, leaving the major religious denominations with declining membership as the 1970s began (*New York Times* 7/16/70:30; 9/12/71:26, 1/9/72:59; 3/27/73:40). But they had also turned away disillusioned from the activist movements of the 1960s. Without either a family or a cause to shelter them, they had become "rootless people." Ultimately, they joined "post-movement" (Foss and Larkin 1978:157) sects and cults to furnish their lives with meaning. For example, the "psychic deprivation" of the followers of the Guru Maharaj Ji led them to worship nonsense, as the only thing that seemed to make any sense.

> Guru Maharaj Ji was worshipped for his seemingly nonsensical and unpredictable behavior. In order to minimize the pain (see Festinger et al., 1956, on psychic pain generated by insupportable reality systems) caused by the conflicting interpretations of reality in "straight" society and from the movement, the Mission systematically stripped its members of all notions of causality and offered its own view of the universe that emphasized formal structure without substantive content. (Foss and Larkin 1978:158)

Even members of the more conservative Catholic Charismatic Renewal (CCR), which retains ties with the Catholic Church, show evidence of "psychic deprivation" prior to their joining. Responding to a questionnaire, 88 percent said that the CCR gave "meaning and order to life" (Johnson and Weigert 1978:166).

Another target population was the poor, especially for groups such as the People's Temple, the Black Muslims, or the Father Divine Church. According to Finney (1978), "income has a relatively strong negative effect on [religious] experience" (partial correlation coefficient of $-.23$ derived from a telephone survey of 500 people). This, he believes, supports Glock's hypothesis of "economic deprivation" as a major source of religious commitment (Glock 1964).

In addition, cults draw their members from special sets of rootless and vulnerable people, whom they single out and approach. Synanon, for example, recruits former drug addicts. The Unification Church, Scientology, Krishna Consciousness, the Divine Light Mission, and the Children of God approach idealistic college students experiencing failure at school or loss of a lover (*US News & World Report* 12/4/78:23-29). People's Temple recruited poor blacks and middle-class white humanitarians, in the civil-rights era of the 1960s (*Newsweek* 12/4/78:38-85; *US News & World Report* 12/4/78:23-29). Scouts from various groups approach apparently disordered young people at railroad or bus stations or near military installations (Train 1979).

Rootless people need somebody to care for them. They lack "an underlying purpose in life, a sustaining power, a cause, a goal drawing men out of their self-centered enclosures and eliciting from them a supreme devotion" (Smith 1979). For example, a former People's Temple member writes,

> From time to time Al and I would ask one another, "What did we do with our lives before we joined this group?" And we would answer that life hadn't seemed worthwhile until Jim instilled a sense of purpose in us and gave us a reason to live. (Mills 1979:131)

To rootless people it is a welcome relief to submerge "their troubled selves into a selfless whole" (Singer 1979). In addition, many of the poor blacks who joined the People's Temple felt that their lives had been materially improved, that they were no longer neglected. They felt that Jones was "helping people become somebody" (*San Antonio Express-News* 5/24/78:10-C).

Sectarian Context

According to Finney (1978), "ritual commitment" cannot be wholly determined by demographic factors such as income, education, marital status, sex, age, or formal church membership ($R^2 = .43$). More than half of a member's commitment is determined, he says, by the effects of associating with other members of the religious group (Finney 1978). The authoritarian form of communal association in a religious cult of the 1950s has been well described by Lofland (1966). This form remained consistently the same for the violent sects of the 1970s as well. In a context of total control, the sect enforces a single version of the truth and unquestioning loyalty to the sect leader, reinforced by a state of isolation and agitation toward the larger society.

Total Control First, the sect exercises total or around-the-clock control over its adherents. In sects such as the Children of God, the Unification Church, Krishna Consciousness, the Divine Light Mission, and the Church of Scientology, members spend hours a day in chanting and meditation. The sect dictates what to eat, what to wear, even how and when to defecate. Some even have their members listen to sermons through headsets while they sleep (Singer 1979; *US News & World Report* 12/4/78:23–29). Sex and marriage are especially regulated. Jim Jones asked each of his followers to voluntarily ban sex from his or her life (Mills 1979:255). Sun Myung Moon chooses each member's marital partner in the Unification Church. In the Krishna Consciousness some members have been so severely restricted that they lapse into a "pre-adolescent stage" of sexual development (*US News & World Report* 12/4/78:23–29). Followers of the "Perfect Teenage" Guru Maharaj Ji in the Divine Light Mission take a vow of celibacy. One "premie" notes

...when the urge came I looked for ways to satisfy it, but the urge just isn't coming. It's not a conscious effort; I just don't feel the need. In an *ashram*, there are 20 or 30 people; if they all were going to bed with each other, it would be havoc. You stop wanting to; there's a higher desire. There was that moment, but it's only a moment. Meditation is permanent; it's more blissful than orgasm. (*New York Times:* 12/9/73:38-VI)

Perhaps more than anything, lack of sleep blurred people's judgment. In People's Temple, members of the governing board often worked all day and then stayed up until 3:00 or 4:00 in the morning, attending meetings. The severe discipline, the lack of sleep, the lack (or control) of sex, the constant work, and the repetitious indoctrination combine to produce what Singer has referred to as an "altered state of consciousness," making people highly suggestible (Mills 1979).

Single Version of Truth The sect leader does not permit independent thought. He provides his followers with tasks and with a purpose, which they may not question. In Synanon, people are allegedly told, "We do your thinking for you." In the Unification Church, "independent thought is labeled as a tool of Satan" (*Newsweek* 12/4/78: 38–85).

In the Divine Light Mission, Guru Maharaj Ji provided an ideology which guaranteed that, through rigorous discipline, members would learn the ultimate meaning of life (Foss and Larkin 1978:61). In Krishna Consciousness, a twenty-year-old woman posed the question,

Why should I go back to college when I have already learned everything there is to know through Krishna? (Johnson 1976:33)

This rigid framework holds particular attraction for people who need and want others to solve their problems of uncertainty.

Loyalty to the Leader The way Jim Jones explained it, certain members of People's Temple executed Congressman Ryan and his party because "They love me. They will do anything for me" (*US News & World Report* 12/4/78:23–29). What he said illustrates how loyalty to a charismatic figure can lead to violence. Newcomers to the sect are typically subjected to "love bombing," an "inundation of demonstrative affection" (Train 1979). One former member of People's Temple describes her second visit to the group.

> Smiles of recognition greeted us as we walked toward the church. By the time we entered the building, all our children had been invited by other children to sit with them. People we didn't remember seeing during our previous visit came by and talked to us, calling us by name. We hadn't written to tell anyone we were returning and I couldn't believe that so many people would remember us. (Mills 1979:128).

Newcomers are greeted with hugs and kisses when they encounter other members. They develop a familial devotion to the group.

Devotion to the group is transferred to its leader. In Krishna Consciousness, octogenarian spiritual master A. C. Bhaktivedanta provided a conduit to the god Krishna (Johnson 1976:39). In the Divine Light Mission, devotion per se to the "Perfect Master and Lord of the Universe" Maharaj Ji was the *raison d'être* for membership in the movement. The youthful followers repudiated or became estranged from the conventional ("straight") interpretation of social reality, as it presented a declining promise of fulfillment.

> Society was therefore something merely factitious, making no sense. Guru Maharaj Ji accordingly represented the ideal embodiment of the universe since he was himself so manifestly preposterous. (Foss and Larkin 1978:159)

Loyalty to the leader is often raised to a higher level during a period of testing and sacrifice. The member is required to sign over his money, or his property, or even his children (*US News & World Report* 12/4/78:23–29).

> This divestment of past pleasures seemed to be a result of a radical transformation of the ego; rather than oneself, the group (as the representation of the deity Krishna) became the reference point for all desires and aspirations. (Johnson 1976:41)

In this way the member becomes totally committed, body and purpose, to the sect. The *loyalty test* is viewed as a critical stage. In his total devotion to the dictates of the sect, the member loses his sense of self. "It doesn't matter if I'm dead," a People's Temple member is quoted as saying (*Newsweek* 12/4/78:38–85). By contrast, members of the *nonviolent* Catholic Charismatic Renewal maintain *divided loyalties*. In a recent survey, while 90 percent of those polled agreed that the institutional Church needs "rebirth," only 12 percent saw CCR becoming a new religious order, and fully 63 percent still believed that the Pope is infallible in matters of faith and morals (Johnson and Weigert 1978:168).

Isolation As the member becomes more involved in the sect, he also becomes progressively more isolated from the society that alienated him to begin with. Physically removed from his family and outside friends, he comes to develop rigid attitudes toward the "uncommitted." Divorced from competing loyalties or competing values, he becomes increasingly vulnerable to collective "hysterical reactions" within the sect, or to any behavior that may seem bizarre to outsiders (Galanter 1978).

Agitation The stages of sect development can be divided into the prophecy stage, the agitation stage, and the consolidation stage (Hashimoto and McPherson 1976). Most of the sect violence in the 1970s seems to have occurred during the middle or agitation stage.

By the mid 1970s, when much of the violence began, the sect movement in America had reached a peak. The Unification Church boasted 2000 members (*New York Times* 6/26/75:3), Krishna Consciousness 5000 members (*New York Times* 12/9/73:38-VI). Scientology claimed 20 central churches plus 100 missions (*New York Times* 7/31/71:20), and the Divine Light Mission was able to assert:

> We're the fastest growing corporation in America. Between January and June of 1973, we grew 800 percent. Our business practices are sound; our accounting practices are sound; our credit and collateral are sound. Dun and Bradstreet has all our financial information. (*New York Times* 12/9/73:38-VI)

As a sign of their prosperity, sects vied with each other to hold rallies at the Houston Astrodome (*New York Times* 12/9/73:38-VI), Madison Square Garden (*New York Times* 6/21/75:3), or Golden Gate Park (Johnson 1976:50).

> ...a three-day festival called Millenium '73 and billed as "the most significant event in the history of humanity" was taking place in the Houston Astrodome. The Astroturf was covered with red carpeting, and the carpeting was covered with thousands of blissed-out followers of the "perfect master," Guru Maharaj Ji, who will be 16 tomorrow. (*New York Times* 12/9/73:38-VI)

On the other hand, none of these movements grew so large or became so well established that it could be considered a "church" in the same league, for example, as Japan's Soka-Gakkai with more than 7 million families (Babbie 1973:240). Instead, the sect movement in America had begun to slow down in terms of membership, even as it gained increasing respectability in the wider society (Slade 1979). With fewer causes of social unrest, the size of the target population dwindled. And the period of major growth passed (Galanter 1978).

> Although the movement is at its largest and most extensive in its history, several factors suggest that ISKCON (International Society of Krishna Consciousness) may have reached the peak of its growth. Most important is the diminishing significance of the college-age drug subculture, the movement's primary recruitment base. (Johnson 1976:50)

Despite their growth and prosperity, most of the sects did not reach the final stage of consolidation or conventionalization. They remained isolated from the wider society and, with some exceptions, had not yet begun to compromise their doctrines. For example, Synanon, the Divine Light Mission, the Unification Church, Scientology, Krishna Consciousness, and the People's Temple had all acquired millions of dollars as well as important political connections, yet with their ideological rejection of worldly affairs, all of these groups maintained residential insulation from the outside world in urban ashrams or missions or temples. Some isolated themselves even further by retreating to camps or communes. In 1971, for example, Hare Krishna began relocating its members to rural settings, such as New Vrindiban in West Virginia (Johnson 1976:50). And in the Children of God

> ...an estimated 1500 members live in about 50 communes, or colonies, throughout America; they visited with their families during Thanksgiving or Christmas to assure them that rumors about the 3-year-old sect were not true... Members, because they seek to devote themselves 100% to the Lord, do not take jobs; they depend on donations from sympathetic or resigned parents and on savings of individual members, who turn over all their possessions upon joining the sect. (New York Times 8/13/72:54)

Synanon is a case in point. As it grew and prospered, instead of joining the mainstream, Dederich began to see his group as an alternative to the outside world (Newsweek 12/4/78:38-85). He and several of his followers settled in an isolated commune in northern California, where the now-notorious head shaving, group sex, and enforced sterilization first began. People's Temple also turned its back on society. When they went into retreat at Jonestown, what began as a missionary farm turned into what one member called a "concentration camp" (*San Antonio Express-News* 12/3/78:16-A). In isolation, sect leaders exact increasingly bizarre requirements from their followers. The bizarre requirements, in turn, lead to increasingly disillusioned members, an increased threat of defection from within or intrusion from without, an increasingly paranoid leadership, and an increasingly distorted view of the outside world.

Most of the conditions outlined above could apply as well to the peaceable monastery as to the violent sect (Hillery and Morrow 1976). Both are religious organizations with total control, authoritarian rule, extreme loyalty, and a degree of power in terms of members and income. Consequently, both are able to require their members to perform behaviors that outsiders may consider extreme or bizarre (Galanter 1978). But violence requires a special explanation because it is a special kind of "bizarre" behavior. And in two regards, violent sects differ from most monasteries. First, most monasteries are not in the agitation stage of sect development. In fact, they are usually not sects at all, but branches of larger faiths. Second, monasteries are not *isolated* in the same sense as the sect, even though they are physically set apart. Their beliefs and practices are still governed by and consistent with the teachings of the wider church. Sects, however, exercise their totalistic control in isolation from, and in opposition to, any wider system. This condition may make them more prone to violence.

Sectarian Beliefs

If we regard religious violence as a "devotional practice," like prayer or Bible reading, then to what extent is this particular practice the result of prior learning? According to "psychological consonance" models (Finney 1978) practice conforms to beliefs, and thus learning the beliefs in the first place is important. On the other hand, according to Durkheim, who views religious behavior as primarily a "collective effervescence," religious practice is the result of conformity to group experience, regulated by mutual surveillance, norms, and sanctions (Finney 1978). In a test of the two positions, Finney found that .09 of the variance in "devotional practice" was directly affected by knowledge of religious beliefs, as compared to the direct effects of ritual (p = .27) and belief (p = .12). This finding suggests that prior learning does not much affect level of devotional practice and it tends to support the Durkheimian position. But the main effect of prior learning may be on the type of practice rather than on the level (see, for example, Smelser 1963 concerning the "generalized belief"). And whether people engage in religious violence, as distinct from bizarre behavior in general, may depend on the beliefs they hold concerning an afterlife, evil outsiders, and homicide or suicide.

Afterlife According to Douglas (1967), in Western civilization a crucial component of suicidal motives is belief in an afterlife (of sorts). When people kill themselves, they want to believe that they are moving on to something *better* (and certainly not to something worse). Therefore, we might expect that suicidal religions would emphasize a favorable view of death. For example, Jones's final peroration repeatedly stressed "death with dignity" and meeting together in a "better place." The transmigration or transcendency of the soul is a tenet of faith in such groups as the Divine Light Mission, the Unification Church, Scientology, and Krishna Consciousness, where members "have renounced the material world in order to find spiritual redemption at death" (*New York Times* 8/5/73:79). The "spacey, vague, cosmic" talk encouraged by many of the new sects may place followers in an otherworldly frame of mind (Singer 1979).

In a study of the effects of intrinsic as distinguished from extrinsic religious orientation of one's view of death, Spilka et al. found that people who were more intrinsically oriented, more *committed*, tended to hold a more favorable view of death. They believed in death "in terms of an Afterlife of Reward and as Courage" (Spilka et al. 1977).

Hostility to Outsiders Hostility to outsiders is an inbuilt feature of sect formation. Sects are, by definition, groups that oppose the dominant beliefs of society (Johnson 1972). Many form in defense of traditional values threatened by a corrupted society (Robbins et al. 1978). Others reject both current and traditional values.

Recruits into the new sects are "reborn." They are given new names, new clothing, new identities, and are made to feel guilty about their previous way of life (*Newsweek* 12/4/78:38–85). Their loyalties to the sect are often reinforced by an uncompromising stance toward the uncommitted and by a view of outgroups as evil. To Manson, for example, blacks were the evil outgroup. To Dederich, it was the government and the news media. To Jones, the evil outgroups were the FBI, CIA, and KKK (*Newsweek* 12/4/78:38-85). In particular, Jones warned about the government as an oppressor of blacks and black-sympathizers, reinforcing his point with films showing tortures and concentration-camp horrors practiced by other "fascist regimes" against their enemies (Mills 1979:251). For practically all of the new sects, one especially evil outgroup is parents.

Children of God is a youthful, rigidly Fundamentalist group of Christians who are disillusioned with the universe and have abandoned family, friends, and society to retreat to isolated communes; it has recently promulgated the doctrine that anyone who does not hate his parents cannot be a disciple of Jesus. (*New York Times* 11/29/72:41)

The member is taught to renounce his old family for the sake of his "new family." In the Symbionese Liberation Army, Patty Hearst began referring to her parents as "pigs." In People's Temple, they were taught that "families are part of the enemy system" (Mills 1979:241). One member of People's Temple told Congressman Ryan that the only way he wanted to see his mother was through the sights of a rifle (*San Antonio Express-News* 12/1/78:5-B).

As much as the sectarian groups hated outsiders, the outsiders seemed to hate them even more. Politicians and parents, theologians and deprogrammers, and legions of others arrayed themselves against the growing sects. The Children of God numbered among their enemies an organization named FREECOG (The Parents Committee to Free Our Sons and Daughters from the Children of God), as well as the Attorney General of New York:

New York State Attorney General Louis J. Lefkowitz charges in a report on an 18-month probe of the Children of God religious sect that the sect has become a fraud-tinged cult whose young converts have been subjected to brainwashing, sexual abuse, and involuntary confinement; he charges fiscal chicanery, obstruction of justice, and alleged physical and mental coercion of followers. (*New York Times* 10/14/72:37)

Facing opposition from orthodox churches, liberal politicians, and parents, the Unification Church was turned down in its second bid to gain membership in the New York City Council of Churches (*New York Times* 6/23/75:71). Twenty major United States airports attempted to bar solicitation by members of Hare Krishna (*New York Times* 12/22/76:31). And the enemies of Scientology include the Food and Drug Administration, the American Medical Association, Fairchild Publications, the *Washington Post*, Delacorte Press, the *Sunday Times* of London, and two members of Britain's Parliament (*New York Times* 7/31/71:20). The history of struggle with outside groups has twisted Scientology's growth as an organization.

The growth of the movement is set within a *deviance amplification* model in which the moral crusades of mental health practitioners and overzealous legislators called forth increased deviance on the part of Hubbard and his followers. Many of the most intriguing characteristics of this fascinating sect have been formed in the struggle with defectors, schismatics, competitors in the field of occult religions, and orthodox churches, medical associations and the State. (Wilson 1977:175)

Homicide and Suicide According to Bandura (1973), forms of aggression are learned in association with certain outcomes. It is not enough that a person harbor feelings of frustration and hostility; he must also learn how to express these feelings through specific violent acts. And violence as a form of aggression, once learned, can be used to express more things than simply frustration or hostility. Thus, learning violence is crucial to its (intentional) performance. And we might expect that religions which specifically condone and engage in either homicide or suicide also teach violence.

Not all of the new religions adhere to violent beliefs. But some do. The Church of Satan teaches, "If a man smite you on the cheek, smash him on the other." An ex-member of the Unification Church reports, "I was drilled and instructed to kill." And Jim Jones, as well as Charles Manson, dwelt on the imagery of war—race war (*US News & World Report* 12/4/78:23–29). Manson saw the coming of war as a time of "Helter Skelter," which his "family" would cleverly manipulate by turning blacks against whites. "Dad" Jones and his particular family did not envision a homicidal role for themselves in the coming war, but instead they adapted the concept of revolutionary suicide from the Black Panthers (Blake 1972). Mark Lane and Charles Garry report that a People's Temple guard exulted on the eve of the mass suicide:

> We're going to die for the revolution, we're gonna die to expose this racist and fascist society. It's great to die for the revolutionary suicide. (*San Antonio Express-News* 11/27/78:13–C)

The Black Panthers and Jones believed in killing oneself as a protest against an oppressive and discriminatory society. Suicide as a form of warfare was deemed particularly appropriate for the reactionary 1970s, after the 1960s had taught the futility of direct confrontation.

The practice suicides that Jones instituted reportedly began as early as 1973, in San Francisco. The first such rehearsal is said to have taken place shortly after the first group of defectors walked out on the

People's Temple (*San Antonio Express-News* 11/26/78:6-C). Jones had called a special session of his People's Council, the governing body of the sect. He began the meeting with the announcement, "Eight people left the church last night." Voicing fears that the defectors might say something to discredit the group, Jones mused, "This might be the time for all of us to make our translation together." The idea was that all Council members would take poison in order to be "translated" to a distant planet where they would live together for eternity (Mills 1979:231). But suicide was not Jones's only response to defection. Reportedly, he announced that anyone who quit the church was a traitor and thus fair game (Mills 1979:323). Other sects also concentrate their homicidal intentions on defectors. For example, the Children of God warn potential defectors that either God or Satan will strike them dead. Scientologists employ a "2–45 solution"— anyone who leaves gets two .45 caliber slugs (*Newsweek* 12/4/78: 38–85). The Moonies reportedly practiced slashing themselves on the wrist to avoid deprogramming—a form of forced defection (ABC-TV 1979).

We maintain that the practice of religious violence presupposes the learning of violent beliefs. Thus, many of the people at Jonestown apparently believed they were killing themselves for the sake of the revolutionary suicide. On the other hand, a second reason that people at Jonestown killed themselves was that they were coerced to do so. That is, they realized that they were faced with the threat of being shotgunned by one of Jim Jones's armed guards. A still further reason seems to be that many of the people did not think they were killing themselves, but that they were undergoing a loyalty test. Jones had conducted rehearsals in the past, and always in the past people had survived them, only to be taught that the "poison" was innocuous, that the purpose of the exercise was to test their loyalty to Jones, and that anyone proven disloyal might be shot.

> Patty Cartmell was the next to react. She started to run out the door, and the guards grabbed her...At a nod from Jim, another guard stepped forward with a rifle and shot her in the arm [from a suicide rehearsal in 1975]. (Mills 1979:311)

Therefore, it is highly possible that beliefs about the desirability of homicide or suicide, per se, may have played an insignificant part in the killings at Jonestown. On the other hand, people who thought they were undergoing a loyalty test, or who felt they were being coerced, were not *technically* committing suicide, if suicide means to kill oneself voluntarily. Our argument, on the other hand, specifically applies to people who do *voluntarily* kill themselves or others, and to the beliefs underlying their behavior.

Thus, the sects that reportedly engaged in homicide or suicide prepared their members beforehand. They did so in practice sessions and through their teachings and proclamations. The violence, both as taught and as performed, was frequently associated with the breaking up of the sect, either through the defection of sect members to the outsider camp or through the forced intrusion of the outsiders themselves. Hostility toward outsiders, who are seen as different and evil, is also a regular component of belief in the violent sect. This hostility both justifies and channels the exercise of violence. Finally, in the case of suicide cults such as People's Temple, death—as an alternative to life among the outsiders—is viewed in a highly positive light.

Conclusion

The beliefs discussed above are all associated with the conditions that foster the development of the sect. The uncohesiveness of society at large, leading to extreme cohesion within the sect and to magnified fears of defection and intrusion, all combine to promote a paranoid milieu. In such a context, it is expected rather than surprising that extreme and distorted themes of alienation and devotion should emerge, channeling people into both extremely hostile and extremely selfless behavior.

2
A Comparison between Jonestown and Other Cults*
James T. Richardson

The tragic mass murder/suicide[1] of more than 900 People's Temple members in Guyana has been one of the most misunderstood events of recent times. Many people have been extremely curious and upset about the People's Temple tragedy, but the profoundly troubling event cannot be completely understood very easily. The typical journalistic media analysis of that tragic episode has been fairly simplistic, and such treatments have not yielded satisfactory understanding of Jonestown and People's Temple. This chapter attempts, through a comparison with a number of the newer religious groups, to furnish a better understanding of the actual organization and functioning of People's Temple and how it could have been involved in such an act of revolutionary suicide.

The particular approach adopted by most people in interpreting the Guyana situation has been a psychologized one—a view that uses psychiatric and psychological concepts and jargon and focuses on individualistic explanations of events.[2] The most simplistic example of this approach is the idea that Jones was "crazy" and all those people were crazy and together they did a tragic but crazy thing. That view is indefensible. Jones may have been insane, depending on how the term is defined, but certainly his followers were not insane, in any kind of technical sense of the term. The frightening thing about most of Jones's followers is that they were amazingly normal.[3]

One other disturbing and misleading aspect of media treatments of People's Temple has been the tendency in nearly all commentaries to treat People's Temple as just one of the large number of new religious groups that have developed in our society in recent years and accordingly to assume that it was like these other groups in important ways. Such discussions usually contain comments on some of the various cults that have started recently, including People's Temple (and the word *cults* is always a negatively connoted term in such discussions).

*Published in somewhat different form in *Journal for the Scientific Study of Religion* 19:3 (September 1980).

Thus a discussion of the People's Temple might include material on the Hare Krishna, the Unification Church (Moonies), the Manson group, and/or the Children of God—lumping several groups together, thus implying, if not explicitly stating, that such groups shared significant features.[4] This assumption is very questionable.

The repeated failure to recognize important differences between People's Temple and the new religious groups of the late 1960s and 1970s has important policy implications. The kinds of images that people have about new religious groups can influence governmental policies of many types toward such groups. Thus it is extremely important that people come to an understanding of what happened in Guyana and of how People's Temple compares with other allegedly similar groups. For example, there may be a growth in the number of deprogrammings that are being done, justified in part by the Guyana tragedy. Deprogramming was already a large business and it may increase under the impact of Jonestown. Ted Patrick claims to have participated in 1600 deprogrammings, and he is now making public statements saying, in effect, "I told you so; we should suppress all these new cults" (see *San Francisco Chronicle* 11/21/78:3). Thus we are seeing what many deem an increase in direct attacks on the First Amendment's guaranteed freedom of religion, an attack given more impetus as a result of the Guyana tragedy.[5] Less dramatic government pressures are also being felt by new religious groups. For instance, the most pervasive social-control agency in our society—the Internal Revenue Service—has also been involved in regulating new religions because most such groups want to be tax exempt, which means they have to follow certain rules and procedures. The IRS has come under increasing pressure to be more stringent in its regulation of new religious groups, and this pressure may increase as a result of the Jonestown tragedy. This chapter furnishes an opportunity to impact such policy questions by outlining key distinctions between People's Temple and other religious groups.

The focus of the presentation will be a comparison between the People's Temple group and other new religious groups that have come to public attention in the past ten years or so—the 1970s. The comparison will be chiefly from a sociological and cultural point of view, and should demonstrate the problems of adopting a psychologized view. In lumping "other new religious groups" together, this presentation is, in a sense, committing the same sin that most news media have been accused of committing by their failing to differentiate between groups. It is obvious, for instance, that the Moon group (the Unification Church) is not like the Children of God in some important ways and that both differ markedly from Hare Krishna. However, since People's Temple was so much different from any of those mentioned (and from most other such groups), perhaps this kind of presentation is justified.[6]

The major differences between People's Temple and most of the new religions fall into eight analytically distinct areas: (1) time and social location of their inception; (2) characteristics of members and potential members; (3) organizational structure and operation; (4) social-control techniques and contact with the outside world; (5) resocialization techniques; (6) theology or ideology; (7) general orientation; and (8) ritual behaviors.

Time and Social Location of Origin

One important difference between People's Temple and the new religious groups is the time and social location of inception. Most of the new religious groups discussed in the media today—groups such as Hare Krishna, the Jesus Movement groups, the Happy, Healthy, Holy Organization (3HO), the Divine Light Mission—developed in America in the late 1960s and some of them were not discussed much until around 1970.

Some new religious groups did have a few members in America in the early 1960s but did not attract a large following at that time. The Unification Church, for instance, was studied in its inception in America by sociologist John Lofland, who wrote about them in *Doomsday Cult*, published first in 1966 (and reissued with an update in 1977). In that book Lofland does not even suggest that the small group he studied would become an important part of a large new movement, as turned out to be the case. The social, demographic, political, and economic conditions of the 1960s combined to produce a situation extremely conducive to the inception of new (at least for our society) religions. The largest generation of young people in America's history—many of whom were shaken loose from the social structure of America by events like the Vietnam War, pervasive racism, and drug experiences—was willing to listen to new messages from the East and to new interpretations of the traditional Judeo-Christian message (see Richardson 1974 for more detail). Many listened and a significant number joined or converted, some looking for new meaning in a world gone mad, others trying to achieve or maintain experiential levels of which drugs had made them aware. This time and social location of origin were profoundly different from those out of which came People's Temple.

People's Temple started in the 1950s in the Midwest in a totally
different milieu, as a reaction to a social and cultural situation that
was extremely racist. Jones was affected by the racism of his area, but
astonishingly he somehow apparently overcame that racism and for a
time developed an interracial and somewhat egalitarian church, with
a mission of helping disadvantaged people. His efforts to form such a
church led to some personal harassment by local citizenry (which may
well have directly contributed to the paranoia Jones felt later in life).
He established an interracial church in a situation not conducive to
such bold acts. Only later did he move his group to California and
even then he was not really a part of the new religions scene.

Member Characteristics

People's Temple started in a different time and a different cultural
milieu from the other new religions. It also started with different
kinds of people and had, up until that fateful day, different kinds of
people in it. Most of the other new religious groups now in the news
are peopled by white individuals of middle-class and upper-middle-
class social origins (see Wuthnow 1976; Enroth et al. 1972; and
Richardson 1977). The level of education is relatively high. One
group that some colleagues and I have studied in depth had an average education of more than 12 years. Members were young, with an
average age around 21 years, and overwhelmingly white. This Jesus
Movement group (described in Richardson et al. 1979) is similar to
most other new religions in this regard (see Wuthnow 1976). The
target population for the new groups was that type of person, and the
type was available in large numbers in the 1960s.

That well-known target population that we are used to reading
about by now was not, however, the kind of persons who made up the
bulk of membership in People's Temple. The People's Temple members were 80 to 90 percent black and from poor and lower-class backgrounds. There were a few whites in the group, and they seemed to
"flow upward" into the upper echelons of the authority structure.
People's Temple was preponderantly a black group (a fact with pro-
vocative implications) even if all the defectors seen on television were
white.[7]

The best analogy that can be drawn between People's Temple and
any other religious group is actually with the Father Divine movement (see Burnham 1979 for a recent study). Father Divine, one of the
most famous leaders of black sects and cults in American history,
developed a very large following in the 1930s and 1940s. Divine, a
black man who achieved national prominence through his religious

activities, set up an organization that looked amazingly like the later organization that Jim Jones operated. Fairly early in his career Jim Jones spent some time studying Divine's methods during a visit to Divine's center of activities in Philadelphia. Jones adopted many of Father Divine's tactics and procedures, and even used some of the hymns in People's Temple services. He built a church that appealed to poor urban blacks, not to the affluent young whites that peopled the other new religions.[8] In fact, People's Temple was not really new at all; it was instead, at least initially, an extension of a long tradition of urban blacks affiliating with sects and cults that offered them some this-worldly relief from the extreme destitution they suffered. The development of black cults promising rewards in this world is described in Joseph Washington's *Black Sects and Cults* (1973). Those desiring to understand People's Temple would be well advised to study Washington's book, as well as that of Burnham (1979).[9]

Organizational Structure

The organization of People's Temple was not complicated at all. Jones set up a relatively authoritarian structure that did not have many layers; one might call it shallow. Jones always kept power well centralized in his hands; he was the absolute authority of the organization and he played a large role in the day-to-day operations.

Below Jones in the organization was a second level, sometimes referred to by him as "the Angels" (a term also used by Father Divine to refer to his immediate advisors). Jones's group was made up of about 15 or 20 people who were his private group of counselors and workers. Most of these were women (also the case with Father Divine), and they tended to be attractive, tall, white women. Very few blacks were in that high-level group. Below the Angels in the group was another organizational level, known as "the Planning Commission," around 100 people who were principal leaders in People's Temple. This was the group before which occurred many of the disciplinary actions that are now so well known. The Planning Commission was responsible for many of the day-to-day chores of operating People's Temple. It was also in charge of the bus pilgrimages to Los Angeles and San Francisco and of other large group activities, such as attending political rallies and voting. About two-thirds of the Planning Commission members were white and one-third were black. At the bottom of the organizational structure were the followers, who were mostly black. Thus People's Temple had a four-level structure, quite shallow considering the number of people involved, and it allowed considerable direct control by Jones.

That Jones also apparently was an extremely charismatic person augmented his structural authority. Some stories from his childhood talk about him as a person who could get other children to obey him. He apparently had a real personal gift of charisma, even if it did go awry during his last few years.

Sharply contrasted to the shallow and greatly centralized People's Temple organization are most of the newer religious groups. Contrary to popular belief, most of the new groups are not nearly so tightly centralized and authoritarian. Especially is this the case for widely dispersed organizations like the Children of God. Research on the Children of God by Davis and Richardson (1976) delineated a twelve-level structure of authority for this worldwide organization, and firsthand experience by both researchers found much evidence for local autonomy on most matters. Christ Communal Organization (a pseudonym), another nationwide Jesus Movement group studied in depth by Richardson et al. (1979), was found to be similar in this regard. With communes and other facets of this well-differentiated organization in nearly thirty different states, centralized control of the kind often attributed to such new religious groups was not possible, even if desired by leaders. Such groups cannot function without decentralization, and without deeper authority structures.

The contrast between People's Temple and other religious groups was made even more distinct with the move to Guyana, simply because this move brought nearly all members of that group together in one location. Some of the smaller new religious groups have most members together in one location, but most of the ones usually compared to People's Temple are not organized in this fashion, as has been indicated. It should also be noted that none of the new religious groups has had armed security guards as a part of the organization, as apparently was the case in Guyana and also possibly while the group was still in America. Having a police force certainly indicates important differences between People's Temple and other groups that perceived no need for such protection.[10]

Social Control and Contact with the Outside World

The kind of spatial arrangements and authority structure just described for People's Temple lends itself very well to considerable social control of members' behavior and even beliefs. Before leaving the United States Jones had much contact with his followers in regularized meeting situations, and he was apparently very gifted at exploiting that forum. He was a skilled orator and plied his talents well with his relatively uneducated followers, who tended to accept what he told them to believe and do. The Planning Commission meetings, where strong disciplinary measures were taken against members who did not please Jones, added a strong element to social control within the group (see Kilduff and Javers 1978:60–65). When the Guyana outpost was established and Jones moved there himself in 1977, the situation was exacerbated. Jonestown was 30 jungle miles from the nearest settlement. Jones told horror stories about tigers and snakes in the jungle and the members actually could not leave anyway since he took their passports away from them, making them virtual prisoners. One or two people did "escape" as is described in some of the instant-book accounts (see Chapter 9 of Kilduff and Javers 1978). Jonestown was virtually a prison camp; no one was allowed contact with the outside world without permission and most outsiders were not welcome either, as Leo Ryan's party found out. Torture was employed as a way of maintaining control of members; adults were sometimes put for a week at a time in a wooden prison called "the box," 3 × 3 × 6 feet, and children were dropped into a water well for even small rule infractions. No other recent religious group of which we are aware visited such terrorizing actions on its members, and this practice represents a sharp and important contrast between such groups and People's Temple.

The social-control situation of People's Temple can be illustrated using a variable that might be labeled "contact with the outside world." For most new religious groups there was a fair degree of deliberate social and even geographic isolation initially, but contact with the outside world increased over time. Sometimes at the beginning this contact may have been as evangelizers, but at least there was contact. Generally, the new groups have become less wary as time has passed about contact with the dominant society and have even institutionalized such contact.

Christ Communal Organization, the Jesus Movement organization described in Richardson et al. (1979), very early in its organization life was negotiating labor contracts, working to establish tax-exempt status, serving as a conscientious-objector camp and a group to which the courts remanded juveniles, operating large agricultural enterprises well integrated into the local economy, and doing many other things. The Children of God's worldwide literature publication and distribution network is another important example, as is the Unification Church with its many properties and business enterprises (which have come under fire from some quarters). See Glock and Bellah (1976) for other such illustrations.

People's Temple seemed to develop in an opposite fashion. Initially and for some time there was more contact with the outside world through all the many service arms of the organization, but over time the organization, under Jones's direction, seemed to withdraw into itself more. Before moving to Guyana it was engaged in fewer such outward-oriented activities and instead had more long meetings, some with Jones speaking to the members and some with Planning Commission disciplinary activities. After the move to Guyana, the members there were almost totally cut off from contact except with group members. This sharp difference between outside contact for most newer religions and for People's Temple can be graphed as in Figure 1.

Figure 1. Contact over time with the outside world for People's Temple and other new religious groups.

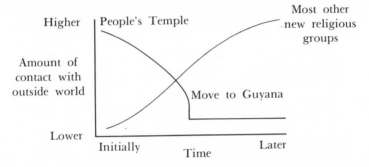

Resocialization Techniques

The actual techniques of resocialization used in People's Temple also appear to differ from those practiced by most new religions (see Richardson 1977). This important fact should be understood, if only because so much attention has been focused on recruitment techniques of new religious groups. The popular images of mind control, brainwashing, and coercive persuasion have, much to the distress of the new religious groups, been associated with joining such groups. Those images have been used to justify punitive actions against certain of the new groups, including, as has been mentioned, deprogramming. The tragedy in Guyana has added to this problem since some deprogrammers and their sympathizers want to lump People's Temple together with other new religions, apparently to help justify deprogramming. It is perhaps worth noting that although this link has been suggested by some deprogrammers, there is no record of anyone being deprogrammed from People's Temple, a fact that may be related to the class and racial origins of most members or to the circumstance that this group was of no concern to those opposed to newer religions until the Guyana tragedy.

There are always some problems of interpretation associated with accepting atrocity tales told by defectors from groups (see Bromley et al. 1979). Defectors may be involved in either conscious or unconscious self-serving behavior when they recount how terrible it was in such and such a group. Even taking this kind of thing into account, one is left with the impression that life in People's Temple was pretty grim during the later years of the organization's history, if media accounts and the instant books on the tragedy can be believed. There is considerable agreement between accounts by different people and sources, and there is some physical evidence of strange activities (such as the self-incriminating letters and "the box"). We read tales of physical punishments of various kinds, of sleep and food deprivation, of the total lack of privacy, and of the systematic development of feelings of guilt and humiliation in members. We read of techniques used to break down normal relationships between family members—the rewarding of children for tattling on their parents and the use of sex (including forced abstinence in married couples) to break down husband-wife ties. The picture that one gets from these accounts is one that shares important facets with the thought-reform model developed by Lifton in his study of resocializing Chinese intellectuals around 1950 in China. Jones was not as systematic as were the Communists in China but perhaps he did not have to be to accomplish his ends with the group with which he was working.

Although there are some charges to the contrary for certain new religious groups, resocialization techniques in most of them cannot easily be classified as thought reform or brainwashing. They *can* be viewed as effective persuasion, but key elements of the thought-reform model (such as physical coercion) are simply not present. Not that the techniques of newer religions are ineffective; indeed they are, as the love bombing of the Unification Church has demonstrated (see Lofland 1977). But well-done love bombing should not be mistaken for physical coercion, and encouraging people to spend a weekend at a country retreat should not be confused with incarceration. Being assigned a brother or sister with whom a new convert is to keep in close contact should not be considered the equivalent of having armed guards to deter desertion.

Theology or Ideology

Most of the new religious groups to which People's Temple is often compared are promoting Americanized versions of theologies that are very old. Predictably, the groups that adopted versions of Western Judeo-Christian theology were generally treated better. Most of the Jesus Movement groups, for instance, were accepted by the greater society and encouraged by it, because they were, after all, espousing new variations of fundamentalist Christianity, "the rock whence we are hewn." Members of such groups may have acted and dressed a little differently but that nonconformity was generally viewed as better than being on drugs (the Children of God seemed to elicit a partial exception to this more tolerant view). Even the Eastern-oriented new groups adopted versions of religious philosophies with long histories even if their histories were not familiar to most in our society. Both the Eastern- and Western-oriented belief systems (and those of eclectic groups such as the Unification Church) were pervaded with individualism and tended to interpret in individualized ways both problems and solutions to problems, even if specific concepts differed among the groups (see Ellwood 1973; Cox 1977; and Needleman 1970).

With People's Temple the theology or ideology was quite different, as has been noted by John Hall in his *Society* paper (1979). For one thing, Jones started out in the middle 1950s building a church around the idea of racial integration, which was initially a major impetus for him. He established a racially integrated church in the Midwest area, which was overtly racist at the time. Thus People's Temple ideology contained an element that is quite muted in other new groups, which are nearly totally Caucasian and which attend directly to race very little. Such groups rarely include many members of racial minorities. But with Jones, racial equality was an integral part of his theology. This feature of his beliefs may well have contributed to Jones's paranoia, since he received considerable abuse for his ideas early during his career in the Midwest.

Another key aspect of Jones's personal theology which is counter to that of recent religious groups is socialism. Why Jones adopted socialism is unclear, but it probably has something to do with his rejecting American society because of racism. Whatever the reason, Jones adopted fairly early in his professional career a socialist-oriented theology or philosophy, and in his own way he set out to implement this view. His adoption of a version of socialism has caused much difficulty for socialists, who do not want to claim Jones as a fellow traveler anymore than do members of newer religious groups. Some socialists have attempted to put distance between themselves and Jones, as illustrated by Moberg's two articles (December 1979) in *In These Times*, a socialist newspaper, which attempts to discredit Jones's brand of socialism.

Jones put together these elements—racial equality and socialism—and earned much criticism for his efforts. This criticism helped encourage a conspiracy theory that became an integral part of his theology and philosophy; there was always some conspiracy by people out to get him, or so he thought. Other recent groups such as the Children of God, the Unification Church, or Hare Krishna have been criticized and challenged by social-control agents and others in our society, and as a result have developed some paranoia. But the causes of the paranoia were different for Jones and his group; they stemmed from Jones's personality and also significantly from America's historical lack of tolerance for racial equality and for socialistic ideas.

One other key aspect of Jones's beliefs that demands attention is his theology of suicide, which offers a sharp contrast with other religious groups of recent times. None of the newer religious groups' theologies view suicide positively. In fact, most such groups negatively sanction suicide. Jones's paranoia may have led him to the idea of suicide, which he integrated into his philosophy later in his life.[11] He talked about "revolutionary suicide" and "dying for a cause." He opposed individual suicide, but advocated collective suicide as a possible positive and logical outcome of being attacked by forces allegedly opposed to his efforts. The idea of suicide for a cause is not, of course, entirely rare. A few examples of large-scale suicides are the kamikaze pilots in World War II; the Jews at Masada or those at York, England, in the 1200s; and the Japanese on some of the islands captured during World War II. But none of these events was recent, and none occurred in such ostensibly inexplicable circumstances.

General Orientation

One can talk of specific beliefs and sets of beliefs such as socialism, racial equality, and suicide, but another area which should be considered in making comparisons is the general orientation of a group. Most of the new religious groups of the 1960s were oriented toward individual evangelism, personal self-development, or both. When such groups focused outward, they did so usually for the express purpose of converting others to the group; usually they were inward oriented and more introspective. People's Temple seems somewhat different in this regard, especially earlier in its history, when Jones displayed a more conscious structural orientation and tried even in a small way to change some structures in society. Many commentators apparently would like to forget that People's Temple was more outward oriented during most of its history, and that it helped many people, especially people who had few resources. But to ignore these facts contributes to the misunderstanding about People's Temple and Jim Jones.

Over the course of its history, People's Temple operated soup kitchens, child-care centers, and infirmaries for the poor. The Temple was engaged in drug rehabilitation programs, legal-aid services, homes for the aged and for delinquents, and other such activities. Some think that all this can be discounted as a facade or as a cover for illicit activities, but to regard it thus is probably a mistake. Certainly such humanitarian activities were later de-emphasized by People's Temple, but much good was accomplished earlier. One must hope that researchers will be able to document more carefully the early activities of People's Temple and help us to understand the shift that apparently occurred in the last few years. Pending this research we should not just dismiss those significant activities that indicated a more humane orientation.

One significant indication of the structural orientation of People's Temple was Jones's interest in political matters. The Unification Church also has shown some interest in political matters (see Nelson 1979 and Horowitz 1979), but this is an exception in the newer religions. Some groups openly deride political involvement of any kind, and most only begrudgingly allow their members to participate in political processes. Such actions generally are not comparable to Jones's efforts to get involved directly in the political processes.

People's Temple members and leaders participated in everything from voting and campaigning to occupying appointed political offices. Jones had considerable contact with politicians, including some on the national scene such as Walter Mondale and Rosalynn Carter. His involvement in San Francisco politics seems a self-serving effort to gain personal power. A more benign view might hold that political involvement would be a natural avenue for someone holding Jones's collectivistic view of the world. He seemed to assume that structural change was best accomplished through political action and political power. His efforts on behalf of a free press also may have derived from a deep-seated belief in the value of a free press for encouraging change, although he may have been interested in direct manipulation of the press as well.

Rituals

No group can exist without rituals, be it a Jesus Movement group or the People's Temple. Even groups that decry ritual behavior and overtly disallow it can be accused of turning their antiritualism into a ritual. This chapter cannot begin to describe the richness of ritual behaviors that pervade new religious movements, but one major point can be made. Usually those rituals have been entered into with great sincerity and with considerable symbolic meaning for the participants. This point should be made for most participants in People's Temple as well, even if there is some evidence that Jones manipulated ritual behavior to accomplish his own ends. According to some reports, Jones claimed to have lost faith in the Christian message several years before his death. He was perhaps cynically using that message with its rich symbolism to conceal his true aims of preaching socialism (see Novak's December 18, 1978, *Washington Star* column). We do know that he incorporated certain aspects of Father Divine's rituals in People's Temple activities. If one accepts accounts of Jones's change of beliefs, and if one posits good will and sincerity on the part of leaders of other recently established Christian-oriented religious groups, then Jones's general use of Christian rituals indicates a difference that may be noteworthy.

Aside from this possible general difference in the way rituals were used in People's Temple and in more recent religious groups, there is one specific crucial ritual used by Jones that bears examination. Accounts of the last few years of People's Temple all refer to group sessions in which those present were required to drink liquids that were said to be poison. If such reports are correct, this suicide-oriented ritual behavior pattern was repeated several times, perhaps often, in the later years. Sometimes the people participating were told the liquid was poison before they drank, and sometimes afterward, but the point is that they were participating in a ritual analogous to one as old as Christendom itself, one with considerable symbolic meaning. When people take Holy Communion, the Lord's Supper, or the Eucharist, they are doing something with important similarities to the behavior pattern developed around People's Temple suicide drills.

Whether or not Jones deliberately planned to incorporate Christian symbolism and ritual so explicitly remains to be proved, but either by accident or design he was tapping into a ritual pattern with tremendous meaning to most people within a Christian culture. Jones seemed to understand the basic fact that ritual is often more important than belief and that behavior usually predates belief. At the very least, the drills were analogous to fire drills for school children practicing what to do in a time of danger. But the significance of these drills was possibly much greater. Anthony Wallace's discussion of the ritual process in *Religion: An Anthropological View* emphasizes the great value of prelearning to that process. "Prelearning" refers to the presence of previously learned cognitive elements. Jones took advantage of the already present elements of drinking a liquid in a religious setting and added new cognitive material concerning revolutionary-suicide interpretations of the event. This recombination of the old and new was essential to Jones's purposes, and he succeeded all too well with his plan to make a thunderous point for his political and social views. Leo Ryan's visit was a catalyst that triggered this most dramatic conclusion to People's Temple, but the stage for this tragic multiple murder/suicide had been set much earlier by Jones himself.

Conclusion

The intent of this chapter has been to demonstrate that most media discussions of People's Temple have been misguided and have contributed to the mounting hysteria about certain religious and pseudoreligious groups. Such hysteria is contributing to significant First Amendment problems in our society. This chapter has pointed to a number of key differences between People's Temple and other religious groups that developed in the 1960s in America and to the value of examining People's Temple from a more sociological viewpoint. Hopefully, the effort will contribute to a better understanding of this group that so tragically entered the pages of history in November 1978 in Guyana.

3
The Apocalypse at Jonestown*
John R. Hall

The events of November 1978 at Jonestown in Guyana have been well documented, indeed probably better documented than most comparable bizarre incidents. Beyond the wealth of facts drawn from interviews with survivors of all stripes, piles of as yet unsifted documents and tapes remain; if they can ever be examined, these may add something in the way of detail. But they are unlikely to change very much the broad lines of our understanding of Jonestown. The major dimensions of the events and the outlines of various intrigues are already before us. But so far we have been caught in a flood of instant analysis; some of this has been insightful, but much of the accompanying moral outrage has clouded our ability to comprehend the events themselves. We need a more considered look at what sort of social phenomenon Jonestown was, and why (and how) Reverend Jim Jones and his staff led the 900 people of Jonestown to die in mass murder and suicide. On the face of it, the action is unparalleled and incredible.

The news media have sought to account for Jonestown largely by looking for parallels "in history"; yet we have not been much enlightened by the ones they have found, usually because they have searched for cases that bear the outer trappings of the event but have fundamentally different causes. Thus at Masada, in 73 C.E. the Jews who committed suicide under siege by Roman soldiers knew their fate was death, and chose to die by their own hands rather than at those of the Romans. In World War II, Japanese kamikaze pilots acted with the knowledge that direct and tangible military results would follow from their altruistic suicides if these were properly executed. And in Hitler's concentration camps, though there was occasional cooperation by Jews in their own executions, the Nazi executioners had no intentions of dying themselves.

Besides pointing to parallels that don't quite fit, the news media have tagged Jim Jones as irrational, as a madman who had perverse tendencies from early in his youth. They have labeled People's Temple a "cult," perhaps in the hope that a label will suffice when an

*Published in somewhat different form in *Society* 16:6 (1979).

explanation is unavailable. And they have quite correctly plumbed the key issue of how Jones and his staff were able to bring the mass murder/suicide to completion, drawing largely on the explanations of psychiatrists who have promoted the concept of brainwashing as the answer.

But Jones was not totally irrational, though he may have been "possessed" or "crazed." Both the organizational effectiveness of People's Temple for more than fifteen years and the actual carrying out of the mass murder/suicide show that Jones and his staff knew what they were doing.

Moreover, People's Temple became a "cult" only when the media discovered the mass murder/suicide. As an Indiana woman whose teenager died at Jonestown commented, "I can't understand why they call the People's Temple a cult. To the people, it was their church" (*Louisville Courier-Journal* 12/23/78:B1). Granted that even if the use of the term *cult* in the current press has been sloppy and inappropriate, some comparisons, for example, to the Unification Church, the Krishna Society, and the Children of God, have been quite apt.[1] But these comparisons have triggered a sort of guilt by association in which Jonestown is deemed a not so aberrant case among numerous exotic and weird religious cults. The only thing stopping some people from "cleaning up the cult situation" is the constitutional guarantee of freedom of religion.[2]

"Brainwashing" is an important but incomplete basis for understanding the mass murder/suicide. There can be no way to determine how many people at Jonestown freely chose to drink the cyanide-laced drink distributed after Jonestown received word of the murders of Congressman Leo Ryan and four other visitors at the airstrip. Clearly more than 200 children and an undetermined number of adults were murdered. Thought control and blind obedience to authority (brainwashing) surely account for some additional number of suicides. But the obvious cannot be ignored: a substantial number of people—brainwashed or not—committed suicide. Insofar as brainwashing occurs in other social organizations besides People's Temple, it can be only a necessary and not a sufficient explanation of the mass murder/suicide. The coercive persuasion involved in a totalistic construction of reality may explain in part *how* large numbers of people came to accept the course proposed by their leader, but it leaves unanswered the question of *why* the true believers among the inhabitants of Jonestown came to consider "revolutionary suicide" a plausible course of action.

In all the instant analyses of Jones's perversity, the threats posed by cults, and the victimization of people by brainwashing, there has been little attempt to account for Jonestown sociologically and as a religious phenomenon. The various facets of Jonestown remain incongruous pieces of seemingly separate puzzles; we need a close examination of the case itself to try to comprehend it. In the following discussion, based on ideal-type analysis and *verstehende* sociology (Weber 1977:4-22), I will suggest that the People's Temple Agricultural Project at Jonestown was an apocalyptic sect. Most apocalyptic sects gravitate toward one of three ideal-typical possibilities: (1) preapocalyptic adventism, (2) preapocalyptic war, or (3) postapocalyptic other-worldly grace. Insofar as the adventist group takes on a communal form, it comes to approximate the postapocalyptic tableau of other-worldly grace. Jonestown was caught on the saddle of the apocalypse: it had its origins in the vaguely apocalyptic revivalist evangelism of People's Temple in the United States, but the Guyanese communal settlement itself was an attempt to transcend the apocalypse by establishing a heaven-on-earth. For various reasons, this attempt was frustrated. People's Temple at Jonestown was drawn back into a preapocalyptic war with the forces of the established order. Revolutionary suicide then came to be seen as a way of surmounting the frustration, of moving beyond the apocalypse to heaven, albeit not on earth.

In order to explore this account, let us first consider the origins of Jonestown and the ways in which it subsequently came to approximate the ideal-typical other-worldly sect. Then we can consider certain tensions of the Jonestown group with respect to its other-worldly existence, so as to understand why similar groups did not (and are never likely to) encounter the same fate as Jonestown.

Jonestown as an Other-Worldly Sect

An other-worldly sect, as I have described it in *The Ways Out* (1978:207), is a utopian communal group which subscribes to a comprehensive set of beliefs based on an apocalyptic interpretation of current history. The world of society-at-large is seen as totally evil and in its last days; at the end of history as we know it, it is to be replaced by a community of the elect—those who live according to the revelation of God's will. The convert who embraces such a sect must, perforce, abandon any previous understanding of life's meaning and embrace the new world-view, which itself is capable of subsuming and explaining the individual's previous life, the actions of opponents to the sect, and the demands placed on the convert by the leadership of the sect. The other-worldly sect typically establishes its existence on the other side of the apocalypse by withdrawing from this world into a timeless heaven-on-earth. In this millennial kingdom those closest to God come to rule. Though democratic consensuality or the collegiality of elders may come into play, more typically a pre-eminent prophet or messiah, legitimated by charisma or tradition, calls the shots in a theocratic organization of God's chosen people.

People's Temple had its roots in amorphous revivalistic evangelical religion, but in the transition to the Jonestown Agricultural Mission it came to resemble an other-worldly sect. The Temple grew out of the interracial congregation Jim Jones had founded in Indiana in 1953. By 1964, the People's Temple Full Gospel Church was federated with the Disciples of Christ (Kilduff and Javers 1978:20). Later, in 1966, Jones moved with a hundred of his most devout followers to Redwood Valley, California. From there they expanded in the 1970s to San Francisco and Los Angeles—places more promising for liberal interracial evangelism than rural Redwood Valley.

In these years before the move to Guyana, Jones engaged himself largely in the manifold craft of revivalism. Jones learned from others he observed—Father Divine in Philadelphia and David Martins de Miranda in Brazil—and Jones himself became a purveyor of faked miracles and faith healings (*Newsweek* 12/4/78:55–56). By the California years People's Temple was prospering financially from its somewhat shady tent-meeting-style activities and from a variety of other petty and grand money-making schemes; it was also gaining political clout through the deployment of its members for the benefit of various politicians and causes.

These early developments give cause to wonder why Jones did not establish a successful but relatively benign sect like Jehovah's Witnesses, or why alternatively he did not move from a religious base directly into the realm of politics as did Adam Clayton Powell from his Harlem congregation to the House of Representatives. The answer seems twofold. First, Jim Jones seems to have had limitations both as an evangelist and as a politician. He simply did not succeed in fooling key California religious observers with his faked miracles. And for all the political support he peddled in California politics, Jones was not always able to draw on his good political credit when he needed it. The ability to sustain power in the face of scandal is a mark of political effectiveness. By this standard, Jones was not totally successful in either Indiana or California; there always seemed to be investigators and reporters on the trails of various questionable financial and evangelical dealings (Kilduff and Javers 1978:23-25, 35-38).

Second, and quite aside from the limits of Jones's effectiveness, the very nature of his prophecy directed his religious movement along a different path from either worldly politics or sectarian adventism. Adventist groups receive prophecy, keyed to the Book of Revelations, about the apocalyptic downfall of the present evil order of the world and the second coming of Christ to preside over a millennial period of divine grace on earth. For all such groups, the advent itself makes irrelevant any social action to reform this world's institutions. Adventist groups differ from one another in their exact eschatology of the last days, but the groups that have survived, like the Seventh Day Adventists and Jehovah's Witnesses, have juggled their doctrines that set an exact date for Christ's return. Thus they have moved away from any chiliastic expectation of an imminent appearance to engage in conversionist activities intended to pave the way for the millennium (Clark 1949:34-50; Lewy 1974:265).

Jones himself seems to have shared the pessimism of the adventist sects about reforming social institutions in this world (for him, the capitalist world of the United States). True, he supported various progressive causes, but he did not put much stake in their success. Jones's prophecy was far more radical than those of contemporary adventist groups: he focused on imminent apocalyptic disaster rather than on Christ's millennial salvation, and his eschatology therefore had to resolve a choice between preapocalyptic struggle with "the beast" and collective flight to establish a postapocalyptic kingdom of the elect. Up until the end, People's Temple was directed toward the latter possibility. Even in the Indiana years Jones had embraced an apocalyptic view. The move from Indiana to California was in part justified by Jones's claim that Redwood Valley would survive nuclear holocaust (Krause 1978:29). In the California years the apocalyptic vision shifted to CIA persecution and Nazi-like extermination of blacks. In California, too, People's Temple gradually became communal in certain respects; it established a community of goods, pooled resources of elderly followers to provide communal housing for them, and by establishing group homes for displaced youth drew on state funds paid to foster parents. In its apocalyptic and communal aspects People's Temple more and more came to exist as an ark of survival. Jonestown, the agricultural project in Guyana, was built beginning in 1974 by an advance crew that by early 1977 still amounted to fewer than 60 people, most of them under age 30. The mass exodus of People's Temple to Jonestown really began in 1977 when People's Temple was coming under increasing scrutiny in California.

In the move to Guyana, People's Temple began to concertedly exhibit many dynamics of other-worldly sects, though it differed in ways central to its fate. Until the end, Jonestown was similar in striking ways to contemporary sects like the Children of God and the Krishna Society (ISKCON, Inc.). Indeed, the Temple bears a more casual (and somewhat uncomfortable) resemblance to the various Protestant sects that emigrated to the wilderness of North America beginning in the seventeenth century. The Puritans, Moravians, Rappites, Shakers, Lutherans, and many others set up theocracies where they hoped to live out their own visions of the earthly millennial community. So it was with Jonestown. In this light, neither disciplinary practices, the daily round of life, nor the community of goods at Jonestown seem so unusual.

The disciplinary practices of People's Temple—bizarre and grotesque though they may sound—are not uncommon aspects of other-worldly sects. These practices have been played up in the press in an attempt to demonstrate the perverse nature of the group and thus explain the terrible climax to their life. But as Erving Goffman (1961) has shown, the physical abuse and sexual intimidation and general psychological terror occur in all kinds of total institutions, including mental hospitals, prisons, armies, even nunneries. Indeed, Congressman Leo Ryan, just prior to his fateful visit to Jonestown, accepted the need for social control: "... you can't put 1200 people in the middle of a jungle without some damn tight discipline" (quoted in Krause 1978:21). Practices at Jonestown may well seem restrained in comparison to practices of, say, seventeenth-century American Puritans who, among other things, were willing to execute "witches" on the testimony of respected churchgoers or even children. Meg Greenfield (1978:132) observed, in reflecting on Jonestown, "the jungle is only a few yards away." It seems important to recall that some revered origins of the United States lie in a remarkably similar "jungle."

Communal groups of all types, not just other-worldly sects, face problems of social control and commitment. Rosabeth Kanter (1972) has convincingly shown that successful communal groups in the nineteenth-century United States often drew on mutual criticism, mortification, modification of conventional sexual mores, and other devices in order to decrease the individual's ties to the outside or personal relationships within the group and to increase the individual's commitment to the collectivity as a whole. Such commitment mechanisms are employed most often in religious communal groups, especially those with charismatic leaders (Hall 1978:225–226). Otherworldly communal groups, where a special attempt is being made to forge a wholly new interpretation of reality, where the demand for commitment is especially pronounced (in a word, where it is sectarian)—these groups are likely to seek out the procedures most effective at guaranteeing commitment. After all, defection from the way of the group inevitably casts doubt on its sanctity, no matter how rationalized among the faithful. Thus, it is against such groups that the charges of brainwashing, chicanery, and mistreatment of members are most often leveled. Whatever their basis in fact, these are the likely charges of families and friends who see their loved ones abandon them in favor of committing material resources and persons to the religious hope of a new life. Much like the other-worldly sects, families suffer a loss of legitimacy in the defection of one of their own.

The abyss that comes to exist between other-worldly sects and the world of society-at-large left behind simply cannot be bridged. There is no encompassing rational connection between the two realities, and therefore the interchange between the other-worldly sect and people beyond its boundaries becomes from the point of view of the sect a struggle between infidels and the faithful, or from the point of view of outsiders a struggle between rationality and fanaticism. Every sectarian action has its benevolent interpretation and legitimation within the sect and a converse devious interpretation from the outside. Thus, from inside the sect, various practices of confession, mutual criticism, or catharsis sessions seem necessary to prevent deviant world-views from taking hold within the group. In People's Temple, such practices included occasional enforced isolation and drug regimens for "rehabilitation" (*New York Times* 12/29/78:A13) akin to contemporary psychiatric treatment. From the outside, all this tends to be regarded as brainwashing, but insiders will turn the accusation outward, claiming that it is those in the society-at-large who are brainwashed. Though there can really be no resolution to this conflict of interpretations, the widespread incidence of similar coercive persuasion outside Jonestown suggests that its practice at Jonestown is not significantly unusual, at least within the contexts of other-worldly sects or of total institutions in general.

What is unusual is the direction coercive persuasion or brainwashing took. Jones worked to instill devotion in unusual ways—ways that fostered the acceptability of revolutionary suicide among his followers. During "white nights" of emergency mobilization, he conducted rituals of proclaimed mass suicide, giving "poison" to all

members and saying they would die within the hour. According to
one early defector, when people did not die in the elapsed time, Jones

> "explained that the poison was not real and we had just been
> through a loyalty test. He warned us that the time was not far off
> when it would be necessary for us to die by our own hands." (Blakey,
> in Krause 1978:193)

This event initially left Deborah Blakey "indifferent" to whether she
"lived or died." A true believer in People's Temple was more emphat-
ic: disappointed by the string of false collective suicides, in a note to
Jones he hoped for "the real thing" so that they could all pass beyond
the suffering of this world (*San Francisco Examiner* 12/6/78:10).
Some people yielded to Jim Jones only because their will to resist was
beaten down; others, including many seniors—the elderly members of
People's Temple—felt they owed everything to Jim Jones, and provided him with a strong core of unequivocal support. Jones allowed
open dissension at so-called town meetings apparently because, with
the support of the seniors, he knew he could prevail. Thus, no matter
what they wanted personally, people learned to leave their fates in the
hands of Jim Jones and accept what he demanded. The specific uses
of coercive persuasion at Jonestown help explain how (but not why)
the mass murder/suicide was implemented. But the special use, not
the general nature of brainwashing, distinguishes Jonestown from
most other-worldly sects.

In addition to brainwashing, a second major kind of accusation
about Jonestown, put forward most forcefully by Deborah Blakey,
concerns the work discipline and diet there. Blakey swore in an affi-
davit that the work load was excessive and that the food served to the
average residents of Jonestown was inadequate. She abhorred the contradiction between the conditions she reported and the privileged diet
of Jones and his inner circle. Moreover, because she had dealt with the
group's finances, she knew that money could have been directed to
providing a more adequate diet.

Blakey's moral sensibilities notwithstanding, the disparity between
the diet of the elite and that of the average Jonestowner should come
as no surprise: it parallels Erving Goffman's (1961:48ff) description of
widespread hierarchies of privilege in total institutions. Her concern
about the average diet is more the point. But here, other accounts
differ from Blakey's report. Maria Katsaris, a consort of Jones, wrote
her father a letter extolling the virtues of the Agricultural Project's
"cutlass" beans used as a meat substitute (Kilduff and Javers 1978:

109). And Paula Adams, who survived the Jonestown holocaust because she resided at the People's Temple house in Georgetown, expressed ambivalence about the Jonestown community in an interview after the mass murder/suicide. But she also remarked, "My daughter ate very well. She got eggs and milk every day. How many black children in the ghetto eat that well?" (*San Francisco Examiner* 12/10/78:9). The accounts of surviving members of Jones's personal staff and inner circle, like Katsaris and Adams, are suspect, of course, in exactly the opposite way from those of people like the concerned relatives of Jonestown emigrants. But the inside accounts are corroborated by at least one outsider, *Washington Post* reporter Charles Krause. On his arrival at Jonestown in the company of Congressman Leo Ryan, Krause (1978:41) noted, "Contrary to what the concerned relatives had told us, nobody seemed to be starving. Indeed, everyone seemed quite healthy." It is difficult to assess these conflicting views.

Beginning early in the summer of 1977, Jones set in motion the mass exodus of some 800 People's Temple members from California to Jonestown. Though Jonestown could then adequately house only about 500 people, the population quickly climbed well beyond that mark, seriously overtaxing the agricultural base of the settlement. The exodus also caused Jonestown to become top-heavy with less productive seniors and children. Anything close to agricultural self-sufficiency thereupon became an elusive and long-range goal. As time wore on during the group's last year of existence, Jones himself became ever more fixated on the prospect of a mass emigration from Guyana; in this light, any sort of long-range agricultural-development strategy seemed increasingly irrational. According to the *New York Times*, the former Jonestown farm manager, Jim Bogue, suggested that the agricultural program at Jonestown would have succeeded in the long run if it had been adhered to. But with the emerging plans for emigration it was not followed, and thus became merely a charade for the benefit of the Guyanese government.

This analysis would seem to have implications for internal conflicts about goals within Jones's flock: for example, Jim Jones's only natural son, Stephen Jones, as well as several other young men in People's Temple, came to believe in Jonestown as a socialist agrarian community, not as an other-worldly sect headed up by his father. Reflecting about his father after the mass murder/suicide, Stephen Jones commented, "I don't mind discrediting him...but I'm still a socialist, and Jim Jones will be used to discredit socialism. People will use him to discredit what we built. Jonestown was not Jim Jones, although he believed it was" (*San Francisco Examiner* 12/10/78:9).

Like other-worldly sects in general (Hall 1978:207), Jonestown did not seek to survive on the basis of patronage, petty financial schemes, and the building of a community of goods through proselytization. Jones had already built up assets valued at more than $20 million. As a basis for satisfying collective wants, any agricultural production at Jonestown would have paled in comparison with this amassed wealth.

But even if the agricultural project itself became a charade, a pretense, it is no easy task to create a plausible charade in the midst of relatively infertile soil reclaimed from dense jungle; to do this would have required the long hours of work that People's Temple defectors described. Such a charade could serve as yet another effective means of social control. In the first place, it gave a purposeful role to those who envisioned Jonestown as an experimental socialist agrarian community. Beyond this, it monopolized the waking hours of most of the populace in exhausting work, and gave them only a minimal (though probably adequate) diet on which to do it. It is easy to imagine that many city people, or those with bourgeois sensibilities in general, would not find this lifestyle acceptable in any case. But the demanding daily regimen, however abhorrent to the uninitiated, is widespread in other-worldly sects. Various programs of fasting, work, and asceticism have long been regarded as signs of piety and routes to religious enlightenment or ecstasy. In the contemporary American Krishna groups, an alternation of nonsugar and high-sugar phases of the diet seems to create an almost addictive attachment to the food communally distributed (Hall 1978:76; cf. Goffman 1961:49–50). And we need look no later in history than to Saint Benedict's monastic order to find a situation in which the personal time of participants is eliminated for all practical purposes, with procedures of mortification for offenders laid out in his *Rule* (c. 525/1975; cf. Zerubavel 1977). Though the concerns of Blakey and others about diet, work, and discipline may have some basis, they have probably been exaggerated and in any case they do not distinguish Jonestown from other-worldly sects in general.

One final public concern with People's Temple deserves mention because it so closely parallels previous sectarian practice: Jones is accused of swindling people out of their livelihoods and life circumstances by tricking them into signing over their money and possessions to People's Temple or its inner circle of members. Of course, Jones considered this a contribution to a community of goods and correctly pointed to a long tradition of such want satisfaction among other-worldly sects; in an interview just prior to the mass murder/suicide, Jones cited Jesus' call to hold all things in common (*San Fran-*

cisco Examiner 12/3/78:16). There are good grounds to think that Jones carried this philosophy into the realm of a con game. Still, it should be noted that in the suicidal end, Jones did not benefit from all the wealth as a good number of other self-declared prophets and messiahs have done.[3]

As with its other disciplinary practices and its daily round of life, the community of goods in People's Temple at Jonestown emphasizes its similarities to other-worldly sects—both the contemporary ones labeled cults by their detractors and the historical examples often revered in retrospect by contemporary religious culture. The elaboration of these affinities is in no way intended to suggest that we can or should defend the duplicity, the bizarre sexual and psychological intimidation, and the hardships of daily life at Jonestown. But it must be recognized that the Jonestown settlement was a good deal less unusual than some of us might like to think: the practices detractors find abhorrent in the life of People's Temple at Jonestown are of the core nature of other-worldly sects and widespread among them, both historical and contemporary. Grant that the character of such sects— the theocratic basis of authority, the devices of mortification and social control, and the demanding regimen of everyday life—predispose people in such groups to respond to the whims of their leaders, whatever fanatic and zealous directions they may take. Even so, given the widespread occurrence of other-worldly sects, the other-worldly features of Jonestown are not in themselves sufficient to explain the bizarre fate of its participants. If we are to understand the unique turn of events at Jonestown, we must look to certain distinctive features of People's Temple—things that make it unusual among other-worldly sects—and we must try to comprehend the subjective meanings of these features for various of Jonestown's participants.

Persecution at Jonestown

If People's Temple was distinctive among other-worldly sects, it is so for two reasons: First, the group was far more thoroughly racially integrated than any other such group today. Second, People's Temple was distinctively protocommunist in ideology. Both of these conditions, together with certain personal fears of Jim Jones (in combination perhaps with organic disorders and assorted drugs), converged in his active mind to give a special twist to the apocalyptic quest of his flock. Let us consider these matters in turn.

In People's Temple, Jim Jones had consistently sought to transcend racism in peace rather than in struggle. The origins of this approach, like most of Jones's early life, are by now shrouded in myth. But it is clear that Jones was committed to racial harmony in his Indiana ministry. In the 1950s, his formation of an interracial congregation met with much resistance in Indianapolis, and this persecution was one impetus for the exodus to California (*Time* 12/4/78:22; Kilduff and Javers 1978:16–17, 19–20, 25). There is room for debate on how far Jones's operation actually went toward racial equality, or to what degree it simply perpetuated racism, albeit in a racially harmonious microcosm (Kilduff and Javers 1978:86–87; Krause 1978:41). But People's Temple fostered greater racial equality and harmony than that of the society-at-large; in this respect it has few parallels in present-day communal groups, much less in mainstream religious congregations.[4] The significance of this interracial communal lifestyle for both blacks and whites in social activities cannot easily be assayed, but one view of it is captured in a letter from a twenty-year-old Jonestown girl: she wrote to her mother in Evansville, Indiana, that she could "walk down the street now without the fear of having little old white ladies call me nigger" (*Louisville Courier-Journal* 12/23/78:B1).

Coupled with the commitment to racial integration, and again in contrast with most other-worldly sects, People's Temple moved strongly toward ideological communism. Most other-worldly sects practice religiously inspired communism—the "clerical" or "Christian" socialism that Marx and Engels (1959:31) railed against. But to date few, if any, have flirted with the likes of Marx, Lenin, and Stalin. By contrast, it has become clear that, whatever the contradictions other socialists point to between socialism and Jones's messianism (Moberg 1978), Jones and his staff considered themselves socialists. In his column "Perspectives from Guyana," Jones (1978:208) maintained, "neither my colleagues nor I are any longer caught up in the opiate of religion. . . . " Though the practice of the group prior to the mass murder/suicide was not based on any doctrinaire Marxism, at least some of the recruits to the group were young radical intellectuals, and one of the group's members, Richard Tropp, gave evening classes on radical political theory (*San Francisco Examiner* 12/8/78:1). In short, radical socialist currents were unmistakably present in the group.

Whether People's Temple was religious in any conventional sense of the term is perhaps more questionable. True, all utopian communal groups are religious in that they draw together true believers who seek to live out a heretical or heterodox interpretation of the meaningfulness of social existence. In this sense, People's Temple was a religious group, just as Frederick Engels (1964a, 1964b) observed that socialist sects of the nineteenth century paralleled the character of primitive Christian and Reformation sects. Clearly, Jones was more self-consciously religious than the socialist sects were. Though he preached atheism, and did not believe in a God who answers prayer, he did believe in reincarnation; a surviving resident of Jonestown remembers him saying, "Our religion is this: your highest service to God is service to your fellow man." On the other hand, it seems that the outward manifestations of conventional religious activity—revivals, sermons, faith healings—were, at least in Jones's view, devices calculated to draw people into an organization that was something quite unconventional. It is a telling point in this regard that Jones ceased the practice of faith healings and cut off other religious activities once he moved to Jonestown. Jones's wife Marceline once noted that he considered himself a Marxist who "used religion to try to get some people out of the opiate of religion." In a remarkable off-the-cuff interview with Richard and Harriet Tropp—the two Jonestown residents who were writing a book about People's Temple—Jones reflected on the early years of his ministry, claiming, "What a hell of a battle that (integration) was—I thought 'I'll never make a revolution, I can't even get those f--ers [sic] to integrate, much less get them to any communist philosophy'" (*San Francisco Examiner* 12/8/78: 16). In the same interview, Jones intimated that he had been a member of the Communist Party of the United States in the early 1950s. In view of Jones's Nixonesque concern for his place in history, it is possible that his hindsight, even in talking with sympathetic biographers, was not in agreement with his original motives. In the interview with the Tropps, Jones hinted that the entire development of People's Temple, down to the Jonestown Agricultural Project, derived from his communist beliefs. This interview and Marceline Jones's comment give strong evidence of an early communist orientation in Jones. Whenever this orientation originated, the move to Jonestown was in part predicated on it. The socialist government of Guyana was generally committed to supporting socialists seeking refuge from capitalist societies, and apparently thought Jones's flexible brand of Marxism would fit well in the country's political matrix. By 1973, when negotiations with Guyana about an agricultural project were initiated, Jones and his aides were professing identification with the world-historical communist movement.

The convergence of racial integration and crude communism gave a distinctly political character to what in many other respects was an other-worldly religious sect. The injection of radical politics gave a heightened sense of persecution to the Jonestown Agricultural Project. Jones himself seems both to have fed this heightened sense of persecution to his followers and to have been devoured by it himself. He seems to have manipulated fears among his followers by controlling information and spreading false rumors about news events in the United States (Moberg 1978:14). With actual knowledge of certain adversaries and fed by his own premonitions, Jones spread predictions among his followers, thereby heightening their dedication. In the process, Jones disenchanted a few, who became Judas Iscariots, in time bringing the forces of legitimated external authority to "persecute" Jones and his true believers in their jungle theocracy.

The persecution complex is a characteristic of other-worldly sects. It is naturally engendered by a radical separation from the world of society-at-large. An apocalyptic mission develops in such a way that persecution from the world left behind is taken as a sign of the sanctity of the group's chosen path of salvation. Though racial and political persecution are not usually among the themes of other-worldly persecution, they do not totally break the other-worldly way of interpreting experience. But the heightened sense of persecution at Jonestown did exacerbate the disconnection from society-at-large which is the signature of other-worldly sects.

Most blacks in the United States experience persecution; if Jones gave his black followers some relief from a ghetto existence (as many seem to have felt he did), he also made a point of reminding these blacks that persecution still awaited them back in the ghettos and rural areas of the United States. In the California years, for example, People's Temple would stage mock lynchings of blacks by the Ku Klux Klan as a form of political theater (Krause 1978:56). And according to Deborah Blakey (in Krause 1978:188), Jones "convinced black Temple members that if they did not follow him to Guyana, they would be put into concentration camps and killed."

Similarly, white socialist intellectuals could easily develop paranoia about their activities; as any participant in the New Left movement of the 1960s and early 1970s knows, paranoia was a sort of badge of honor to some people. Jones fed this sort of paranoia by telling whites that the CIA listed them as enemies of the state (Blakey, in Krause 1978:188).

Jones probably impressed persecution upon his followers to increase their allegiance to him. But Jones himself was caught up in a web of persecution and betrayal. The falling out between Jones and Grace and Tim Stoen seems central here. In conjunction with the imminent appearance of negative news articles, the fight over custody of John Victor Stoen—Grace's son whom both Jones and Tim Stoen claimed to have fathered—triggered Jones's July 1977 decision to remove himself from the San Francisco Temple to Guyana (Krause 1978:57).[5]

We may never know what happened between the Stoens and Jones. According to Terri Buford, a former Jonestown insider, Tim Stoen left People's Temple shortly after it became known that in the 1960s he had gone on a Rotary-sponsored speaking tour denouncing communism (*New York Times* 1/1/79:35). Both sides have accused the other of being the progenitors of violence in People's Temple (*San Francisco Examiner* 12/6/78:1; *Louisville Courier-Journal* 12/22/78:5; Blakey, in Krause 1978:189). To reporters who accompanied Congressman Ryan, Jones charged that the Stoen couple had been government agents and provocateurs who had advocated bombing, burning, and terrorism (*San Francisco Examiner* 12/3/78:14). This possibility could have been regarded as quite plausible by Jones and his staff, for they possessed documents about alleged similar FBI moves against the Weather Underground and the Church of Scientology (*New York Times* 1/6/79:16; *Columbia (Mo.) Tribune* 1/6/79:6). The struggle between Jones and the Stoens thus could easily have personified to Jones the quintessence of a conspiracy against him and his work. It certainly intensified negative media attention on the Temple.

For all his attempts to garner favor from the press, Jones failed in the crucial instance: the San Francisco investigative reporters gave a good deal of play to horror stories about People's Temple and Jones's custody battle. Jones may well have been correct in his suspicion that he was not being treated fairly in the press. After the mass murder/suicide, the managing editor of the *San Francisco Examiner* proudly asserted in a letter to the *Wall Street Journal* (1/15/79:21) that his paper had not been "morally neutral" in its coverage of People's Temple.

The published horror stories were based on the allegations by defectors, the Stoens and Deborah Blakey foremost among them. We do not know how true, widespread, exaggerated, or isolated the reported incidents were. Certainly they were generalized in the press to the point of creating an image of Jones as a total ogre. The defectors also initiated legal proceedings against the Temple. And the news articles began to stir the interest of government authorities in the operation. These developments were not lost on Jones. The custody battle with the Stoens seems to have precipitated Jones's mass suicide threat to the Guyanese government (Blakey, in Krause 1978:190). Not coincidentally, according to Jim Jones's only natural son, Stephen, at this point the first "white night" drills for mass suicide were held (Stephen Jones connects these events with the appearance of several negative news articles) (*San Francisco Examiner* 12/17/78:5).

With these sorts of events in mind, one can easily see how Jones came to feel betrayed by the Stoens and the other defectors, how he felt persecuted by those who appeared to side with the defectors—the press and the government foremost among them. In September 1978 Jones went so far as to retain well-known conspiracy theorist and lawyer Mark Lane to investigate the possibility of a plot against People's Temple. In the days immediately after he was retained by Jones, Mark Lane (perhaps self-servingly) reported in a memorandum to Jones that "even a cursory examination" of the available evidence "reveals that there has been a coordinated campaign to destroy the People's Temple and to impugn the reputation of its leader" (*New York Times* 2/4/79:1, 42). Those involved were said to include the United States Customs Bureau, the Federal Communications Commission, the Central Intelligence Agency, the Federal Bureau of Investigation, and the Internal Revenue Service. Lane's assertions probably had little basis in fact: though several of the named agencies independently had looked into certain Temple activities, none of them had taken any direct action against the Temple, even though they may have had some cause for doing sò. The actual state of affairs notwithstanding, Lane's assertions as a widely touted theorist of conspiracies substantiated Jones's sense of persecution.

The sense of persecution that gradually developed in People's Temple from its beginning and increased markedly at Jonestown must have come to a head with the visit there of Congressman Leo Ryan. The State Department has revealed that Jones had agreed to a visit by Ryan, but withdrew permission when it became known that a contingent of concerned relatives as well as certain members of the press would accompany Ryan to Guyana (*San Francisco Examiner* 12/16/78:1). Among the concerned relatives who came with Ryan was the Stoen couple; in fact, Tim Stoen was known as a leader of the concerned relatives (Krause 1978:4; *New York Times* 1/1/79:35). Reporters with Ryan included two from the *San Francisco Chronicle*, a paper that had already pursued investigative reporting on People's Temple, as well as Gordon Lindsay, an independent newsman who had written a negative story on People's Temple intended to be (but never actually) published in the *National Enquirer* (Krause 1978:40). This entourage could hardly have been regarded as objective or unbiased by Jones and his closer supporters. Instead, it identified Ryan with the forces of persecution, already personified in the Stoens and the investigative press, and it set the stage for the mass murder/ suicide that had already been threatened in conjunction with the custody fight.

The ways in which People's Temple came to differ from more typical other-worldly sects are a matter more of degree than of kind, but the differences together profoundly altered the character of the scene of Jonestown. Though the avowed radicalism, the interracial living, and the defector-media-government "conspiracy" are structurally distinct from one another, Jones drew them together into a tableau of conspiracy that was intended to increase his followers' attachment to him, but ironically brought his legitimacy as a messiah into question, undermined the other-worldly possibilities of the People's Temple Agricultural Project, and placed the group in history by reference to the apocalypse.

Jonestown and the Apocalypse

Other-worldly sects by their very nature are permeated with apocalyptic ideas. The sense of a decaying social order is personally experienced by the religious seeker in a life held to be untenable, meaningless, or both. This interpretation of life is collectively affirmed and transcended in other-worldly sects, which purport to offer heaven-on-earth, beyond the effects of the apocalypse. Such sects promise the grace of a theocracy in which followers can sometimes really escape the living hell of society-at-large. Many of Jones's followers seem to have joined People's Temple with this in mind. But the predominance of blacks and the radical ideology of the Temple, together with the persistent struggle against the defectors and against the alleged conspiracy that formed around them in the minds of the faithful, all gave the true believers' sense of persecution a more immediate and pressing rather than other-worldly cast. Jones used these elements to heighten his followers' sense of persecution from the outside, but this device itself may have drawn into question the ability of the supposed charismatic leader to provide an other-worldly sanctuary.

By the middle of October, a month before Congressman Ryan's trip in November 1978, Jones's position of pre-eminent leadership was beginning to be questioned not only by disappointed religious followers but also by others more important—by previously devoted seniors who were growing tired of the ceaseless meetings and the increasingly untenable character of everyday life and by key virtuosi of collective life who felt Jones was responsible for their growing inability to deal successfully with Jonestown's material operations.

Once those who were dissatisfied circumvented Jones's intelligence network of informers and began to establish solidarity with one another, the conspiracy can truly be said to have taken hold within Jonestown itself. Jones was like the revolutionary millenarians described by Norman Cohn (1970) and Gunther Lewy (1974). Rather than successfully proclaiming the postapocalyptic sanctuary, Jones was reduced to denouncing the web of "evil" powers in which he was ensnared and to searching with chiliastic expectation for the imminent cataclysm that would announce the beginning of the kingdom of righteousness.

Usually, other-worldly sects have a sense of the eternal about them: having escaped this world, they adopt the temporal trappings of heaven, which amounts to a timeless bliss of immortality (Hall 1978:72–79). But Jones had not really established a postapocalyptic heavenly plateau. Even if he had promised this to his followers, it was only just being built in the form of the Agricultural Project. And it was not even clear that Jonestown itself was the promised land: Jones did not entirely trust the Guyanese government and was considering seeking final asylum in Cuba or the Soviet Union. Whereas other-worldly sects typically assert that heaven is at hand, Jones could hold it out only as a future goal and one that became more and more elusive as the forces of persecution tracked him to Guyana. Thus, Jones and his followers were still within the throes of the apocalypse, still, as they conceived it, the forces of good battling against the evil and conspiratorial world that could not tolerate a living example of a racially integrated American socialist utopia.

In the struggle against evil, Jones and his true believers took on the character of a warring sect—fighting a decisive Manichean struggle with the forces of evil (Hall 1978:206–207). Such a struggle seems almost inevitable when political rather than religious themes of apocalypse are stressed, and it is clear that Jones and his staff at times acted within this militant frame of reference. For example, they maintained armed guards around the settlement, held "white night" emergency drills, and even staged mock CIA attacks on Jonestown. By doing so, they undermined the plausibility of living an other-worldly existence. The struggle of a warring sect takes place in historical time, where one action builds on another, where decisive outcomes of previous events shape future possibilities. The contradiction between this earthly struggle and the heaven-on-earth Jones (1978) would have liked to proclaim, as in "Perspectives from Guyana," gave Jonestown many of its strange juxtapositions—of heaven and hell, of suffering and bliss, of love and coercion. Perhaps even Jones himself, for all his megalomaniac ability to transcend the contradictions others saw in him (and for which they labeled him an opportunist), could not endure the struggle for his own immortality. If he were indeed a messianic incarnation of God, as he sometimes claimed, presumably Jones could have either won the struggle of the warring sect against its evil persecutors or else delivered his people to the bliss of another world.

In effect, Jones had brought his flock to the point of straddling the two sides of the apocalypse. Had he established his colony beyond the unsympathetic purview of defectors, concerned relatives, investigative reporters, and government agencies, then the other-worldly tableau perhaps could have been sustained with less repressive methods of social control. As it was, Jones and the colony experienced the three interconnected limitations of group totalism which Robert Jay Lifton (1968:129) has described with respect to the Chinese Communist revolution: diminishing conversions, inner antagonism (as of disillusioned participants) against the suffocation of individuality, and increasing penetration of the "idea-tight milieu control" by outside forces.[6] As Lifton noted, revolutionaries are engaged in a quest for immortality. Other-worldly sectarians in a way short-circuit this quest by the fiat of asserting their immortality—positing as the basis of their everyday life the timeless heavenly plateau that exists *beyond* history. But under the persistent eyes of external critics, and because Jones himself exploited such persecution to increase his social control, he could not sustain the illusion of other-worldly immortality.

On the other hand, People's Temple could not achieve the sort of political victory that would have been the goal of a warring sect. Since revolutionary war involves a struggle with an established political order in unfolding historical time, revolutionaries can attain immortality only in the wide-scale victory of the revolution over the "forces of reaction." Ironically, as Lifton pointed out, even the initial political and military victory of the revolutionary forces does not end the search for immortality: even in victory, revolution can be sustained only through diffusion of its principles and goals. But as Max Weber (1964) observed, in the long run it seems impossible to maintain the charismatic enthusiasm of revolution; more pragmatic concerns come to the fore, and as the ultimate ends of revolution are faced off against everyday life and its demands the quest for immortality fades and the immortality of the revolutionary moment is replaced by the myth of a grand revolutionary past.

People's Temple could not begin to achieve revolutionary immortality in historical time, for it could not even pretend to achieve any victory against its enemies. If it had come to a pitched battle, the Jonestown defenders—like the Symbionese Liberation Army against the Los Angeles Police Department SWAT (Strategic Weapons And Tactics) team—would have been wiped out. But People's Temple could create a kind of immortality that is really not a possibility for political revolutionaries: the members could abandon apocalyptic hell by the act of mass suicide. This would shut out the opponents of the Temple: the enemy could not be the undoing of what was already undone and there could be no retaliations against the dead. The suicide could also achieve the other-worldly salvation Jones had promised his more religious followers. Mass suicide bridged the divergent public threads of meaningful existence at Jonestown—those of political revolution and those of religious salvation. It was an awesome vehicle for a powerful statement of collective solidarity by the true believers among the people at Jonestown—that they would rather die together than have the life that was created together subjected to gradual decimation and dishonor at the hands of authorities regarded as not legitimate.

Most warring sects reach a grisly end: occasionally they achieve martyrdom, but if they lack a constituency, their extermination is used by the state as proof of its monopoly on the legitimate use of force. By comparison, revolutionary suicide is a victory. The event can be drawn upon for moral didactics, but these cannot erase the stigma that Jonestown implicitly places on the world its members left behind. Nor can the state punish the dead who are guilty, among of other things, of murdering a congressman, three newsmen, a concerned relative, and however many Jonestown residents did not willingly commit the suicide.[7] Though they paid the total price of death for their ultimate commitment, and though they achieved little except perhaps sustenance of their own collective sense of honor, still those who won this hollow victory cannot have it taken away from them. In the absence of retribution, both the government's search for living guilty and the growing widespread outcry against "cults" take on the character of scapegoating (*Washington Post* 12/16/78:3; *New York Times* 12/27/78:A23). Those most responsible are beyond the reach of the law: unable to escape the hell of their own lives by creating an other-worldly existence on earth, they instead sought their own immorality in death and left the apocalypse they unveiled to be pondered by others.

Part Two
Concepts Illuminating
the People's Temple Movement

Part Two focuses on questions of particular concern: What motivated Americans in the 1970s to join extremist cults, and how did these cults manage to radically transform the people who joined them? Chapter 4 by Zurcher addresses the question of motive by underlining the need for a stable identity. The vortex of changes during the 1970s created a "me generation," a time of panic for people desperate to know "Who am I?" Such people, according to Zurcher, fled into the arms of weight reducers, or plastic surgeons, or pop gurus, or any groups or people that provided them with a solid and simplified identity, including the cult. Zurcher's article implies that the decision to become a cultist is not well thought out, but made in a panic. Cult members themselves, naturally, would probably disagree with this view and maintain that their decision came after much soul searching.

While Chapter 4 focuses on the self of the cultist, Chapter 5 instead examines the environment of the cultist. It is a contradiction-free environment, according to Mills. But without contradictions it is difficult for individuals to maintain their personal autonomy. This difficulty partly explains the radical transformation that persons undergo when they enter a cult. Redlinger and Armour in Chapter 6 refer to this process as "changing worlds." How does the antiwar pacifist turn into the zealot killer? Gradually—according to Redlinger and Armour, who outline the conditions that make cult life compelling.

4

A Self-Concept
for Religious Violence
Louis A. Zurcher

This chapter is based on the assumption that contemporary American society is undergoing rapid social and technological changes. The changes have disrupted people's sense of identification with standard and previously stable social organization, or at least have caused people seriously to question the efficacy of those identifications. The result has in part been a decrease in social solidarity within American society, especially among such traditional institutions as work, the family, orthodox religion, and community. The tenuousness of social relations is associated with, some scholars argue causally, the emergence of the "me generation" in the 1970's. Individuals have turned inward, developed an obsessive concern with their own psyches, their own gratification, and their own personal growth.

Ralph H. Turner (1976) has reported a recent shift in people's self-concepts from institutional to impulse orientation. In other words, there has been a change, according to Turner; from primary identification with social organizations and with the kinds of external controls such identification engenders to a locus of identity centered in the person himself or herself. That locus is characterized by egotism, selfishness, narcissism, and general alienation from responsibility to society-at-large. Similarly, I have observed and reported a shift among Americans from what I call the "social self" to the "reflective self."

In this chapter I will argue that those individuals who have been thrust into reflective self-concepts by rapid social change (and thus by the erosion of familiar social self-concepts) often scurry to resolve the discomfort of identity dislocation. Some of those persons resolve the discomfort by joining highly cohesive religious cults.

Membership in such cults provides previously dislocated persons with a solid and simplified social self-concept. "Who am I? I am a member of the XYZ church, or temple, or commune, or fellowship."

Should the cult be threatened by outside elements, or should it be thought to be threatened, the use of violence by members would not be exceptional nor without sufficient precedent. The election of violence by cult members would be particularly likely if their social

selves (based in allegiance to the cult) were also linked to an "oceanic" component of self (an ideological basis for self-concept) that
espouses violence toward own person (suicide) or toward other persons (homicide) as a legitimized defense of values or lifestyles.

The characteristics of the cult-violence self-concept will be discussed in this chapter, as will the genesis of that sort of self-concept. A
two-step model for the emergence of religious violence will be presented.

At the conclusion of the chapter I will contrast the self-concept for
religious violence with what I have called the "mutable self"—a more
healthy and not destructive alternative for persons experiencing rapid
social change.

The theoretical orientation of the analysis will be social-psychological. More specifically, the analysis will be guided by the perspective
of symbolic interactionism (Blumer 1969; Meltzer, Petras, and Reynolds 1975). The discussion will also be in part drawn from my book,
The Mutable Self: A Self-Concept for Social Change (1977).

A Definition of Self-Concept

Gordon (1968:116) has argued that

> The self is not a thing: it is a complex process of continuing inter-
> pretive activity—simultaneously the person's located subjective
> stream of *consciousness* (both reflexive and nonreflexive, including
> perceiving, thinking, planning, evaluating, choosing, etc.) *and* the
> resultant accruing *structure of self-conception* (the special system of
> self-referential meaning available to the active consciousness).

Turner (1968:105) focused his definition on the *self-conception* of
self:

> The self-conception consists of a selective organization of values and
> standards, edited to form a workable anchorage for social interac-
> tion. Typically, the self-conception is a vague but vitally felt idea of
> what I am like in my best moments, of what I am striving toward
> and have some encouragement to believe I may achieve, or what I
> can do when the situation supplies incentive for unqualified efforts.
> The individual function of self-conception is to supply stable and
> workable direction to action by providing a criterion for selective
> attention to the social consequences and reflections of ego's behavior.

In this chapter I will emphasize conscious self-conception, though I
will also be interested in the underlying processes that generate the
content of self-conception as applied to religious violence.

The Evolution of Self-Concept

People in significant part define themselves according to the way they think other people perceive them. This social-psychological truism is assumed in "measures" of self-concept such as the Twenty Statements Test (TST). The TST asks each respondent to answer the question "Who Am I?" 20 times on a sheet of paper (Kuhn and McPartland 1954). One of the most instructive protocols for scoring the TST was developed by McPartland, Cumming, and Garretson (1961; see also McPartland 1965). The TST responses are assigned to one of four categories: A, B, C, or D. Each category represents a position on a continuum of self-conception references which are seemingly more or less abstracted from social structure and social interaction.

"A" statements are those by which a person identifies self as a physical entity (I am 5 feet 10 inches tall; I weigh 145 pounds). They are the most concrete of self-references and reveal only indirect inference to social interaction or to identification with social structure.

"B" statements locate the self in established statuses, usually within a social institution (I am a vice-president; I am a student). The self is shown to be enmeshed in a network of structured interactions, rules, rights, responsibilities, and expectations (Mead, 1934). Identity is thus rather externalized.

"C" statements indicate moods, attitudes, and personally characteristic ways of behaving or feeling in social settings (I am an enthusiastic person; I do not like racists). They imply evaluation, reveal self-concept to be relatively situation-free, and show only a loose identification with social structure.

"D" statements reveal self-conception to be removed from social interaction, at least in the sense of being located in institutionalized social structure. The statements are vague, nondifferentiating, and imply no attitudes, feelings, or behavior specific to the social network (I am one and whole; I am part of the cosmos).

Most TST respondents make at least one more statement (a modal response) in some one of the four categories than in the other three. Consequently, it is possible to identify self-concept types as A mode, B mode, C mode, or D mode and to classify the respondents accordingly. Descriptive labels can be assigned to the four modes. The A mode indicates a person who manifests primarily a *physical* self. The B mode indicates a person who manifests primarily a *social* self. The C mode indicates a person who manifests primarily a *reflective* self. The D mode indicates a person who manifests primarily an *oceanic* self. These categories, and the method by which they are derived, are not precise. But they do yield a framework useful for exploring the kinds

of self-concepts that might lead to or might be associated with participation in religious violence.

Most descriptions of human socialization present socialization as
beginning with some notion of a physical self, a bodily image, to
which is added a social self. The latter is shaped by social interaction,
especially by role playing. Adolescence is represented by role confusion and an unsettled relation between self and roles—chosen or
imposed. Adults generally have assembled a fairly stable set of roles
that form the foundation for a social self. However, the necessity to
choose from among a wide array of roles, to discard obsolete ones and
add new ones, and to accommodate conflict among roles can be difficult even under ordinary conditions. Challenge to an accustomed role
can be experienced as challenge to self-concept. The person is caused
to examine his or her own self-concept and to judge its appropriateness. During these times of appraisal, evaluation, and change the person manifests the reflective self. Anxiety or at least some degree of
disequilibrium is characteristic. This self-concept mode is temporary
for most people in conditions of relatively stable social structure.
They adopt a new role or modify an old one and reformulate new
social selves. Anxiety abates until the next need for an examination of
self.

Some people remain fixed in reflective selves, chronically and
unhappily discontented with social roles in general. Occasionally,
such people are labeled by others as alienated, maladjusted, or
neurotic.

Other people attempt to resolve anxiety associated with reflection
and reappraisal by in effect dissolving self-concept. They abstract
themselves away from social interaction and find what they deem true
self in another world of beliefs, ideologies, or philosophies. They are
pronouncedly oceanic selves. Those persons might be labeled by others as saints, prophets, weirdos, or odd balls.

In the last phase of the human life cycle, when people are aged or
infirm, the physical self-concept might again be dominant, urged by
the pains and failures of the body. People in this phase may successfully be urged by others to accommodate the social self of "old person" or "dying person." They may enter into a confused reflective self
or transcend their immediate social situation by emphasizing an
oceanic self.

The transitions people make among self-concept types are part of
the routine of everyday life. Which of the four self-concept modes
(physical, social, reflective, or oceanic) is most healthy or most desired
depends upon the interpretations and orientations of the observer. If,

for example, the social self is considered to be the preferred or normal self-concept, then departures into physical or oceanic self would, unless only temporary, be considered odd. Departures into reflective self would be seen primarily to have value insofar as social self is modified or improved.

But it could be argued that a self-concept based solely on external social roles would be restricting, conformist, and narrow. It would be centered on the *content* of identity and detached from the processes of identity formation (which seem to be apparent to the reflective self). The rigidity of a primarily social self might also mitigate opportunity for experiencing productive transcendent states through the oceanic self. And what if the social structures and the patterned interactions upon which the social self is based are themselves for some reason made unstable? People would be thrust into an enforced reflective self from which they might, because of being used to a solid social self, scramble for a new dominant role, any dominant role, that would seem to provide some kind of relatively permanent identity.

The Impact of Rapid Social Change

"The times," Bob Dylan urgently proclaimed in the 1960s, "they are a-changin'." Dylan was less a prophet than a keen observer; indeed the times were dramatically changing then. Rapid change continued in the 1970s. Apparently, technological and social change will accelerate throughout the next several decades. The writings of futurists rather consistently characterize twenty-first-century society in terms of impermanence, transience, emphemerality, marginality, instability, novelty, and conflict of values. According to futurists, there will be dramatic development in mechanical, electronic, chemical, and medical technology, all of which will affect the quality and diversity of lifestyles. Work and work organizations will become less driven by an ethic for material achievement and will be more influenced by considerations of personal well being and service to society. To move voluntarily from job to job within a trade or profession, or to change trade or profession several times, will become acceptable and accepted. The guarantee of minimum annual income and the implementing of shorter and variable work periods will afford people more leisure time, which they will fill with physically and psychologically stimulating experiences. The pressures of population growth (or transformation), the changes in work structure, the development of rapid and inexpensive transportation, and the trend toward renting rather than owning living spaces will escalate geographical mobility. The traditional nuclear family structure will be found wanting in the face of mobility, the changing role of women, and medical developments concerning reproduction. There will be widespread experimentation with alternative domestic units. Organizations will restructure so as to be less hierarchical, and will be oriented less toward stability and more toward change. Education will be more individual-centered, with greater emphasis upon experiential learning. The trend toward megalopolis will continue, with accompanying crowding, lack of privacy, noise, pollution, and other forms of urban pathology.

The change in technology and social organization will have a marked impact upon the values, norms, roles, and statuses that are supported by and are supporting of the older technology and social organizations. Conversely, the changes in values, norms, roles, and statuses will encourage further modifications in technology and social organization. The sum total of the changes moves American society toward what Kahn and Weiner (1967) described as an "empirical, this-worldly, secular, humanistic, pragmatic, utilitarian, epicurean, or hedonistic culture."

In the midst of this vortex of changes, the person will be challenged to organize his or her life around transience, to endure its discontinuities and disjunctions, and to withstand ego-flooding from an environment explosive with sensory stimulation. His or her personality will evolve toward greater orientation for change. Time perspective will become oriented more toward the present, interpersonal contacts will be briefer, and spontaneity of emotions will be highly valued. The person will be urged to continue cherishing freedom, but the sense of obligation or responsibility will be less affixed to social forms outside of primary contacts and more toward commitment to community as a whole. The person will be influenced to become oriented less to doing and more to being.

All of those changes are pressing on us *now*. How are we responding? Not very well, according to many observers. We are panicking, running amuck psychologically and socially. Toffler (1970) advises us that we have fallen into an unproductive condition of future shock. *Time* magazine (1977) diagnoses us as having developed chronic narcissism, a pathological preoccupation with ourselves. Rosen (1978) warns us that we have fallen prey to "psychobabble," frantically looking for gurus who would make us well again. Back (1971) suggests that we have made the self-awareness movement into a secular religion in an attempt to protect us from changes we do not understand or with which we cannot otherwise cope. Schur (1976) reports that we have fallen into an awareness trap, compulsively seeking supposedly deeper but essentially insignificant understandings of ourselves.

The social self has in the past been seen as the dominant self-concept among members of American society. Other modes generally have been taken to be quite secondary for most people, more often than not merely serving as temporary states during shifts from one form of social self to another. More recently, however, there is evidence that the reflective self is becoming dominant, at least in part because the bases for the social self are now less stable (or are perceived to be less stable) than before (Turner 1976; Spitzer and Parker 1976; Hartley 1977; Zurcher 1977). If that shift actually is becoming widespread, what does it mean for individual adjustment? Where does the person go from reflection, given that the reflective self is usually uncomfortable and tentative? To a physical self? To a new social self? To an oceanic self? Is there another alternative—the mutable self—by which the individual integrates all four modes into a purposeful and adaptive wholeness?

Problematic Personal Adaptations to Social Change

Some individual reactions to rapid social change can impose important limitations on the person. He or she actually is diminished by the coping strategy. Problematic adaptation of this kind can be seen when a person enacts one of the self-concept modes in a compulsively exaggerated manner such that other self-concept modes are inaccessible.

The Exaggerated or Exclusive Physical Self-Concept Some people escape the uncertainty of social change and the anxiety associated with forced reflection essentially by withdrawing into their physical shells. They may compulsively practice what they consider inward meditation, looking deeply within themselves—perhaps with the aid of drugs. They may develop a consuming concern with their physical appearance, seeking the perfect tan, the perfect body shape, the perfect wardrobe, or the perfect face. They may become preoccupied with physical performance, for example, diligently jogging hours and miles per week in order to tune or tame the body.

Granted, there is nothing wrong with meditation, attention to physical appearance, or a regimen of physical exercise. But when these activities are pursued to the exclusion of other endeavors, when the physical self obscures the social, reflective, and oceanic selves, the person cannot be whole.

People with rigid and compulsive physical self-concepts are prey for those who would sell them youth, beauty, health, and vitality. In other words, they are candidates for the messages advertisers advance concerning the "right" nostrums, perfumes, deodorizers, diets, appearance, and definition of well-being. Since some flaws and weaknesses can always be perceived in the body, persons with compulsive physical selves are consistently vulnerable to exploitation disguised as helpful prescription.

The Exaggerated or Exclusive Social Self-Concept Another way of escaping the anxiety associated with being dislocated from an accustomed social self is to find a new one. In itself, that is a healthy adaptive process. However, some people are so traumatized by the dislocation, as perhaps during rapid societal change, that they virtually race to the nearest available source of social identity. Having found a refuge, then if again dislocated they race to another. Such individuals can be seen among those who are chronic joiners of organizations or associations. They can never have too many memberships, or a long enough consecutive series of memberships. They feel psychologically naked without the accoutrements of belonging, such as, status and other identifying symbols or perquisites. They are exaggerated or exclusive social selves, and have cut off access to the other components of self. Fundamentally, they are opposed to social change, since their self-concepts are wholly defined by memberships that will not endure except by maintenance of the status quo. Such persons not only seriously restrict their own lives but also insist upon restricting the lives of others. Rigid social selves need consistently to validate their worth by comparing their memberships to those of others, or by comparing themselves to nonmembers (of different socioeconomic, ethnic, religious, educational, sex-role, regional, or lifestyle classes and groups). Inevitably, the comparison is one of "better or worse than me," thereby generating stereotypy, prejudice, discrimination, and other forms of invidious distinction.

Society needs members to whom belonging is important and in whom social self is functioning. The survival of a society hinges upon the commitments of its members. But rigid social selves do neither society nor themselves a service. They impede productive change (although change sometimes needs to be resisted, delayed, or avoided) in society and in themselves. They deny physical, reflective, and oceanic selves.

People with exaggerated or exclusive social self-concepts are prey for those who would sell status and, in order to do so, create artificial hierarchies. They promise to put their clients, customers, converts, colleagues, or comrades at the top of those hierarchies. People with exaggerated or exclusive social self-concepts also are prime targets for hatemongers who would enhance their status so long as they agree to demean the status of some other people.

The Exaggerated or Exclusive Reflective Self-Concept The compulsively reflective self-concept is a psychological paradox. The person attempts to escape the anxiety of change-produced uncertainty by embracing uncertainty, skepticism, and cynicism. The individual adapts a personal style of chronic reflection, evaluation, and assessment to such a degree that he or she cannot experience physical, social, and oceanic self except for judging them. Such people are alienated not only from most social structures but from their own potential wholeness. Often they are crisis personalities, rushing from one trouble to another, whether their own or someone else's. They thrive on negation and conflict, not necessarily toward some constructive purpose but rather for the sake of negation and conflict.

Societies and individuals need reflective selves. Societies need people with them so that the usefulness of its current status can be continuously assessed. Individuals need to draw upon their reflective selves in order to appraise their own development. They also thereby importantly question the personal and social benefits of their interactions with others and their memberships in societal institutions. Productive social and psychological change is not possible without the application of reflective selves. But reflection compulsively pursued as a defense, and resulting in the denial of physical, social, and oceanic components of self, contributes little to societal or individual well-being.

People with rigid reflective selves are prey to those who would sell so-called insight as if it were toothpaste. All sorts of awareness groups, encounter sessions, and instant devices for "getting in touch with yourself" are available, many of them doing nothing more for participants than perpetuating a chronically reflecting self. Those people move from one device to another, always finding yet another segment of their psyche that needs evaluation (unfortunately often by the device inventor's rather arbitrary standards).

The Exaggerated or Exclusive Oceanic Self-Concept Some people withdraw from change-generated uncertainty and the accompanying anxiety by losing themselves in notions of time, space, and existence beyond the mundane, painful, or rejected everyday life. Those notions are contained in certain theologies, philosophies, or belief systems, especially if oriented toward mystical or other-worldly phenomena. The experiences might be sought through expansive meditation or through drug use. Whatever sort of altered consciousness the person of rigid and compulsive oceanic self pursues, he or she has little or no use for physical, social, or reflective selves. Those components of self-concept are transcended, perhaps even seen as having to be denied in order to attain transcendence.

Deeply spiritual experiences are beneficial to people and to society. Transcendence can revitalize societal and individual values and can generate fresh ones. On a less lofty plane, the oceanic self provides the individual with a sense of purpose, of perspective, of reason for being. Though occasionally some humans are called upon to sacrifice other aspects of self for oceanic validations (martyrs, for example), most of us must live in this world. To do so fully, we need the transcendent experiences of our oceanic selves, but not to the exclusion of our physical, social, and reflective selves. Those also are psychological and social realities.

People with exaggerated and exclusive oceanic selves are prey for self-styled pop gurus who promise to take the novice to a world apart or beyond. When the idol is discovered to have feet of clay, the compulsive oceanic selves look for another seemingly charismatic savior. This is not to say that all gurus and saviors, or that all social movements with an oceanic orientation, are fraudulent and deceptive. It is to say that the individual with a rigid oceanic self has difficulty determining the difference between being saved and being exploited.

The Self-Concept and Religious Violence

Which of the problematic personal adaptations to social change exemplifies the self-concept process of an individual who elects to perform religious violence? It would be incorrect to assume absolute homogeneity of self-concepts among members of violence-oriented religious groups, just as it is incorrect to assume homogeneity of motivational characteristics among members of any social movement. Though there may be some commonality in identifying one's self as a member of the religious group, it is difficult to determine, except on a case-by-case basis, how deeply each member has internalized the definitions of self offered by the group. People become members for varying reasons and at different times in their life cycles and in the life cycle of the religious group. It is probably correct to assume that each group member does affiliate in order to resolve some change-related sort of uncertainty or anxiety, but those strains include many different types of personal and social problems. One recruit might have been experiencing an unhappy love affair, another a disenchantment with organized religion, another a repugnance for parental arbitrariness, another a painful sense of personal failure or rejection, another disgust with societal hypocrisy and injustice, and so on. They learn about the new religious group, usually from a friend or acquaintance although sometimes through the proselytizing efforts of strangers, and conclude that membership probably will solve their problems or the problems they perceive in society.

Given these cautions against undue simplification of convert selves, I still wish to speculate about the usefulness of the four-component model (physical, social, reflective, and oceanic) for understanding religious violence.

I will start, consistent with the arguments I presented earlier in this chapter, with the assumption that people are experiencing rapid social and technological change. Many of them, if not most, find the experience unsettling, especially insofar as it jars them from what had been relatively stable identities in relatively stable social structures. Whereas they had been primarily social selves, they now are primarily reflective selves, and are not content with that circumstance.

Some Corroborating Views

Various authors, writing specifically about the proliferation of religious groups in American society, describe the phenomenon in terms which suggest the operation of reflective self-concepts among prospective converts. Bellah (1976), for example, pointed to the role of contemporary social malaise in generating cults. Marty (1977) described the "rootless" people who were ideal candidates for cults. Barnes (1978), Ahlstrom (1978), and Wuthnow (1976), among others, have offered the experience of rapid social change as at least a significant part of the explanation for convert behavior. Glock (1964) observed what he termed "psychic deprivation" among cult recruits. The literature on cults in the 1960s and 1970s nearly always depicts cult recruits as being dislocated, alienated individuals. They are seen to be reacting to, withdrawing from, or fighting against what they perceive to be a confusing, errant, painful, or hopeless social situation. They are described as seekers of meaning, of certainty, of a place in an acceptable (to them) social institution. The language in the literature on new religious groups suggests that recruits are reflective selves and do not find that experience a happy one.

The New Religion as the Answer Why do some people choose cult membership as a means to "solve" the uncertainty and anxiety associated with having been thrust into self-reflection? If it is true that many if not most people in American society are experiencing the traumata of rapid social change, why don't they all rush to join cults?

Cults are only one option among the scores available to people who are looking for the security of new and more stable social roles upon which to frame an identity. It is likely that most people who choose the religious option do so because it is convenient (Snow 1977). They live in an area that has proximity to new religions, or they have friends who are members, or they have had previous membership in organizations related to the religions or from which the religions were derived by schism. Had the opportunistic factors been different, the convert might have found comfortable social roles in such alternatives as a political social movement, or an activist civic group, or a secret society, or a secular commune. It is important to acknowledge that the choice to join a new religion in order to embrace a new social self manifests a role-selection process not different from any other role selection. The person who elects to become a convert in order to allay anxiety and to gain a sense of stability is essentially acting in the same manner as the person who elects to become a Rotarian for those reasons. The implications of the role choice may be dramatically different, but the selection process is fundamentally the same, as indicated by the following diagram:

As I mentioned above, though the process of role selection might be similar in electing to become a cultist or a Rotarian, the implications of the choice can be quite different. A cult is a new religious group, characterized by its opposition to values widely accepted in its social environment. It is one of the most extreme role selections that a person searching for a stable social self can make. The conditions of membership are usually quite rigorous. They often demand total commitment to the role, the clear dominance of the cult role over other components of the member's role set, and a detachment of the person from society-at-large. The cult role also usually is associated with a guiding ideology that must be embraced categorically. The cult leaders often are charismatic and require total fealty; the rules of the cult are to be obeyed without question.

Consequently, the cultic religion demands a great deal from the member. But it gives a great deal in return. Few social groups offer so powerful a sense of member cohesion and belongingness. Few offer such a straightforward identity, albeit one that often is rigid and over-simplified. The member is expected to yield self to the cult, but in return is provided a new self, one defined by the cult.

The problem with yielding self in order to find self is that the mediating social structure can become devastatingly authoritarian. The more members depend upon cult leaders for self-definition, the more the members can be manipulated. Bellah (1976) has shown manipulation to have happened in several of the contemporary cults he studied. Lofland's (1966) classic analysis of a doomsday cult revealed the process of burgeoning authoritarianism. A vicious circle prevails. Members acquiesce to a leader in order to gain a stable social self. The leader becomes more powerful and dictates requirements intended to make the group more cohesive and the members more committed. Members oblige, and thereby further increase the power of the leader. Eventually, neither the leader nor the followers can satisfy each others' requirements, and the cult transforms—new goals, new strategies, new requirements for member commitment, or new leader.

The authoritarian character of the cultic religion generates a fragile social self for members. Though cult membership (having a powerful element of group cohesion) affords in the short run a quite clear identity, that identity is based on a rigid social self. Membership, and accordingly member self-concept, is an all-or-none proposition. "You are a member or you are not. You are with us or against us." To sustain such a self-concept demands much personal energy for denial, selective perception, and suppression of individual proclivities. It is a difficult self-concept to maintain. Cult cohesion depends to a large extent upon the maintenance of group boundaries by an us-versus-them mentality. Out-groups must be numerous and their members readily labeled as hateful, misguided, inferior, or somehow stereotypical. The out-groups at any time can use their power to destroy, neutralize, or co-opt the cult. The cult members once again find themselves in a painful condition of reflection, searching for a new social self.

A Two-Step Model of Religious Violence The progression of cult members toward violence, it can usefully be hypothesized, is characterized by two major steps. First, the recruit becomes a member; second, the recruit concludes that violence is an appropriate strategy for the cult.

Becoming a member brings with it the fragilities of a rigid social self, as I discussed above. It is likely that few people form cults for the specific and singular purpose of engaging in violent behavior against some out-group. If a cult does espouse violence, the candidate probably is at least ambivalent about its use, but learns how to justify it in terms of the cult's ideology. Still, the recruit must become a *member* first (and undergo the appropriate initiation) before becoming a violent member.

Inclination to participate in violence may be a condition for membership in cults already established as violent. The more common occurrence seems to be that a cult originally was not violent but becomes so. Recruits had initially no proclivity for violence as a strategy. Leaders may deliberately have desensitized members to violence against themselves or others by drills and rehearsals (example, the suicide drills in Jonestown). Or perhaps the leaders, caught in the vicious circle of power over and demands by members, in order to maintain their authority, finally must call for the ultimate in member commitment—violence to themselves or to others. It would not thereafter be a great behavioral leap for members who have sacrificed themselves psychologically for the group to sacrifice themselves physically—a sort of death spiral. The phenomenon of cognitive dissonance certainly would be apparent in the move toward violence (Festinger 1957; Festinger, Riecken, and Schacter 1956). Members would have defined themselves as cult members and oriented themselves toward cult leaders. They would have engaged in behaviors that validated those definitions and orientations. When the new expectation that a good member engages in violence is put forth, the odds are it would be embraced, especially if violence drills had been held or if there had been a phased desensitization to violence.

The two major steps leading to religious violence are quite complex. I suggested above that the recruit usually first becomes a cult member and then accommodates to violence as a condition of the membership in which he or she has embedded a rigid social self-concept. The agreement to be violent is another price for a seemingly consistent social self.

Members can also engage in violence if they perceive outside forces to be threatening the life of the cult. The threat can be to the cult's espoused ideology, group cohesion, or freedom to operate—any element which if removed or thwarted would weaken the basis for the cultist's social self. Defending the cult is actually defending self. If it takes violence, so be it.

Smelser's (1962) stages for the development of collective behavior are useful for understanding the complexity of the two steps toward religious violence. The stages are: structural conduciveness (it must be physically and socially possible to engage in religious violence); structural or psychological strain (within the context of conduciveness there must be some social or social-psychological disequilibrium, inconsistency, or conflict); growth and spread of a generalized belief (the strain must be articulated and its source identified and labeled); precipitating factors (an event or situation must focus the generalized belief more clearly, or give evidence that the source of the strain is correctly identified and labeled); mobilization of participants for action (events and leaders must develop and implement a course of action based on the generalized belief, action seen as able to alleviate the strain); the operation of social control (counterdeterminants to the first five stages must be activated which shape the form, direction, and intensity of the collective behavior).

The first of the two steps toward religious violence, becoming a cult member, can be outlined using the Smelser stages. It must be structurally conducive for the recruit to become a member. That is, he/she must know about the cult and have access to it. There must be some sort of strain working on the recruit which he/she would like to alleviate. The strain, for example, can be as severe as a deep antipathy for the noncult society or as seemingly minor as pressure from a friend to join. The recruit develops the generalized belief that cult membership will resolve the strain, whether it be as profound as taking action to change society or as simple as satisfying a friend's urging. A precipitating factor occurs, perhaps a sharpening social problem or a favor from the friend, which convinces the recruit that joining the cult is right and should be done now. He or she mobilizes for action and becomes a member. During this entire decision process, the constraints of social control have been minor enough to permit recruitment. The cult is not under such direct attack from hostile forces that it has become fractured or pushed so deeply underground that it is nearly impossible to join. Now a member, the individual has the opportunity to construct a pervasive social self-concept as a cultist.

The second of the two steps toward religious violence, electing the violence, can also be outlined using the Smelser stages. It must be structurally conducive for the cult to engage in violence. The members must have the tools and the potential target for violence. There must be sufficient precedent for violence in comparable situations and with comparable groups. The member must feel a severe psychological strain. Most probably it would be associated with an external threat to the cohesion of the cult, and thus to the social self of the member. He/she develops the belief (often prodded by cult leaders) that specific individuals or outside groups are responsible for the strain and ought to become cult targets for punishment or for elimination by violence. An alternative belief would be that all is lost, that the outside forces will destroy the cult, and that the members ought to eliminate themselves. This generalized belief is greatly facilitated if the cult member is in the mode of a rigid social self-concept that is complemented by an oceanic component accepting of violence (I shall elaborate upon this self-constellation below). Some precipitating factor must occur which convinces the member that the generalized belief is indeed correct. The cult *is* gravely threatened, and violent action is called for, *now*. The member mobilizes for action and engages in the violence, following the example or the urging of the cult leaders. Throughout the process of evolving toward violent action, the cult has been influenced by social-control forces in two ways, crucial but not mutually exclusive: (1) the agents of social control had created, exacerbated, or been blamed for the strains felt by the cult members; (2) the agents of social control could not prevent the violent action by the cult members.

Smelser intended his formulation of the stages of development to be used for the analysis of collective behavior, not of individual behavior as I have used it here. It would have been more appropriate, from Smelser's standpoint, to use the stages to understand a specific collective episode: for example, the mass suicide at Jonestown or the violence against the United States embassy personnel in Iran. However, the application of the stages to the two-step model for religious violence, though the model is phrased in terms of the individual member, is nonetheless helpful. It reveals the complexity of the evolution of religious violence. The cult is clearly shown to be part of a social network, the character of which can determine the feasibility or likelihood of violence. Strain experienced by the cult members does not result in religious violence unless other important conditions are met (unless the other Smelser stages are operational). The types of cult members, though I have made much of them in this chapter, have meaning for action only in the broader social context. For example, the cult member with a rigid social self-concept will not engage in violence unless he/she experiences the appropriate strain and develops the appropriate belief about how to handle it. Leaders and social control agents, as well as specific precipitating events (contrived or accidental), affect the strain and the kind of action taken. Self-concept is only one piece of the puzzle, albeit an important one that not only is influenced by but also influences other factors leading to religious violence.

The Rigid Social-Oceanic Self The kind of self-concept ideally suited for religious violence, and which ideally emerges from the two-step model of religious violence, can be characterized as a hybrid of social and oceanic rigidity. The cult member's identity is wholly embedded in the cult and is dictated by the normative prescriptions pronounced by the cult leaders. The greatest fear the member has, and therefore the most powerful device for social control of the member, is that he or she might be ostracized by leaders and other members. The loss of membership means loss of self.

The rigid social self of the cult member rests in a belief system that holds membership somehow to be sacred insofar as it is total, complete, and exclusive. Members are deemed to have been specially inspired, chosen, or identified by cult leaders who represent a supernatural force or a transcendent ideology. Both the social self of membership and the oceanic self reflecting the belief system are accepted rigidly and without question as right, righteous, and rewarding. The rigid social self and rigid oceanic self interact and reinforce each other, reciprocally maintaining the rigidity. Categorical membership needs a categorical belief to support it. A categorical belief needs the protection of a categorical membership to sustain it. The reflective self is absent or minimized—evaluation of the member role and the belief system is neither proper nor done. When justification for violence is among the beliefs, the physical self is absent or minimized. Personal safety is eschewed. The member who is harmed when engaged in violence for the sake of the cult, or who suffers death for its cause, is blessed. Violence against others is the expectation of an angry god, the requisite for cult survival, the duty to ancestors or predecessors, the ultimate pledge to cult leaders and followers, the fullest manifestation of dedication to ideology, or the consummate victory over one's tormentors.

The Mutable Self The mutable self is a self-concept that affords the individual: (1) full recognition of the four components of self (physical, social, reflective, and oceanic) and, consequently, an openness to the widest possible experience of self; (2) an awareness of the interaction among the four components of self in varying social settings; (3) an awareness of the process experiences as well as the content changes within and among the four components of self in varying social settings; (4) the flexibility to move among the four components, at will, with purpose, naturally, without rigid fixation on any component; (5) the ability to integrate the four components and to accept the productive dialectic among them, a dialectic that provokes personal growth; (6) understanding, tolerance, acceptance of, and empathy with other human beings who manifest mutable selves and with those who do not; (7) the ability to accommodate, control, or resist rapid sociocultural change and its concomitants, without need to affect defensive stances in, or denial of, any of the four components of self (Zurcher 1977:34-35).

The mutable self is an alternative response to the dislocations of identity engendered by rapid social change. Rather than reacting to change by rigidly adopting one of the components of self (or a hybrid rigidity of two of them), the person draws upon and perhaps even develops all four components. Such a person would be unlikely to join a cult out of a compulsive need for membership. The operation of the reflective self, allowing the individual to assess his or her own membership in any social organization, supports a greater sense of autonomy. The mutable self does not depend upon any one social source of identity. The oceanic component of the mutable self can be quite profoundly representative of a philosophy, theology, or other belief system, but is open to evaluation and modification. This is not to say that the person with a mutable self does not sometimes reject aspects of society-at-large, and with vehemence like that of a cultist acting to change, eliminate, neutralize, or escape those aspects. The mutable self can pursue those efforts without having to become rigidly wedded to an exclusionary membership or ideology and without having to yield autonomy.

It is possible, but it is not likely, for a person with a mutable self to engage in violence. Premeditated violence demands a degree of rationalization that would be difficult for someone whose views of situations or other people are modulated by all four components of self. The mutable-self person might, as any human might, precipitously act with violence when under extreme duress. If he or she were to do so, the mutability of self might be lost, at least for a time, during the period of rationalization after the act.

The more people in a rapidly changing society develop mutable selves, the fewer the people who will be candidates for membership in any kind of exclusionary group. There are better ways of dealing with the changes in society, and with the injustices in society, than those that necessitate the restriction of human capabilities.

5
Cult Extremism: The Reduction of Normative Dissonance
Edgar W. Mills, Jr.

Although holy wars, ritual sacrifice, and self-flagellation are well-known uses of violence by religious groups, the appearance of any violence in a religious context remains shocking to contemporary Americans. It is clear, however, that physical violence may indeed become a property of a religious group and be a highly probable experience for the majority of its members. In discussing this matter, let us at the beginning eliminate from consideration both isolated instances of individual violence and the situations created by a leader's sudden shift to violent behavior, since these, though often having social sources, constitute individual deviance rather than group violence. Instead, we will concentrate upon the conditions under which a group may develop so that to be a member is to have a high probability of engaging in violent behavior, even though both the individual's early socialization and the group's ethical norms and values eschew violence.

In particular, I will discuss how normative dissonance serves as a source of order and a constraint upon extreme behavior in groups, in addition to giving individuals a significant degree of moral autonomy. The reduction of normative dissonance, which interferes with the full working out of goal-directed rationality in groups, removes this constraint and reduces individual autonomy.

Beginning with a summary of recent findings on the Jonestown incident of November 1978, I will examine several converging discussions of normative dissonance that illuminate the more general phenomenon as it affects groups and organizations. At the end I will return with a further application to People's Temple.

Violence at Jonestown

A plausible account of sources of the suicide/murder debacle of People's Temple may be developed from the news reports and analyses of late 1978 as well as from more recent discussions by social scientists and other investigators.[1]

People's Temple certainly was more than anything else an extension of the beliefs, plans, and needs of its charismatic leader, Jim Jones. Conflicting tendencies in the organization, present almost from its inception, interacted with changes in Jones's own mind and leadership style and were exacerbated by events in the surrounding society to produce the desperate situation of early November 1978 in Guyana. The processes involved may be grouped under six headings.

Recruitment of Vulnerable People Jones's members came largely from three groups: blacks, the elderly, and alienated or confused young whites. Each group has experienced in the larger society some degree of discrimination and deprivation, and many responded to Jones's emphases upon social structural change and amelioration of need. People with deprivation backgrounds, even when attracted by an activist program, are probably more susceptible than most people to conspiracy interpretations and to the trapped feelings that led to Jones's retreatist strategies. Further, as Coser (1975) and others have shown, the encouragement of intellectual flexibility needed to exercise independent judgment

> is directly associated with status position. Those who occupy high-status positions are expected to use their judgment, to weigh alternatives, and to be guided in their actions by moral principles, cognitive assessment, and commitments to goals. Those who occupy low [status] positions have much less leeway and fewer options...; for them specific activities are more frequently prescribed in detail, and their relation to a goal is not always clear. (p. 252)

Coser cites evidence regarding both speech and behavior patterns to show that not only low status but traditional, less complex social structures are associated with low autonomy and high behavioral conformity. Thus the elderly and minority recruits generally came from segments of the population most vulnerable both to Jones's conspiratorial theories and to his absolutist control policies.

Isolation Increasing control over the exchange of information with the outside world, coupled with suppression of internal dissent, created prolonged intellectual isolation of People's Temple members. Melton (1979:15) regards this isolation as necessary for "the internal logic of a paranoid world view...to work itself to a conclusion." At the same time, especially after the move to Guyana, lack of contact with any outside sources that might have reinforced variant views or action tendencies left members entirely dependent upon the leadership group for value and norm confirmation. In this setting the elaborate resocialization processes undertaken by Jones (both with his central leadership group of 100 and with the larger membership) could proceed with little fear of contradiction and the cultural standards internalized during childhood socialization could be easily eroded.

Undermining Trust Relationships The series of moves, from Indiana to California to Guyana, along with increasing residential isolation, cut members off from extended family contact and from friendships formed prior to joining. The disruption of such external ties paralleled the fracturing of family relationships within People's Temple. Proscription of normal sexual contact between spouses, mutual observation and reporting of deviance to leaders, redirecting the sexual activity of women to Jones, separation of children from family environment, and other techniques undermined the normal family bonds that would have provided a base of independence from People's Temple and its leader.

Heightening of Frustration In addition to promoting the disruption of relationships and isolation from the outside world, Jones's policies gradually increased the frustration level within the group. Intense demands for service to the organization, all-night meetings, physical exhaustion, overcrowding of living quarters, the contrast between members' privation and Jones's privilege, anxiety about loved ones, fear of arbitrary power—all combined to heighten frustration, which in turn made aggressive behavior more likely.

Suppression of Alternatives Safety valves such as internal criticism, democratic procedures, and even voluntary departure from the group were increasingly forbidden. The powerful emphasis upon loyalty was, by the Guyana period, couched in absolutist terms which neither brooked significant deviation nor gave opportunity to influence events. With the heightening of frustration, the blocking of normal relationships, and the suppression of both voice and exit alternatives, the potential for violence grew steadily.

Legitimation of Violence Both precept and example made violent means more and more acceptable within People's Temple. Jones's feelings of persecution led to greater reliance on weapons and security measures. The resocialization and disciplinary techniques within the group became quite harsh. Moreover, both real and imagined harassment from without lent plausibility to Jones's interpretation of narrowing options and the closing noose of fascist hostility. Finally, the concept of revolution was given fresh power by the co-optation of a central Christian symbol (taking the cup together) to express a violent rejection of the persecuting world. Revolutionary suicide became acceptable not only through conceptual integration but also through repeated rehearsals that took away its shock value and added legitimacy to the act.

The probability of violence directed either outward or inward is maximized by these six groups of processes. When we are confronted with the Jonestown murder/suicides it is relatively convincing to adduce these as reasons for the tragedy. Yet we have not thereby understood the breakdown of normative order within the group which could lead ostensibly religious, humane, normal people to mass destruction.

Sometimes it helps to stand an issue on its head. Let us, instead of asking "Why violence in Jonestown?" ask the opposite question: "Why not violence in every group?" In view of the aggressive tendencies in every human being and the probability that one person's aggressiveness will excite another's, why does violence *not* break out in every group? What is it that restrains violence in most situations and whose absence or breakdown allows violent behavior to emerge in the rare instance? An account of the sources of normative order is essential to understanding how it fails under conditions such as those described above. The remainder of this chapter discusses a major source of normative order in groups and illustrates how its breakdown can create conditions in which the probability of violent action is very high.

Legitimated Inconsistency

Let us begin with another effort to turn a familiar view around. Kanter declares that in utopian communities "the problem of securing total and complete commitment is central" (1972:65). Beginning with this premise, she offers an impressive conceptual framework from which are derived six mechanisms for building commitment. Our question, however, is whether more commitment is always better. Granted that too little commitment in a group leads to its failure, is there such a thing as too much commitment? I suggest that in most groups the commitment mechanisms are damped and inhibited by the interplay of complex and partially inconsistent norms and values of the group and of its environment. Loss of this damping process leads to a kind of supercommitment in which autonomy, both in moral judgment and role behavior, is replaced by unquestioning obedience, even to participation in violence.

We exist morally within a value space whose boundaries are set by the varied and partly inconsistent values and norms of our reference orientations, including our own standards internalized through earlier socialization. Our moral decisions are made in relation to these boundaries so as to keep us always within this space legitimized by norms and values to which we give some loyalty. This is not a simple equilibrating or homeostatic process consisting of tension reduction and return to a quiet state. Rather it corresponds more to the dynamic life space described in Kurt Lewin's field theory of behavior (1936). As he points out, psychological forces are properties of the environment rather than of the person and moral forces belong to the valuative and normative environment to which each of us refers his or her own inner standards.

The most important fact about this value space is the inconsistency of the various positions that form its boundaries. That is, we accord to several normative sources some degree of legitimacy, and by balancing their credibility, using one set of values or norms to counter another, we create a measure of moral autonomy for ourselves. Individuals thus can make independent decisions without forfeiting group approval or incurring severe guilt because full agreement does not exist within our value space. Its absence is not due simply to interpersonal disagreement about values and norms but also to our own intrapersonal conflicts between normative expectations. The phenomenon of conflicting norms as a fixed characteristic of social systems has been noted by many writers, though not always as a source of autonomy in decision making. One of the most famous of these writers is Robert S. Lynd, who regarded "contradictions among assumptions" as sources of "extreme complexity, contradictoriness and insecurity" for Americans (1940:59,105). Lynd cites as conflicting assumptions of American life the following, among others:

> 5. Everyone should try to be successful. *But*: The kind of person you are is more important than how successful you are.
> 15. Children are a blessing. *But*: You should not have more children than you can afford.
> 20. No man deserves to have what he has not worked for. It demoralizes him to do so. *But*: You cannot let people starve. (1940: 60–62)

He further cites psychoanalyst Karen Horney on the same point: "These contradictions embedded in our culture are precisely the conflicts which the neurotic struggles to reconcile" (1940:102, cited from Horney 1937:289).

Although Horney thus views contrasting assumptions as harmful to individuals, Lynd comes close to pointing out the practical usefulness of such contrasting pairs:

> One [assumption] may be thrown into the scale as decisive in a given situation at one moment, and the other contrasting assumption may be invoked in the same or a different situation a few moments later. It is precisely in this matter of trying to live by contrasting rules of the game that one of the most characteristic aspects of our American culture is to be seen. (1940:59)

Both Lynd and Horney were so focused upon a rational model of decision making and upon self-consistency as essential to mental health that they did not see the utility of legitimated inconsistency for retaining personal autonomy.

A more perceptive analysis of contrasting norms and values is found in Robert K. Merton's treatment of "sociological ambivalence." One of the earliest and best examples is his discussion of the physician's role as

> a dynamic alternation of norms and counternorms...[which] call for potentially contradictory attitudes and behaviors.... This alternation of subroles *evolves* as a social device for helping people in designated statuses to cope with the contingencies they face in trying to fulfill their functions.... *Only through such structures of norms and counternorms... can the various functions of a role be effectively discharged.* (1976:58)

Here contrasting norms (of which Merton lists 21 pairs; see 1976: 67–69) are not the stuff of neurosis nor of insecurity but rather are means for preserving role effectiveness under widely varying conditions of practice. We might generalize that a measure of autonomy in the physician's role thus is rooted in legitimated normative inconsistency, and it makes possible resistance to extreme pressures by invoking contrary norms without loss of role or status.

Contrasting norms and values, however, are not only mechanisms by which role consistency and autonomy may be retained in spite of rationally contradictory behavior. They also are definers of the situation, and in particular they are dampers of commitment. If, for example, a group member holds as a supreme value the good of the group, or perhaps the divine perfection of the leader, the member's family may suffer severely unless the increasingly extreme demands from the group trigger in the member a countervalue of family welfare. This countervalue causes the member to limit his or her commitment to group or leader and to balance their demands against those of the family. By the same token, of course, commitment to the family's welfare is damped by the value placed upon the group's needs. What is important in the example is not the role conflict engendered but the opportunity, indeed the necessity, to choose between commitments that are mutually limiting yet both legitimate for group members. One retains role and status by honoring different loyalties under differing conditions.

To eliminate one side of this contrasting value set is both to decrease the ground for role autonomy and fundamentally to alter the member's commitment by removing the damper. For the group to destroy family ties and refuse legitimacy to the needs of spouse and children (or to provide for those needs in an entirely separate way) effectively releases commitment to group needs from one significant limiting countervalue. As group demands become more extreme there is less basis for refusing them. Thus (to the degree that a member accepts the redefined value structure), as commitment to group needs grows more complete and less damped by countercommitments, role autonomy declines. The consequences for the group include both the loss of a source of criticism and correction (the member with multiple loyalties) and the greater possibility of unquestioning obedience to demands for extreme behavior such as violence to self or others.

An important consequence is that agents of violence or other antisocial behavior need not actually approve their own actions to engage in them. It is sufficient that their inhibiting or damping norms or values be reduced in effectiveness. That is, the ordinary morality of individuals is sustained by their contrasting loyalties to inconsistent standards, with the consequent necessity to keep correcting their behavior whenever allegiance to one norm threatens severe violation of another (thus we refer to "healthy skepticism"). The loss of this damping effect thus releases behavior from its principal inner restraint and allows group influence to carry the individual far beyond what he or she would ordinarily approve.

The observed tendency of leaders to surround themselves with lieutenants who support the leader uncritically likewise greatly reduces the operation of contrasting value sets and leaves the leader vulnerable to extremes of behavior, which can then have dire consequences for the group.

Explanations using legitimated inconsistency are common in the social sciences. Roger Brown (1965:704–706) summarizes social psychological research on the "shift to risk" phenomenon, in which individuals become more likely to take risks after participating in group discussions of the issues. He finds that the findings cannot be explained by a theory based on a single value but rather:

> We value both risk and caution, according to the circumstances. At present we can only say that a story-problem involving risk may engage either the value on caution or the value on risk. The group decision will be more extreme than the individual decision, in the direction of the value engaged, whichever that direction may be. (705)

Broad, culturally based values thus act in opposite directions and may be engaged at different times. I am suggesting that such values receive social support external to the individual through his or her reference orientations, and that the elimination or discrediting of a varied reference set causes the individual to lack an effective range of counterbalancing values that can serve as dampers upon potentially extreme behavior.

In sociological theory, the introduction of pattern variables by Parsons and Shils (1951:76ff.) was an attempt to systematize the choices in human behavior. Heading their discussion "Dilemmas of orientation and the pattern variables," Parsons and Shils sketched a "system of choices" resembling the value space described above and defined by five continua whose poles constitute the pattern variables. Like Brown, they failed to state clearly the function of these variables in maintaining individual autonomy but the "dilemma" character of the choices suggests both their role in self-determination within the larger sociocultural system and the damping effect that each pole has upon tendencies toward its opposite.

Yet a third example suggests legitimated inconsistency as useful in managing normatively ambiguous problems. Some recent research on attitudes toward abortion (Barnartt and Harris 1980; Arney and Trescher 1976) suggests that attitudes fall empirically into two subsets that differ in the type of reason given for an abortion. The hard or physical concerns involve circumstances (mother's health endangered, probable deformed child, pregnancy due to rape) in which a woman is forced to become a mother under unfair conditions that are not her fault. The soft or social subset of attitudes consists of elective options (do not want more children, feel they cannot afford more, parents not married) in which the possibility of abortion arises not from coercive circumstances but from a rational decision not to complete what seems to have been voluntarily begun. I believe these two subsets invoke different cultural values that constitute a contrasting pair (in Merton's sense): the hard or coercive reasons refer to the value placed on freedom of action and a mother's right to decide without being forced, and the soft or elective reasons engage the value placed on personal responsibility to see through a task one has begun, regardless of preference. Abortion is thus approved or disapproved depending on which of the two values is primarily heeded. Both values are held by most Americans, with each serving to damp extreme tendencies either toward liberalism or toward unfair coercion. Both are valued, as Brown says, but "according to the circumstances."

Rationality and the Generation of Slack

Just as normative dissonance allows individuals to create autonomy for themselves by means of legitimated inconsistent behavior, so at the social-system level the presence of contrasting norms and values assures a ferment of differences that both encourages innovation and interferes with system efficiency. In moderation this dynamic protects against supercommitment and undamped tendencies to extreme behavior.

Alvin Gouldner, discussing reciprocity and autonomy in functional theory (1959), points out the need of individuals (as parts) to maintain a degree of functional autonomy from the larger system. Further, he says,

> a need of systems, which possess parts having degrees of functional autonomy, is to inhibit their own tendencies to subordinate and fully specialize these parts. In short, they must inhibit their own tendencies toward "wholeness" or complete integration if they are to be stable. The system model...is not one in which the system is viewed as a "plunger" playing an all-or-none game, but as a minimax player seeking to strike a federalizing balance between totalitarian and anarchist limits. (159-160)

Later, Gouldner says:

> It is of the essence of social roles that they never demand total role involvement by the actors but only segmental and partial involvements. [The significance of] the part's involvement in multiple systems [is]...not only that such a functionally autonomous part will be refractory to system steering but that it will tend to oscillate and initiate changes. (162)

What Gouldner describes in social-system terms can be restated in the language of cultural norms and values. Multiple reference orientations ally a group member with socially legitimated values and norms that are somewhat at odds with each other, making the individual refractory to behavioral steering by a single loyalty and inducing him or her to "oscillate and initiate changes." As a result, stable groups (religious and otherwise), even those with strong orthodoxies, tend to allow degrees of lukewarmness and to develop a tolerance for what Everett Hughes called "the rhythms and cycles of birth, growth, and decline and death" (1958:21). The balance that groups thus strike between Gouldner's "totalitarian and anarchist limits" arises from members' own multiple loyalties.

It is but one step more to recognize that these indeterminacies by which individual moral autonomy and group stability are sustained are inimical to any hard-headed rationality that seeks to bring all of life under a single principle rigorously and unswervingly applied. Therefore, the value space within which an individual exercises freedom of choice, which is protected by his or her multiple reference loyalties, is constantly in danger of being reduced by leaders who aspire to total rationality, to complete devotion to a cause. Reduction of value space (and thus of moral autonomy) to a unidimensional line, in which obedience rather than decision making is called for, deprives the group of the alternative criteria by which potentially extreme forms of behavior are inhibited. Thus the larger system becomes vulnerable to mobilization of its obedient parts into violent action undamped by contrasting norms. As Kanter says, "All human groups may need to strike balances, for social life is full of such trade-offs" (1972:234).

The tension between thoroughgoing rationality and the moral autonomy of individuals is also illuminated by economist Albert Hirschman's *Exit, Voice, and Loyalty* (1970). Noting the classical economic model of perfect competition, he evokes "the image of a relentlessly taut economy" in which "society as a whole produces a comfortable... surplus, but every individual firm considered in isolation is barely getting by, so that a single false step will be its undoing. As a result, everyone is constantly made to perform at the top of his form..." Classical economic theory thus idealizes the taut economy and regards slack as fault or failure.

Yet, as Hirschman shows in some detail, slack is constantly generated both in economic and in organizational terms. Performance (judged on rational, goal-oriented grounds) is continually being undermined in a kind of social entropy. "Firms and other organizations are conceived to be permanently and randomly subject to decline and decay, that is, to a gradual loss of rationality, efficiency, and surplus-producing energy, no matter how well the institutional framework within which they function is designed" (1970:15). Hirschman's comments evoke echoes of Hughes, Gouldner, and others who find that the goal-oriented organization is difficult to maintain at full rigor and gradually evolves into a more complex system. The white heat of total commitment is replaced by softer demands that recognize both the legitimacy of individual needs and also the importance of the "cycles and turning points" of the calendar as regulators of fluctuating commitment. Like these sociologists, Hirschman finds that "slack fulfills some important, if unintended or latent, functions." It acts "like a reserve that can be called upon," offering a degree both of stability and of emergency resources to an organization which, if always taut, would be much more volatile and vulnerable to environmental changes.

Normative dissonance likewise may be seen as slack by goal-oriented leaders, since it legitimates inconsistent behavior by members. Yet it both protects the organization from extreme volatility and produces for it a level of collective wisdom not available to fully taut groups with supercommitted members.

Conclusion: The Slide toward Violence

The idea of normative dissonance has led us in several directions. At the level of the individual, the presence of contrasting sets of norms and values creates a degree of autonomy and develops skill in weighing alternatives, charting one's own course among them, and managing inner dissonance arising from multiple reference orientations. Members of groups may thus legitimately behave inconsistently, invoking differing standards at various times. Retaining some degree of commitment to contrasting norms provides a natural damper upon tendencies to extreme behavior and thus protects the individual from demands for supercommitment in any direction.

At the group level, the presence of multiple loyalties in a broad value space among members may, depending upon the leader's ideology, be perceived either as slack interfering with pursuit of group goals or as breadth and depth that members contribute to the group's wisdom in decision making. In either case the strict rationality of goal-oriented behavior is modified by slack that diverts energy and subverts efforts to rationalize commitment. Since this kind of slack is constantly being generated in an open group, drastic measures must be taken by leaders if they are to achieve a taut organization with supercommitted members. Such measures characterize totalitarian societies, thought-reform or brainwashing programs, extreme militant cults or movements, and many tightly run mission-oriented organizations. The summary of reasons for the Jonestown tragedy earlier in this paper reflects just such measures: physical and social isolation, control of information flow, undermining trust relationships, suppression of alternatives. Without them, the moral field of the group, with its natural normative dissonance, would have made impossible the legitimation and use of violence by the majority of members. These measures served to destroy the damper effect upon which member autonomy rests and so to prepare the group to slide toward violence.

I want to emphasize that the violence itself came from Jim Jones and the leadership cadre, through their use of the mounting frustration they generated among followers. The relative absence of normative dissonance within a group does not in itself produce violence— many examples exist of wholehearted and unquestioning devotion to a cause or leader that does not issue in violence. Rather, the absence of this natural damping process robs the group and its members of their principal protection against demands for supercommitment, for unquestioning obedience. Further, this happens more easily among religious cults than sects, since the latter are rooted in longstanding traditions which themselves contain normative dissonance and serve to define norms and values that effectively damp tendencies to extreme behavior. Among cults, however, the absence of a nurturing tradition within their environing society leaves their members more susceptible to the demand for total obedience to leader commands. (See Stark and Bainbridge 1979 for a useful discussion of sects and cults.)

A final comment may help to place this discussion within the larger context of theories of social behavior. I am clearly presenting yet another member of the family of dissonance or incongruence theories. Cognitive dissonance and balance theories among sociologists are familiar members of this family. The dynamic for behavior in most such discussions (and thus their explanatory power) is based on the individual's effort to *reduce* dissonance and to re-equilibrate his or her inner life to a normal or tolerable level. They are essentially homeostatic theories of behavior motivated by the attempt to reduce dissonance. While they are surely sound in part, I am proposing that individuals also learn to *value* dissonance and to cultivate it as a source of autonomy in the face of demands for conformity or commitment to group goals. Thus normative dissonance, like the role complexity of which Coser has written in similar vein (1975), offers opportunity for self-directed change and management of group loyalty precisely by sustaining the dissonance rather than reducing it. People who are unwilling or unable to tolerate such dissonance, or who are caught up in groups that destroy the social supports for multiple reference orientations, are likely to become collaborators in the reduction of their own moral freedom to reluctant obedience. While the slide toward violence is not thereby made inevitable, the way is opened for an entire group to act in ways that each individual in it would have abhorred.

6
Changing Worlds: Observations on the Processes of Resocialization and Transformations of Subjective Social Reality

Lawrence J. Redlinger and Philip K. Armour

How was Jonestown conceivable? This chapter presents an analytic framework aimed at understanding the process whereby persons abandon currently held belief systems, normative structures, and subjective realities for new or reformulated realities.

In this resocialization process, persons usually strive for some degree of consistency between past, present, and future beliefs even though such connections may appear to be quite superficial and tenuous. One reason for this striving is that resocialization (even in its total form of conversion) is never quite complete; intrusions of memory into present circumstance dictate reinterpretation of past events, but they cannot be forgotten (Berger 1963:61). Secondly, as Berger and Luckmann note:

> Typically, the transformation is subjectively apprehended as total. This, of course, is something of a misapprehension. Since subjective reality is never totally socialized, it cannot be totally transformed by social processes. At the very least, the transformed individual will have the same body and live in the same physical universe. (1967:157)

For the majority of people, social life presents innumerable opportunities to modify their lives by dropping and adding clusters of activities as well as a vocabulary of motives and a conversational format for discussing the value of such change. In the following, however, we discuss a most extreme form of resocialization from the following perspective: What are the necessary (ideal) conditions for prompting and sustaining almost total transformations of subjective social reality and personal identity?

Orienting Perspectives

We believe the ideal elements in this resocialization process are five in number. Before we discuss these, several orienting considerations must be kept in mind.

First, not all resocialization experiences contain all elements nor do organizations mandated to resocialize use all these means (Wheeler 1966). Indeed, formal organizations designed, licensed, and mandated to resocialize people may do a very poor job, and while the person may be changed it may not be in a desirable direction.

Second, a few individuals transform themselves in almost total fashion without, virtually, any aid from other human beings. Examples can be found in the histories of almost any religion: Saul of Tarsus, Joan of Arc, Joseph Smith. Yet these cases are extraordinary and usually involve the leaders of movements prior to the routinization of charisma (Weber 1947:363–374). The mass of followers do not see the light in this fashion. What we present below refers more to the mass of followers, or converts, than to leaders.

Third, cults, or organizations attempting to attract and convert (resocialize) others, attempt to control external variables that might intrude into the converting process. They do so in order to reduce uncertainty about what recruits will experience and their interpretations of that experience. However, there is a tension between isolation of recruits and members and the broadening of the movement. In order to enlarge the movement, one must continue to recruit more and more members who, at some point, are socialized not by the inner circle but by other followers. This change can and often does lead to new interpretations of the movement and to incipient counterdefinitions of the new world by virtue of the placement of the socializer and the convert in the developing hierarchy of the movement. Aside from the problems associated with enlargement of the cult or movement, virtually no movement is totally self-sufficient and thus the members must compromise and determine how they will structure their contacts and exchanges with the outside world. In the case of some movements this need has meant that members virtually go underground and adopt identities which disguise them as members.[1] Further, the outside world is interested and curious about the movement. As information about it spreads, outsiders come to scrutinize what is going on. Such scrutiny is often a crisis for the movement and obviates the movement's ability to control information given to recruits as well as that spread to outsiders in general.

Fourth, we wish to point out that the elements we discuss in the remainder of the chapter are not necessarily stages. Indeed, they can and often do occur simultaneously, varying in their sequencing and degree, are repeated, and can be continuous or one-time events. A series of small changes may move a person toward a movement or to a set of new ideas and reality, or a singular big event can change the person. And even once changed, a member of a cult or secret society can slide back and forth between old and new worlds (sometimes called sinning) until the new world firmly takes hold (and a person is lost from the old world forever). In some cases, the transformed can even leave and years later come back (e.g., Castaneda 1968:7, 1972a:7, 1972b:7).

I. The Necessity of a Plausibility Structure

For a person to accomplish resocialization, or to be resocialized, an alternative, plausible, and credible social world must be present. As Berger and Luckmann indicate:

> A "recipe" for successful alternation has to include both social and conceptual conditions, the social, of course, serving as the matrix of the conceptual. The most important social condition is the availability of an effective plausibility structure, that is, a social base serving as the "laboratory" of transformation. (1967:157)

There are four major aspects to a plausibility structure, that is, to the set of believable typifications and recurrent patterns of interactions established by means of them (Berger and Luckmann 1967:33; cf. Holzner 1972:69–84):

1. a way of interpreting events that can be made to appear superior to the person's currently employed way
2. a conversational apparatus and language that can be employed and that is different from old systems
3. a social setting that allows for the trying out of the new ways without recrimination
4. a specific set of procedures designed to generate commitment to the new ways

Together these four culminate in the person's being resocialized, "seeing" the new way as more genuine than the previous social reality. Typically, the neophyte is introduced into the new way of seeing by others who at first *imply* that such a way exists. The pathway to violence, as Zurcher states in Chapter 4, is a gradual one. The opening foray is designed to assess whether the person is a seeker and has any affinity toward the group (cf. Matza 1969).

Lofland (1966) indicates that three predisposing factors comprise the affinity of a potential convert: tension; predilection toward a religious problem-solving perspective; and religious seekership. The tension "is best characterized as a felt discrepancy between some imaginary, ideal state of affairs and the circumstances in which they actually [see] themselves"; yet such tension does not necessarily produce seeker behavior because there are a variety of ways of reducing it. Thus, to become a seeker one must have some affinity for magicoreligious or nonsecular interpretations of events. Finally, conventional rationales and religious ideologies must either not be explored or be found wanting (Lofland 1966:33–49). Thus, the person becomes an active seeker when there is some turning point in his or her life:

> The significance of these various kinds of turning points lies in their having produced an increased awareness of and desire to take some action on their problems, *combined with a new opportunity to do so.* Turning points were circumstances in which old obligations and lines of action had diminished, and new involvements had become desirable and possible. (Lofland 1966:51; emphasis in text)

The way must be revealed slowly in steps that are deemed logical. Initial assumptions must be learned first before a more comprehensive reference frame can be generated. Toward this objective the neophyte must be introduced to a new language system and specific ways of talking and responding. The apparatus must contain a systemized set of rules about how things fit, rules that can be employed on a more or less continuous basis to typify the external world and internal social reality. For example,

> In the first two weeks in Oregon, 1975, I had the feeling that the original group at that time would be going through what I called a "feeling out process." In a camp meeting the question was put before the group, "Would you be willing to bear arms for this cause?" And a little shudder goes up, so Bo covers it very quickly by saying, "We don't mean to kill; we mean to incite people to kill us. If they saw you carrying guns, then that would give them cause to bear arms against us. And it might come to that. It might take that to get us killed." (Personal communication 1979)

A new social setting that allows for trying out new ideas is a key feature that lends power to the new way. Neophytes and seekers, when trying out new ideas, must be able to do so without current or past-life significant others present. The danger lies in the neophyte not being able to sufficiently dissociate from previous life experience. In cases described by Lofland (1966) the seekers of new identities were already quite isolated; however, in other cases we believe that recruits will not be so isolated. Conditions of alienation, for example, can prompt seeker behavior; and when sects can provide positive attachments for those alienated, and a social setting in which such attachments can be rooted, they go a long way toward winning a recruit (cf. Felton 1972). Furthermore, individuals need not feel a profound searching to become neophytes to movements. They simply need not have definite life goals, or they can be drifting socially through encounters set up by the demands of the social structure within which they live (Erikson 1968:107–134, 142ff.; cf. Keniston 1960:84ff.).

By providing a plausibility structure and a setting in which to try it out that is removed from everyday entanglements, sects produce two effects. First, the person is removed from his or her other-directed identity with its encapsulating demands; this can lead to a variety of emotions from revitalization to depression. Second, such removal makes the person particularly vulnerable since he or she lacks conventional reference frames for self and other evaluations. Typically, the sect can remove the seeker from the immediate geographical area and temporally isolate him or her on a communal farm, a cooperative ranch, or other setting.[2] When the potential recruit is encouraged to and does try out the new way, the tryout occurs within the context of the new social reality and removed from old social supports. Moreover, it is positively reinforced by these new others who are almost always extremely friendly, supporting, and loving.

The fourth aspect of a plausibility structure refers to the organizational capacity to generate and sustain commitment. Ideally, this is to be exercised without overt maneuvers that can be discerned by the recruit. The neophyte is to voluntarily make greater and greater investments in the new way of life that parallel the investments made by the organization in the recruit. Kanter (1972:66) says that commitment links the "self to the requirements of social relations that are seen as self-expressive." She goes on to note that

> Commitment thus involves choice—discrimination and selection of possible courses of action. It rests on a person's awareness of excluded options, on the knowledge of the virtues of his choice over others. A person becomes increasingly committed both as more of his own internal satisfaction becomes dependent on the group, and as his chance to make other choices or pursue other options declines. (1972:70)

Commitment, of course, can vary from a temporary investment of self to a total embracing of a new identity, and can be achieved only through situational reinforcement and incremental legitimacy. By this we mean that the investment accretes over time. As resocialization agents positively reward novices for their new behavior, and as old significant others question this growing new set of influences, a gradual breakdown in old interaction matrices and reference frames arises. New "side bets" are developed that bind the neophyte to the new way. As one side bet, the guides provide a way to interpret dubious friends so that they can be seen in the "proper" context. Another set of side bets is to link eating, playing, and similar activity to the new way, specifically doubling and tripling side bets to slowly encapsulate the person in the new way and gradually shut out the old (cf. Becker 1960).

Wheeler (1966) surveys the entry procedures and finds that recruits feel their way through as agents size up recruits; some have elaborate indoctrination procedures while others leave initial learning to chance. Cults trying to attract members are not likely to leave things to chance. Ideally, procedures are formalized and coordinated. Programs should be developed precisely because commitment to organizational goals cannot be assumed, and the new way is essentially a novel and different set of procedures and vocabulary for recruits (cf. Wheeler 1966:86). Finally, formalized indoctrination procedures are designed to generate commitment from recruits; these procedures identify the recruit as a person "without knowledge" and point to the guides of the cult or movement that will impart the new knowledge. This treatment bonds the recruit to a new set of soon-to-be-significant others, and this bonding is a key stage in the development of commitment to the new social world (cf. Kanter 1972:103ff.).

II. Replication of Childhood Dependencies with New Significant Others

Letters to "Dad" (Jones) were found strewn among the dead bodies at Jonestown. They illustrate how the process of destroying and altering old subjective normative structures and replacing them with a new way is made relatively easy when the recruit can be placed into a socially and psychologically dependent state. Lofland (1966) describes such a process when examining the conversion experience of members of the DP (Divine Precepts) sect. He notes that "the development or presence of some positive, emotive, interpersonal response seems necessary to bridge the gap between first exposure to the message and coming to accept its truth" (Lofland 1966:51–52). In the case of Divine

Precepts converts, they were, in addition, often "social atoms": that is, while acquainted with outsiders, they knew no one intimately enough for that person to intervene in the conversion process—in effect, recruits had no outside significant others. If old significant others exist, it is best for the cult to attempt to isolate and alienate the neophyte from them. This step may not always be taken because the neophyte may already be a "seeker" and may have already isolated his or her self from old significant others' influence. In the case of the Lyman family, drugs were a convenient way of establishing dependencies (cf. Felton 1972). Castaneda's (1968) description of the world he was put in by Don Juan provides another example; unable to proceed by conventional rules, Carlos was thrown back on rituals and procedures known only to Don Juan. Events became reinterpreted, and Carlos became extremely dependent upon Don Juan. This dependency was accomplished not only through isolation from others but also by the use of mind-altering substances. In psychotherapy this development is called transference and means that affective ties and dependencies from childhood (some of which may have remained unresolved) are replicated in the new situation and feelings are transferred (Cameron 1963:752–754). Ideally, if there are dependencies that remain unresolved, the new way presented by resocialization agents should offer resolution, but in a unique way. The resolution should establish a convert independent within the cult ideological structure, but helpless without it. Obviously, the earlier in life one gets recruits, the less likely that one will have problems with transference and replication of dependencies; for this reason young children are ideal recruits.

Kanter (1972) identifies another aspect of this process: mortification. She views it as an essential technique that seeks to extract greater commitment from the inductee. She says:

> Mortification processes provide a new set of criteria for evaluating the self; they reduce all people to a common denominator and transmit the message that the self is adequate, whole, and fulfilled only when it lives up to the model offered by the community. (1972:103)

By stripping away the previous identity and normative structure, the resocialization agents seek to increase the dependence of the inductee upon the group (cf. Goffman 1961).

Finally, the maintenance of these dependencies occurs best under conditions of charismatic leadership where strong affective ties of inductees are linked to a living person who embodies the movement rather than to an abstract set of principles. As Kanter (1972:113) notes, many utopian communities that have employed resocialization mechanisms were founded by charismatic leaders: Ann Lee of the Shakers, John Humphrey Noyes of Oneida, George Rapp of Harmony, to mention just a few. Yet personal charisma as a basis for institutional commitment is notably unstable (cf. Weber 1947:358–373).

In the place of loyalty to a person a cult can attempt to create "institutionalized awe."

> It is an extension of charisma from its original source into the organization of authority and the operations of the group, but not necessarily attached to a particular office (status) or hereditary line. (Kanter 1972:113)

This institutionalized awe can provide a person with the meaning as well as the order and predictability necessary for the resocialization process. These being achieved, followed by surrendering to a charismatic leader or to institutionalized awe, a person undergoing resocialization can be more fully integrated into and committed to the group (cf. Shils 1965).

III. Embodied Models of the World

Once the neophyte is socially and psychologically dependent upon a new set of significant others, these become the embodied role models of the new social reality. In addition, these new role models perform important activities as guides to the new world that is being simultaneously acted out and revealed to the neophyte. As guides, they mediate the outside world and offer what in the context of resocialization are highly credible explanations. The explanations comprise two broad groups. One is those dealing with the new reality (its logic, myths, imagery, rituals, and the like) as it becomes known to the inductee. The second is those focused on the problem of dismantling, altering, destroying the previous normative structure of subjective reality (Berger and Luckmann 1967:157).

Expressions such as "what you were doing in your past life" become lead-ins to causal explanations of behavior within the new structure. These explanations provide a contextually more powerful way of viewing and critiquing past behavior. Coupled with the present role models (upon whom the neophyte is dependent), this whole process becomes a most potent tactic. These role models are teachers. Also, provided the sect is large enough to afford such a division of labor, the main members of the sect (groups and the like) also provide visible models. That is, the specific contents of the new reality find form in the fostered identities as they are sustained and maintained through characterizations and presentations of self of the guides and leaders. They must be "in role" or "in character" in the presence of the neophyte—the role models must (1) be in the proper setting and (2) their presentation must conform to the timetable of the organization.[3] Control of the setting obviously aids in fostering credibility because it lends to the character of the person a plausible place. As Berger and Luckmann note:

> The individual's world now finds its cognitive and affective focus in the plausibility structure in question. Socially, this means an intense concentration of all significant interaction within the group that embodies the plausibility structure and particularly upon the personnel assigned the task of resocialization. (1967:157-158)

We agree with Richardson (Chapter 2) that there are large variations in the content, ideology, message, and mission of various sects and cults,[4] but there is also a generic process that underlies the recruitment and retention of members and it is to this process we refer in this chapter. All charismatic figures or their designates must serve as guides to the new reality and represent it actually and symbolically, living and interpreting it so that the recruit will learn it and adopt it as his own (cf. Weber 1964:138-206).[5]

One can argue that conversion experiences need not take the form we are describing, but can occur with the person in isolation and by means of either an internally generated or an externally generated mystical experience (Stace 1960; cf. Brim 1968).[6] We do not disagree with the conversion-in-isolation model but we argue that for such experience to continue to change the converted's way of life there must be a social context, a community of others, willing to believe in the person's experience. Moreover, such a community may make it a point to provide the means for such experiences to occur. If the recruit has already had a conversion experience, the task of resocialization is so much the easier, but the community is essential (cf. Weber 1964: 156).

> To have a conversion experience is nothing much. The real thing is to be able to keep on taking it seriously, to retain a sense of its plausibility. *This* is where the religious community comes in. It provides the indispensable plausibility structure for the new reality. In other words, Saul may have become Paul in the aloneness of reli-

gious ecstasy, but he could *remain* Paul only in the context of the Christian community that recognized him as such and confirmed the "new being" in which he now located his identity. (Berger and Luckmann 1967:158)

Weber (1964) concurs on the social aspect of the conversion process. While he notes the fact that a new personality may be a product of divine grace, a new self can also be created by charismatic community:

> ...a religious total personality pattern may be envisaged as something which may in principle be acquired through training in goodness. Of course this training will consist of a rationalized methodical direction of the entire pattern of life, and not the accumulation of single, unrelated actions. (Weber 1964:156)

He goes on to state that "perfecting of the self is of course equivalent to a planned procedure for attaining religious consecration" (Weber 1964:456).

IV. Isolation and Segregation from the Past in a Community of the Present

The alteration and destruction of past frames of reference is made much easier if the neophyte is physically, socially, and psychologically isolated from past reference frames. This segregation is crucial during the initial stages of indoctrination since the strength of the old world is greatest at this time. Where the ratio of teachers to recruits is low, the dependency that can be developed is perhaps greater than that where recruits have a high ratio as compared to teachers (Wheeler 1966). In the latter case it is wise for the cult or sect to have a general social cause that binds the recruits to the organization irrespective of their bond to specific figures, even though such figures embody the cause. Thus the cause of racial equality bound together the people at Jonestown and also distanced them from what they viewed as a racist America.

The community of the present provides continuing validation for the identity and self of the new members through both behavior and conversation. Socializers must be sure that strangers (and persons from the recruits' past) are not allowed to converse with them until, at the very least, the new social world has set or congealed. After this has occurred, "circumspect relations with outsiders may again be entered into, although those outsiders who used to be biographically significant are still dangerous" (Berger and Luckmann 1967:159). One resource the community of the present can use is a set of rules about persons to whom one reveals his or her "true" identity. In conversation with outsiders one is to be careful and avoid confrontations that might challenge the new system. But since encounters with outsiders cannot be completely avoided, ways must be provided to neutralize and repudiate outsider views. These can be seen as therapeutic devices that keep the new reality intact and provide therapy in the event of backsliding.

The community of the present also provides the convert with a new name that signifies the new relationships of the person to the world. This name change places emphasis on the threefold nature of the conversion to and life in the new way. First, it gives the convert a new sense of identity cut off from old identities; in the extreme this can be viewed as a death of self and subsequent rebirth. Second, the new name signifies the relationship of the convert to a new set of significant others and community; it places in context role relationships, statuses, rights, and obligations. Finally, it supersedes the old community and emphasizes the legitimacy of the denial of all old commitments, investments, and debts; in this way the new community becomes the cultural reference point for all actions, its procedures the guiding rules for action. The community for its part validates the new identity and only that identity, leaving all other references out of conversation or ignoring them if they arise.

Kanter discusses this process from another perspective: de-individuating mechanisms employed by communities to fix a new identity on the recruit. She says:

> De-individuating mechanisms are strategies for removing the individual's sense of isolation, privacy, and uniqueness. They change his identity so as to anchor it in things that are communal rather than personal. (1972:110)

Among these mechanisms used by resocializing agents are communal living, eating, and sleeping arrangements. Uniforms, hair styles, and badges have also been obvious devices that attack the unique forms of adornment and seek to replace them with those of the collectivity.

While this de-individuating concept is useful, its emphasis on the breakdown of individual identities can obscure the fact that successful resocialization agents provide their charges with new identities that fit ideals favored by the cult, community, or movement. This concept also does not capture the active embracement of a new identity by the converts to these new social worlds.

Davis (1968) describes the doctrinal conversion of student nurses in a manner similar to our analysis. However, the situation he examines does not involve religious attachment, but rather a subjective change in view and ways of proceeding. Student nurses come to the school imbued with and attached to a lay imagery of nursing. Subjectively, during the course of their stay they are converted through a subjective reality change to new doctrine. According to Davis, students simulate the role they need to play, find validation, provisionally internalize the new subjective focus, and finally stabilize this internalization of their new subjective reference frame (Davis 1968:235-251; cf. Becker et al. 1961).

V. Reinterpretation, Alienation, and Fabrication of Past Events

The entire resocialization process as well as the outcome of the transformation must be legitimated. Such legitimation requires nullifying old realities, branding them as false, and alienating the neophyte from the old world; in addition, the legitimating process must include conversational ways of reinterpreting the past biography of the convert in terms consonant with the new way. Both these processes must exist for the legitimating apparatus to be successfully employed; they usually occur together interwoven in a mix of conversational validation of the new way, denial of the old way, and the alternation of past biography to place it in context:

> The old reality, as well as the collectivities and significant others that previously mediated it to the individual, must be reinterpreted *within* the legitimating apparatus of the new reality. This reinterpretation brings about a rupture in the subjective biography of the individual in terms of "B.C." "A.D.," "pre-Damascus" and "post-Damascus." Everything preceding the alternation is now apprehended as leading toward it (as an "Old Testament," so to speak, or as *praeparatio evangelii*), everything following it as flowing from its new reality. This involves a reinterpretation of past biography *in toto*, following the formula "Then I *thought*...now I *know*." (Berger and Luckmann 1967:159-169)

In addition, preconversion biography is cast into a negative, nullifying light that aids in alienating the convert from the past while

simultaneously reinterpreting it! That is, the two events are synchro-
nous. The past is seen as a life of evil—greedy, avaricious, "capitalist," or the like. The past is viewed as being one of confusion and
association with the dark side of the world (according to the legitimating apparatus of the new reality). Thus the past and present are
ripped apart from each other and the convert's biography does not
flow evenly and continuously but is ruptured along lines of good and
evil.[7]

The rupturing of events creates some problems and the necessity for
reinterpretation of the past. Data about the past must be rearranged,
particularly data about past significant others. While some events and
places can be simply forgotten, others stand out vividly in view, and
these must be altered to conform to the new vision:

> What is necessary, then, is a radical reinterpretation of the meaning
> of these past events or persons in one's biography. Since it is rela-
> tively easier to invent things that never happened than to forget
> those that actually did, the individual may fabricate and insert events
> wherever they are needed to harmonize the remembered with the
> reinterpreted past. (Berger and Luckmann 1967:160)

Such fabrication cannot be seen as the telling of lies because the
new plausibility structure with its legitimating apparatus allows for
bringing the past into line with the new way of seeing things. Thus
the person and the new community aiding him can be seen to be
doing a sincere job of reducing the dissonance between past and present. In another context, Goffman has described similar procedures as
"passing." Individuals possessing a social stigma who wish to be
viewed as normal can pass by changing biographical others and
learning (resocializing themselves) the normal point of view. The
passer must always be attentive to the possibility of being discredited
or found out as a passer; one way of handling this risk is to leave old
biographical others behind and assume, with a new identity, a new
biography and set of friends (Goffman 1963:73–91; cf. 1961). As Berger
and Luckmann (1967) note, old significant others often do not wish to
be seen in a new light and have their relationship to the convert
recast. Instead, they resist attempts to be seen as part of one's misguided past. "This is the reason prophets typically fare badly in their
hometowns, and it is in this context that one may understand Jesus's
statement that his followers must leave behind them their fathers and
mothers" (Berger and Luckmann 1967:161).

Concluding Comment

In this chapter we are describing the ideal-typical conditions of the generic processes that pervade socialization and resocialization. We realize that empirical case studies of specific movements engaging in active resocialization will reveal deviations from the model we have explicated herein. Specific studies of such movements reveal their ability to develop unique solutions to the problems of resocialization (Zablocki 1971:70ff.; Carden 1969; Felton 1972).

We have also been drawing our examples from the extraordinary movements, cults, sects, and the like, and this emphasis upon the deviant social phenomenon may mislead the reader for the following reason: this conceptualization of the stages of resocialization is not only useful for the examination of the extraordinary but also helpful in describing and explaining the processes of resocialization employed by business corporations, the military, traditional religious orders, and some professions and crafts.

For example, many corporate employers attempt to use some of these processes to gradually (or sometimes not so gradually) and subtly (and sometimes not so subtly) encapsulate their employees within a web of affiliations and identifications with the community. Top management becomes the cadre of employees attempting to foster an identification with the company and to promote the company view of the world as a view that should be held by all employees (Barnard 1971:215ff.; Whyte 1956:69-154). Thus cults and sects are only extreme examples of this resocialization process and their study ought to reflect the universal nature of resocialization techniques.

Further, like Perrow, we draw the reader's attention to the power of premise setting in the construction of social control in the resocialization process that can be undertaken in corporations:

> We are content to speak of socialization, or culture, or community norms, thus making it both sanitary and somehow independent of the organization. But we could just as well label premise setting as indoctrination, brainwashing, manipulation, or false consciousness. (Perrow 1979:152)

In the corporate world such premise setting is a powerful tool that can assist the agents of resocialization in their task for forging company identification among employees.

Finally, we stress the necessity of viewing cults and sects within the generic culture context and process that exist sociohistorically. The dominant view of cults as unique and extreme, as deviant and strange, obscures the common cultural elements that are shared by cults and the dominant culture that gave rise to them. These linkages are sometimes difficult to grasp and often are are threatening to the sense of normalcy of the dominant cultural realm. By revealing these elements in the career of cultists, and pointing to their commonality with the usual processes of socialization undertaken by society, we hope that we have made a contribution to the understanding of the world of deviant social experiences as well as the world of normal social life.

Part Three
Understanding the Reactions to Jonestown

Parts One and Two have examined violent cults and the people in them. But the general public is also vitally affected by religious violence. How should we respond to it, what can we do about it, what can we do to prevent it? In the 1970s the most visible response to the cult phenomenon was the anticult movement, the subject of Chapter 7 by Shupe and Bromley. They outline the history of the anticultists' efforts to organize themselves and to oppose cultic groups through the courts and the legislatures. The anticult movement illustrates some of the dangers of overreaction, legally by violating First Amendment rights and conceptually through simplistic notions such as brainwashing, which Robbins and Anthony consider in Chapter 8. On a more philosophic level, Erde in Chapter 9 examines our emotional response to Jonestown. Should the death of 900 people be deemed any more horrible than the death of one? And why should Americans take Jonestown as a personal tragedy? Finally, in Chapter 10 Hauerwas raises the difficult moral question of whether Jonestown should be considered "an extraordinary challenge to our moral convictions." After all, isn't every true believer expected to die for what he believes in?

7
Shaping the Public Response to Jonestown: People's Temple and the Anticult Movement

Anson D. Shupe, Jr., and David Bromley

During the late 1960s and the first years of the 1970s a number of "new" religious and quasireligious movements representing both Oriental and Judaic-Christian traditions emerged in the United States amid a more widespread revival of religiosity. These included Scientology, the Children of God, the Divine Light Mission, Transcendental Meditation, the Unification Church, and the Hare Krishna.[1] Almost simultaneously a parallel countermovement, which we shall refer to as the anticult movement (hereinafter ACM), arose in direct opposition to these new religious phenomena. Since, as we shall show, the Unification Church became regarded as the archetypical cult and the most potentially dangerous and exploitive of the new religious movements, it thereby became the focal point of ACM efforts. Public awareness of the ACM grew largely out of its sensational and well-publicized tactic of coercive deprogramming. As we shall demonstrate, the ACM achieved only moderate success during most of the 1970s in its professed goal of discrediting and eradicating those groups it defined as "cults."[2] In fact, by 1978 the ACM was clearly foundering despite repeated attempts at centralization and reorganization. The tragic events surrounding Jonestown in November of that year reinvigorated the ACM's campaign, at least for a time, and both revitalized its membership and boosted its credibility in the larger society. Indeed, we shall argue that Jonestown constituted a potent symbolic event that served as a catalyst in its broader attack on all of the controversial new religious movements.

The Development of the ACM

Organization The anticult movement in the United States began in 1971 out of the experiences of individual families whose young adult offspring joined the Children of God, a fundamentalist sect in the larger Jesus Movement. The group's uncompromising ideology, its radically communal lifestyle, and the subsequent intense commitment generated in its members alarmed parents who often tried unsuccessfully to dissuade their children from remaining in the Children of God. In the process of expressing grievances to public officials and media reporters, often charging outright kidnaping or psychological manipulation by the Children of God, individual parents and relatives gradually became aware of others around the country who shared their concerned sentiments and who recounted similar stories. Establishing contacts with one another, they developed a network of communication that coalesced in 1972 into the first major ACM organization: the Parents Committee to Free Our Sons and Daughters from the Children of God (FREECOG). Two years later, after some trial and error, FREECOG expanded its concerns to other marginal religions besides the Children of God, such as the Unification Church and the Hare Krishna sect, as it grew into a more sophisticated organization on the west coast named the Citizens Freedom Foundation.

Elsewhere we have described in detail the history and organizational development of the ACM (see Shupe and Bromley 1980, 1979; Bromley and Shupe 1979; Shupe, Spielmann, and Stigall 1977a, 1977b). For the sake of brevity its growth and expansion can be summarized as a series of repeated attempts by regional citizens' groups (composed almost exclusively of parents and relatives of persons in "cults") such as FREECOG and the Citizens Freedom Foundation, each of which emerged autonomously, to unite in a single effective national organization. A first major attempt at centralization in 1976 foundered due to understaffing of the central office and lack of finances. A second attempt the following year also fell through, revealing the regional factionalism and unwillingness of local groups to surrender completely their separate identities, resources, and structures. By mid-1977 the ACM took on the form in which it was to exist for the remainder of the decade: as a coalition of like-minded decentralized groups loosely coordinated by regional representatives of a tenuous anticult confederation.

Ideology The ideology developed by the ACM during the first half of the 1970s had to deal with two salient facts. First, in a statistical sense relatively few young people actually joined the controversial religious groups and consequently only a small number of families were affected by this predicament. Second, most of the young individuals involved in the cults were legally adults. Actions of parents and relatives to remove their offspring forcibly from religious groups therefore constituted at the very least abrogations of the latters' civil rights and potentially involved assault and kidnaping. Thus the ACM's ideology had to portray cults as larger than they actually were (or at least of potentially menacing size). Furthermore, the constitutional/legal implications of calling for religious repression and possibly illegal activities (specifically kidnaping) had to be legitimated. Our research (Shupe and Bromley 1980) has shown that this ideology emerged gradually sometime after anticult organizations had been in operation. In its mature mid-1970s form, the ACM's ideology could be seen to be based on four pivotal assumptions:

1. Such cults as the Unificiation Church were actually profit-making ventures run by egomanic charlatans and adopted the cloak of religion only in order to gain tax-exemption privileges and hide behind the protection of the First Amendment.

2. Those youths who became involved in these allegedly pseudoreligions did not undergo true conversion experiences but rather had fallen victims to deceptive, seductive, and/or deliberate manipulative (mind control) processes that destroyed their free will and left them submissive pawns to be exploited for the cult leaders' benefit.

3. The results of such programming were physically, mentally, and socially injurious to members as well as to American institutions such as the family, Judaic-Christian religion, and democracy.

4. Persons so programmed were unable to leave cultic groups voluntarily and were even capable of desperate violent resistance against their families; therefore the only hope for restoring them to conventional, productive lifestyles and reestablishing their personal integrity was to undo the cult programming, that is, to have them deprogrammed.

Given a belief in this purportedly irresistible power of cults to lure young men and women and to command their obedience, it was not difficult for ACM spokespersons to offer (and themselves believe) exaggerated estimates of the number of young adults involved in such groups.[3] Moreover, it was imperative for the ACM to produce such figures, not only to lend the cult problem a gravity worthy of official action but also to substantiate claims that such groups could recruit with great effectiveness. It was also imperative for the ACM to remove the conflict over young adults' religious affiliations from the context of civil liberties and First Amendment rights. By positing temporary mental incompetence (a presumed product of systematic indoctrination and/or brainwashing techniques) and an external cult control over members' lives that resembled possession (see Shupe, Spielmann, and Stigall 1977b), the movement's ideology attempted to legitimate, foremost, removal of family members from cults and, second, to harass cults in their economic enterprises and membership recruitment.

This ACM ideology was associated with two broad strategies directed against cults: deprogramming and various lobbying and public-relations activities. The former strategy involved freeing individuals from cults by tactics ranging from pastoral or family counseling to the more spectacular abductions and more or less forcible deprogrammings. The latter strategy involved attempts to shape media portrayals of the new religions and to influence a variety of other groups and institutions with the ability to invoke social control and sanctions. This two-pronged ACM strategy had achieved mixed successes by the mid-to-late 1970s. The deprogramming tactic had several consequences: (1) Enough individuals were forcibly deprogrammed to constitute a real threat to the Unification Church, (2) a number of these deprogrammed persons subsequently became outspoken participants in the ACM's brainwashing ideology, and (3) more than simply hurting morale among Unification Church members as they saw former friends now issuing scathing condemnations of their church, deprogrammings fostered a siege mentality that increased apprehensiveness and mistrust toward outsiders and even toward family members.

The lobbying and public-relations efforts also had a number of detrimental consequences for the Unification Church: (1) It was refused membership by legitimating organizations such as the New York City Council of Churches and the National Council of Churches. (2) It faced considerable difficulty in establishing chapters of its student organization on college campuses, which in turn hurt its recruitment. (3) Its seminary was denied accreditation by the New York Board of Regents. (4) Chambers of commerce and citizens' groups in communities such as Gloucester, Massachusetts, and Bayou La Batre, Louisiana, attempted to block the establishment within their communities of fishing and canning operations owned by the Unification Church. (5) Educational and religious groups developed special information packets and workshops/seminars designed to warn youth and their parents about the Unification Church and other cults. (6) Numerous municipalities passed ordinances designed to hinder its fund-raising teams. (7) By mid-1974 media coverage of the Unification Church had become overwhelmingly negative. Allegations and atrocity stories by former members were routinely and uncritically repeated in the media, and newspapers and magazines competed with one another in publishing sensational cult exposés.

While this string of victories was in certain respects impressive and did impede Unification Church development, they did not completely thwart it. The Church retained its tax-exempt status and continued to amass large sums of money; it continued to attract new members despite its negative public image and high rates of turnover; it undertook court fights to defend its right to raise funds and proselytize; deprogrammers increasingly ran the risk of jail sentences, fines, and law suits; and finally, while atrocity tales continued to be reported in the press, a lack of new revelations left the ACM with declining means of further arousing public indignation. There was even some evidence that the Unification Church might be rebounding. In addition to legal defenses that blunted the ACM's direct attacks, the extremism and heavy-handedness of deprogrammers brought the Unification Church a certain amount of sympathy. Indeed, in some instances it became identified as the underdog in this controversy and some observers began to ask if the deprogramming cure might not in fact be far worse than any alleged cult menace. Increasingly the struggle between the Unification Church and the ACM took on the look of a mortal combat between fanatical opponents, neither of which any longer had untarnished credibility. In this context editorials in newspapers across the nation began to ask whether the Moonies did not possess certain basic rights that were being abridged by their overzealous, even if well-meaning, adversaries. Consider the following brief sample of editorial titles from the late 1970s:

"Leave the Moonies Be" (1/27/77)
"Whose Rights Next?" (8/26/76)
"Religious Freedom Applies to All" (10/16/77)
"Who's Crazy Here—Moonies or Judges?" (4/13/77)
"The Right to Be Moonstruck" (4/17/77)
"Defending Your Right to be Weird in America" (3/17/77)

In sum, then, the ACM appeared to have reached its zenith by the mid-1970s and despite its accomplishments was even seeing its victories erode. Particularly when much of the ACM's strategy depended upon keeping the cult issue in general and the Unification Church in particular in the forefront of public attention, the fact that its allegations became old news caused it to lose much of its journalistic appeal. It was at this point that events at Jonestown provided the ACM with rejuvenation. These events served to rekindle and intensify public fears and apprehensions about cults. For Jonestown, as it came to be portrayed by the anticultists, raised the specter not just of persons robbed of their individuality but also and more importantly the prospect of a series of mass suicides/massacres.

People's Temple and Events in Jonestown

The Background of People's Temple In 1953 Jim Jones founded his first church, the interdenominational Christian Assembly of God and later the Indianapolis People's Temple Full Gospel Church, which was affiliated with the Disciples of Christ denomination. Jones had been a fundamentalist preacher at least since 1950, and in 1964 he was ordained as a Disciples of Christ minister. In 1965 he and more than 100 members of his Indianapolis People's Temple migrated to northern California as a result of his vision of an impending nuclear holocaust to occur in 1967. (California was apparently to be spared bombing and nuclear fallout.) In the years that followed he established churches in both Los Angeles and San Francisco while continuing to maintain his Indianapolis congregation. He attracted a large following of poor inner-city blacks as well as whites to whom his group's fundamentalist religion, liberal politics, and charitable services had great appeal. He also assiduously cultivated political influence in San Francisco. For example, he donated $4400 to twelve newspapers in 1973 as support for "defense of a free press" and contributed $6000 to the San Francisco Senior Assistance Program. San Francisco Mayor George Moscone appointed Jones to the city's Housing Authority in 1976 (Jones became chairman the following year). In 1975 Jones was named one of 100 "most outstanding" clergymen in America by one interfaith group, Humanitarian of the Year in January 1976, and recipient of the Martin Luther King, Jr., Humanitarian Award in 1977. It was during this period of aggressive expansion, in December 1973, that Jonestown was established as a foreign colony of the People's Temple in Guyana.

Jones, along with hundreds of his followers, moved to Guyana during the summer of 1977 after the controversial death of a defector and publication by *New West* magazine of an investigative article critical of the authoritarian lifestyle in People's Temple (Carroll and Bauer 1979). Jones had known beforehand that *New West* intended to publish the article but neither he nor friendly local politicians could prevent it. Soon after publication, Jones resigned from the city's Housing Authority under threat of investigation and of impending lawsuits by apostates, then took up permanent residence in Jonestown. Jonestown was meant to be a community self-sufficient and remote enough to discourage what Jones interpreted as persecution from officials and the media.

Although some families of individual members, concerned or angry with People's Temple over what was regarded as totalistic control over their relatives, banded together into a local opposition group, they were not integrated into the organization or network of communication of the national ACM. Indeed, until the Jonestown events ACM leaders had never been alert to Jones or his church. There are two salient reasons for this relative lack of controversy over the group. First, Jones maintained close ties with important civic and political leaders in San Francisco and was involved in a number of community service projects that offset negative publicity. Second, Jones was an ordained minister of the Disciples of Christ denomination. Thus the group was simply not defined as a cult, a fact that, as Barbara Hargrove (1979) observed, explained the relative lack of attention to People's Temple by social scientists of religion and other professional observers prior to its spectacular demise.[4]

The Jonestown Tragedy This chapter does not attempt to explain the causes for events at Jonestown and the dynamics of the relationship between People's Temple and the larger society. The significant fact is that People's Temple became increasingly controversial in the months following the publication of the *New West* article, the publicized death of an outspoken apostate, and lawsuits. Even though much of this controversy was reported in only the regional media, certain public officials and media representatives became increasingly disturbed about stories describing activities within the church. Jones became increasingly convinced that his People's Temple was the object of a concerted campaign of harassment by state and federal officials.

In the context of this mutually perceived hostility, in November 1978, Congressman Leo J. Ryan, his assistants, and a party of news people visited Jonestown to investigate reports. These had been directed to Ryan by disgruntled family members of Jones followers, twelve of whom were from his own congressional district, and alleged that residents of the settlement were subject to excessively authoritarian and sometimes brutal treatment and were even being held against their will. After what at the time seemed a fairly upbeat visit, with a plethora of positive testimonies by members on behalf of Jim Jones and the settlement's lifestyle, Ryan and a party that included a small number of disgruntled members made preparations to leave by private

airplane. On November 18, while they were waiting at the Port Kaituma airfield to depart, a carload of heavily armed Temple members
pulled up to the plane and in a sudden burst of gunfire killed, among
others, Ryan and well-known television reporter Don Harris. In all,
five persons died and twelve were wounded in this ambush.

Meanwhile, in Jonestown proper a macabre ritual communion
began. Convinced that their community was about to be invaded and
destroyed by the outside world, People's Temple members, under
Jones's orders and (up until the end) persistent encouragement,
assembled to participate in a collective gesture of defiance by committing suicide. In the pattern of previously rehearsed drills, members
queued up as Dr. Lawrence Schacht, the settlement physician, and
two nurses administered a flavored drink laced with cyanide, first to
infants and small children and then to adults. The extent to which
this "suicide" act was voluntary for residents has not been resolved. A
tape recording made during the actual poisonings, widely reported in
the media shortly after the tragedy, documented the chaotic din of
loud sobbings by adults, children screaming, and Jones repeatedly
pleading with parents to "die with dignity" and to "control your children." The dozen or so survivors told of armed guards ringing the
settlement's central pavilion and forcing all to drink the deadly mixture, later arranging the corpses in concentric circles and posing them
in fraternal embraces. However, whether the deaths were voluntary
suicides or not, the fact remains that when the United States Department of Defense flew approximately 200 troops to Guyana to search
the camp and rescue survivors, they made an incredible body count of
more than 900 corpses. Only a handful of members had escaped or
been overlooked.

Reaction of the ACM

It took some time for public reaction to Jonestown to emerge, owing
to the piecemeal process through which information trickled into the
hands of the media. Reports on the extent of the tragedy (even on
such basic matters as the death count) were mixed, incomplete, and
sometimes confusing. As Weincek (1979:2-3) noted, it was not until
the following Tuesday (November 21) that even the broad outlines of
the tragedy appeared in newspapers, largely dealing with background
stories on Jones and People's Temple. More descriptive articles
quickly emerged, but Weincek's survey of the media found few interpretive or analytic articles before December 1, almost two weeks later.
Weincek chronicled this sequence of reporting as:

(1) this is what we know about Jim Jones and the People's Temple; (2) this is what happened in Guyana; (3) this is what people tell us about those who belonged to the People's Temple; and (4) this is why and how such a tragedy could occur.

After the immediate deluge of media attraction to the Jonestown phenomenon had subsided, a steady flow of interpretive articles, editorials, reports, and books on the subject continued. These included: a number of books by former members of People's Temple and journalists (such as, Mills 1979; Theilmann 1979; White 1979; Krause 1978; Kilduff and Javers 1978); a United States Government staff report (U.S. Government 1979); and papers and articles by academic scholars (such as, Weincek 1979; Melton 1979).

Immediately after the tragic events at Jonestown the ACM was as much shocked as the public at large. The ACM's ideology portrayed cult leaders as egomanic, manipulative charlatans who brainwashed their followers and reduced them to a position of servile disciples or zombies. However, the thrust of the ACM's accusations against cults had been that followers were duped or coerced into providing cult leaders with wealth, power, and even sexual favors for the latters' personal aggrandizement. While there were occasional hints that such total devotion and subservience by followers might include fighting (and in this context dying) for the cult, there was no indication that individual or mass suicides had been seriously contemplated by the ACM. Soon, however, the ACM was to assimilate the events of Jonestown into its ideological world view and a few spokespersons would even claim that they had expected it. Yet even before this long-standing crusade against cults incorporated Jonestown into its ideology, the combination of Leo J. Ryan's murder and the deaths of more than 900 of the Jones followers regalvanized the ACM and increased its resolve. For some time Ryan had maintained close ties to the ACM as an outspoken critic of the cults in American society. In May 1977 he and Connecticut Congressman Robert N. Giaimo had requested the Justice Department to investigate charges of brainwashing and physical abuse in certain religious groups (a request "rebuffed" by the Justice Department on the grounds that such investigations would violate those groups' First Amendment rights—see *New York Times* 11/23/78), and Ryan had been instrumental in helping at least one ACM group (the Citizens Freedom Foundation, located in California) eventually obtain tax-exempt status as an educational foundation (personal interviews, 1978). Moreover, Ryan had been a member of the Fraser Committee (the House Subcommittee on International Organizations), which had extensively probed the role of the Unification Church in the scandal that became known as "Koreagate" (see U.S. Government 1978). He was eulogized in their publications. For example, the Citizens Freedom Foundation announced in an issue of its newsletter that it was initiating a Leo J. Ryan Memorial Fund to be "dedicated to preventing another Guyana while preserving our unalienable rights to life, liberty and the pursuit of happiness" (Citizens Freedom Foundation 1978). The Foundation's president pledged:

> Leo Ryan was our ally, friend and champion. CFF can and will continue his battle with courage and compassion for those who are unwilling victims through brainwashing by fanatical cult leaders.

Ryan's murder did more than take from the ACM his influential voice. More importantly, it provided the ACM with its first major martyr figure. In ACM members' eyes, Ryan as their spokesperson had fallen victim to a ruthless religious cult's revenge (a possible consequence of such activism which, several ACM figures confided to us, never could be completely dismissed), and the obvious sacrificial theme in his death was not overlooked. Beyond Ryan and the other victims in his investigative party, moreover, the entire population of Jonestown became transformed into a legion of misdirected martyrs who represented a tangible and dramatic referent for the most extreme claims of ACM spokespersons. The presence of more than 200 children, many preadolescents and even some infants, among the dead accentuated the image of Jones as the archetypical megalomanic cult leader about whom ACM groups had been protesting for the better part of a decade.

More significant in terms of the ACM's impact on public-opinion formation, however, was the linking of the tragic events at Jonestown to the ideology the ACM had already constructed regarding the cult menace. Jonestown both objectified the anticultists' own worst fears about the destructive potential of cults and provided a concrete referent to which they could point as evidence in their appeals to the public and to political officials. Thus by early 1979 the ACM was engaged in a vigorous campaign to reinstill general concern over cults. ACM proponents now felt vindicated by events in Jonestown and clearly adopted an I-told-you-so posture in their new aggressive campaign. They sounded the theme that the Jonestown tragedy could have been averted if government leaders had been responsive to long-standing ACM claims and less concerned with civil liberties, a theme to be repeated often during 1980 in public forums and in ACM publications. For example, one newsletter (Individual Freedom Foundation 1979a) stated:

> News of the mass murder-suicide in Guyana has shocked the entire world and especially the American people. It is now obvious that groups such as IFF have not been exaggerating in our allegations as to the severe consequences of cult involvement. The tragedy in Jonestown is concrete evidence that large groups of people can be controlled by charismatic leaders who manipulate their lives even to the point of death. As you know, our purpose has been to reveal to the public the potentially destructive activities of groups such as People's Temple and to urge our government to take the necessary steps to protect cult victims and to provide avenues for their rescue.

What in effect the ACM attempted to create was a perspective that can be termed a "Guyana complex." This perspective centered around the pre-eminent conviction that events in Guyana could, without much difficulty or extension of the imagination, be recapitulated in other groups in the United States. It was a conviction grounded in a three-step syllogism: (1) Jones, the charismatic and megalomanic leader of the People's Temple communal settlement, exercised complete control over the wills and behaviors of his members through fear and other mind-control techniques; (2) the mass suicide of more than 900 persons in Jonestown was the result of his paranoid will, not theirs; and (3) similar cult leaders in the United States with like control over their followers might, given the right provocation, order their followers to commit parallel acts of violence. This perspective was clearly articulated by Ted Patrick, the aggressive practitioner of deprogramming, in an interview published in early 1979 in *Playboy* magazine (Siegelman and Conway 1979:60). Patrick's statements summarized much of the fear of imminent disaster held by ACM members:

> *Playboy*: Do you think the potential for Guyana-type violence exists in other cults?
> *Patrick*: Unquestionably. The potential exists in the Moonies, in Krishna, in Scientology—and they are much larger and much better organized than the People's Temple.
> *Playboy*: Do you think we could have a tragedy here in this country on the scale of what happened in Guyana?
> *Patrick*: I think they're going to start happening like wildfire.
> *Playboy*: Murders and mass suicides?
> *Patrick*: Yes. Those organizations are multimillion-dollar rackets, and if Congress is forced by the public to do something, the cults are not just going to give up their paradise without a fight. . . . The

> Jonestown suicides and murders weren't anything compared with
> what's going to happen. There's going to come a time when
> *thousands* of people are going to get killed right here in the
> United States.

Although Patrick's interview made mention of numerous groups, it
was clear from the patterns in ACM rhetoric and activity that the
Unification Church had been singled out as a primary target. As early
as January 1979 a link was constructed between the Jonestown "mass
suicide" and the potential for similar extremism in the Unification
Church. In the *New West* magazine issue of that month an article
(Carroll and Bauer 1979) entitled "Suicide Training in the Moon
Cult" quoted five apostates from it, all of whom claimed to have participated in or attended lectures and discussions encouraging suicide
as a last-resort resistance tactic taught systematically by the Unification Church to cope with outsider harassment, particularly when
members were kidnaped by deprogrammers. All five had joined the
Oakland Family branch of the Unification Church operating in the
San Francisco Bay area in 1976 or thereafter. One apostate, Eve Eden,
claimed to have been a member of the "initial staff that conceived of
the suicide idea" in 1976 though she conceded that "we didn't exactly
use that word...." After Eden left, the article alleged that "instruc-
tion in suicide methods" began to be systematically given by December 1976. Apostate Virginia Mabry recounted how she had attended a
lecture at that time in the San Francisco center that contained "anat-
omy lessons on where to cut with the razor if the time came." Mabry
said that Moonies were encouraged to compete with each other in a
sort of kamikaze contest of loyalty by devising new suicide methods
and described her own contributed idea:

> I decided I would go to the bathroom where the deprogrammers
> were holding me, unscrew the light bulb, stand in the sink and stick
> my finger in the socket....

In that same article another apostate, Pat O'Shea, alleged that she
attended a 300-member meeting in the Berkeley center "where a
Moonie nurse demonstrated how to slash a wrist." Two other former
members, one of whom eventually went on a nationally televised talk
show to tell her story, also reported receiving similar instructions.
Sensational relevant excerpts from one of Moon's more hyperbolic
speeches printed in *Master Speaks*, the Church's insider collection of
Moon's sermons, were presented later in the article to establish an
affinity between Moon's calls for loyalty to the death if necessary (in

fighting communism, Satan, and so forth) and Jim Jones's commands to drink the cyanide-flavored drink. Moon had once stated:

> "Have you ever thought that you may die for the Unification Church? ... will you complain against me at the moment of death? Without me on earth everything will be nullified. So, who would you want to die, me or you?"[5]

The article went on to offer other apostates' anecdotes and intimations that suicidal violence was a definite possibility in the movement as a whole.

Thus, in early 1979 the Unification Church suddenly came to be labeled by the media as a suicide cult; pictures of Sun Myung Moon were paired with those of Jim Jones when the motives of the Jonestown participants were mulled over by experts (so billed) on television talk shows; journalists compared quotations and excerpts from speeches of the two men to imply a common paranoia; Church leaders found themselves on the defensive against reporters, politicians, and government officials who in large part were spurred by such suicide stories to renew investigations of Moon's movement. That suicide instructions were actually given in a specific locale at a specific time seems conceivable though not definitely established. That such instructions were a movement-wide or systematic feature of the Unification Church seems extremely dubious. Our own participant observation and study of the Church over a several-year period revealed no evidence of suicide training, the allegations of apostates not withstanding. Further, in our own three years of researching the ACM and being exposed to the most vitriolic accusations imaginable made against the Unification Church we never heard a single disgruntled defector breathe a word about receiving suicide instructions *before* the Jonestown tragedy occurred. Finally, even outspoken ACM leader Rabbi Maurice Davis acknowledged in the *New West* article (Carroll and Bauer 1979) that in his five years of working with Moonies, he had never heard of anyone being given specific suicide instructions. Irrespective of their accuracy, however, such reports served to anger and frighten an already unsympathetic press, a hostile countermovement, and a confused corps of public officials under pressure to do something before it would be too late.

Although, as we shall show, the ACM was successful in raising the specter of future episodes of violence comparable to Jonestown, at the same time some voices were raised against attributing a mass violence potential so simplistically to all new religious groups. On December

1, for example, two weeks after the Jonestown tragedy, President Jimmy Carter publicly resisted requests to probe cults as unconstitutional government interference, stating:

> I don't think we ought to have an overreaction because of the Jonestown tragedy by injecting government into trying to control people's religious belief and I believe we also don't need to deplore on a nationwide basis the fact that the Jonestown cult—so called, was typical of America—because it's not. (*Ft. Worth Star-Telegram* 12/1/78)

Soon after, Dean M. Kelley, a liberal Protestant theologian and civil-liberties advocate, likewise forewarned in an essay entitled "Beware 'Open Season' on Cults":

> The tragic suicides of over 900 Americans in Guyana may have even grimmer repercussions in this country if they cause people to declare "open season" on new and unconventional religious groups. (1978b)

Nevertheless, the ACM made every attempt to capitalize on the shock value and public uncertainty over Jonestown, reiterating its standard atrocity claims to the general public, to governmental officials, and to its members. Jonestown, Ryan's death, and the imminent possibility of such violence being repeated in the United States became dominant themes in anticult lobbying and public-relations efforts.

ACM Influence in the Aftermath of Jonestown

As we have already noted, before the tragedy at Jonestown the ACM had lost much of its momentum despite its sometimes effective harassment of the Unification Church. The number of substantive victories the ACM had been able to achieve was limited and some of the most important potential sanctions it sought to have imposed (for example, large scale abduction/deprogramming and revocation of the Church's tax-exempt status) proved elusive. Events at Jonestown did not significantly alter this state of affairs. Although there appears to have been an immediate but short-lived resurgence on the number of deprogrammings following Jonestown, the basic tactics of battle were unaltered (suits and countersuits; appeals to the media by both sides). Powerful institutional interests were committed to defending state monopoly on the legitimate use of force, separation of church and state, the rule of law, and preservation of constitutional rights sharply constricted the substantive sanctions that could be imposed on cults. What had changed was a growing feeling that perhaps the danger cults posed had been underestimated among a substantial segment of the public and some public officials.

Given the growing level of concern and anxiety over this previously unrecognized threat, political institutions permitted and even supported certain stronger initiatives against the cults than had been allowed previously. However, these new initiatives were symbolic rather than instrumental. The very real constraints on lines of action preferred by the ACM, coupled with a heightened motivation to act, led to a concerted effort to utilize the political institution, as the repository of public interest, to effect a public designation of morality. Specifically, what took place at the federal and state levels was a series of legislative hearings and investigations that had as their objective the elevation of ACM-supported values and the denigration of values associated with the Unification Church and other cults. From the outset there was no real hope that legislative hearings and investigations would eventuate into law. Legislators were well aware of the opposition that would be aroused once such bills were reported out of committee, of their fundamental unworkability, and of their virtually certain unconstitutionality. Thus the issue never really was one of creating law; rather, such hearings and bills served (1) to cool out ACM pressure groups to which legislators could not respond with meaningful legislation and (2) to allow government forums and personnel to be used as a means of asserting the content of public morality. In this sense such hearings and investigations constituted rituals in which the fundamental incompatibility between cult values and dominant American values was stressed. The fact that these value preferences were not and could not in fact be defended in an instrumental way was both cause for and compensated by their symbolic defense. In the following sections we shall discuss the more important of these symbolic events (see Gusfield 1963).

Federal Hearings In February 1976, Robert Dole, Republican senator from Kansas and vice president during the administration of Gerald Ford, showed sympathy for the ACM and in the latter's eyes became an ally in the mold of Leo J. Ryan by holding hearings in the Senate Building at which ACM members were given the opportunity to voice complaints about the Unification Church to various federal officials. Following the Guyana incident, Dole once again came to the forefront as he had in 1976 with public support for investigations of new religious movements and a thinly disguised suspicion of their legitimacy. In early December 1978, shortly after the first reports of the Jonestown massacre, Dole called for an examination of all cults' tax-exempt statuses. In a letter to Senator Russell B. Long, Chairman of the Senate Finance Committee, he explicitly linked this proposed investigation of cults (in particular Moon's) to Jonestown:

> The question surrounding the Jonestown incident and the continuing activity of the Unification Church require action.... The public needs protection from unscrupulous operations that flout the law for their own purposes.... The committee should review the criteria for determining if an organization is engaging in a bona fide pursuit and not a practice which undermines the laws and morals of the country. (*Dallas Times Herald* 12/2/78)

Though Senator Long did not respond, Dole quickly took a prominent role in presiding over a second major public inquiry in Washington, D.C., this time with a departure from the format of the earlier 1976 hearings. On this second occasion cult spokespersons were invited and permitted to speak.

The inquiry to consider "The Cult Phenomenon in the United States" (technically a public information meeting) was held on Monday, February 5. On late Sunday afternoon, February 4, ACM leaders conducted a special memorial service for Leo J. Ryan at the First Baptist Church (the church of President Jimmy Carter and family) in Washington. Attended by several hundred ACM members from across the country (including the Ryan family), the service featured four different clergymen as speakers, among them Rabbi Maurice Davis and Reverend George Swope of the Committee Engaged in Reuniting Families (IFF newsletter 1979b). The sacrificial meaning of Ryan's death was reinforced for participantts, as also was the irony that more than 200 children had been murdered in the International Year of the Child.

Thus regalvanized with determination, ACM representatives and supporters went to the Senate Office Building early the following morning to press their requests for government action against cults in a three-hour public forum. Before the inquiry began the large caucus room was packed from wall to wall with partisans, government officials, and media reporters as well as scheduled speakers. The audience was noisy (segments of it later loudly applauding or booing in sympathy with particular speakers) and doubtless excited by the presence of luminaries from both the Unification Church (such as President Neil Salonen) and the ACM (such as deprogrammers Ted Patrick and

Joe Alexander, Sr., and numerous prominent anticult-association activists). "Moonies" and civil-liberties advocates wore anti-Dole badges and buttons and displayed placards. Many ACM members could not find standing space or even entry into the room. According to American Family Foundation reports (for example, 1979b), more than 1000 members of the Unification Church had spent much of the previous night singing, praying, and queuing up at the entrances to the building in subzero weather.

Dole, like many of the public officials who spoke, was careful to preface his remarks with a stipulation as to the constitutional implications of his meeting, stating:

> ...this is not a hearing, not an inquisition, not a witch hunt, but an effort to try to learn something. (American Family Foundation 1979a:8)

However, individual statements quickly took on an accusatory tone. Commenting on the efforts of (among others) the Unification Church, the American Civil Liberties Union, and various conventional denominational religious leaders to discourage the holding of the meeting, Dole said:

> I think it is about time some of us in government at least took a look. We shouldn't all run the other way because of protests or because someone puts on the pressure. There has been a great deal of pressure. I can think of a couple of my colleagues who decided it was better not to show up here this morning. (AFF 1979a:20-21)

Dole went on to speak of the government's obligation to investigate accusations of tax fraud and the possibility that the government "by granting a tax exemption for certain groups, actually is subsidizing activities prohibited under our tax laws" (AFF 1979a:23).

After opening statements by Dole and Senator Mark Hatfield (who alluded to experiencing deceptions in his own dealings with the Unification Church), the Guyana theme surfaced repeatedly in subsequent presentations and gradually became dominant in discussions of other cults. Congressman Richard Ottinger, for example, stated:

> The Jonestown massacre I suppose illustrates the extremes of dangers that can be presented by the cult phenomenon. But we have had accusations made by parents that their children have been coerced into entering cults, that once they were there they have been physically and mentally abused, subjected to drugs; they have been

physically prevented from returning to society; that immigration laws have been violated; that the laws with respect to weapons have been violated; that the tax laws have been violated. These were all very serious matters that I don't think we can, as a government, ignore because *they are attempted to be cloaked in religious activity* ....(AFF 1979a:11-12; italics ours)

Senator Edward Zorinsky mixed imputation with disclaimer when he noted: "There is a duty, too, it seems to me, to ask questions about the Unification Church, though I do not wish to imply that it and the People's Temple are in any way similar." Zorinsky then went on to refer to some of Moon's followers ("the extreme cases") as "little more than automatons" and likened the idealistic civilization aspired to by Moon and to which Moon "has committed the massive financial resources of his diverse and far-flung business, political and religious enterprises" to the Roman Empire (AFF 1979a:13-14). Other officials made no overt connection between the Unification Church and Jonestown but alluded to possible violations of laws that might remove them from First Amendment protection. Thus Congressman Robert Giaimo warned:

I am convinced...that a distinction must be made between religious beliefs and certain actions taken in the name of religion. Our society must tolerate unorthodox beliefs; that's a basic component of freedom; but society cannot tolerate all actions taken in the name of religion. (AFF 1979a:16)

Subsequent speakers on behalf of the ACM showed little restraint in their accusations against current American cults. Others showed little compunction in lumping the Unification Church and other religious groups together with People's Temple as insidious, exploitive, and menacing to both members and larger society. Thus Robert Boetcher, former staff director for the Fraser Committee which had conducted an extensive investigation of the Unification Church's role in recent controversies involving South Korea's relations with the United States, testified that "we are witnessing a perversion of freedom of religion by leaders of cults who think they have special license to violate laws" (AFF 1979a:31). Boetcher vehemently denounced the Unification Church as a multinational "greedy business conglomerate" with subversive ties to the South Korean Central Intelligence Agency, "an army of brainwashed, obedient servants," and an "antidemocratic, brainwashed political party"; he went on to characterize Moon as a power-lusting "menace." Dr. John Clark, psychiatrist and assistant clinical professor at Harvard Medical School, compared alleged mind-control powers of People's Temple leaders to similar alleged abilities of the Symbionese Liberation Army, the Manson cult, and the Nazi party (what Clark termed the "classic cult"). Clark then proceeded to list clinical symptoms of the psychological cult syndrome and physical stigmata (glassy eyes, stunted linguistic abilities, impaired reasoning) that he claimed characterized the typical "maimed" personality of a cult member. These were accusations that had long been directed at the Unification Church. Such a cult personality was, according to Clark, a second personality. He stated:

> Their minds are split.... The same changes can result from disease processes and are seen as evidence of injury.... Their highly manipulated minds are effective only under total control and are less able to manage the unexpected without resorting to psychosis, suicide, or uncontrolled violence toward others. (AFF 1979a:41)

Clark linked these allegations against current cults to Guyana ("our holocaust," in his words) and summed up his argument in a statement that drew on the favorite atrocity-tale themes of suicide and parricide:

> These cults or groups are armies of willing, superbly controlled soldiers who would not only kill their parents or themselves, but are ready to act against anyone. (AFF 1979a:43)

Similarly Flo Conway and Jim Siegelman, authors of *Snapping*, referred to the alleged personality changes accompanying conversions to the supposed expanding number of new religious movements in this country as the result of a "covert form of hypnotic suggestion" and labeled the latter a "mental health problem with far-reaching medical, legal, and social implications." Specifically naming the Unification Church as one among the groups they investigated, Conway and Siegelman lauded deprogramming as "a new and valued form of mental health therapy" for a problem "quite outside the bounds of diagnosis and treatment used in psychiatry and other mental health disciplines." They likened the "cult problem" ("the systematic destruction of the individual and his human right to freedom of thought") to a critical threat to "the substance of this society and our democratic process" (AFF 1979a:45–52).

Most importantly, the theme that Jonestown could be and would be repeated unless the federal government acted soon was reiterated by ACM speakers. For example, Jackie Speier, former legal counsel to

Leo J. Ryan and a victim of the Port Kaituma airstrip ambush, stated in her testimony that the "major religious cults in the United States show surprising similarities" to characteristics of the People's Temple group as she had observed it firsthand; she specified the presence of a charismatic figure "who had the ability to mesmerize his followers," behavior in members that is "devoid of normal emotion," "monosyllabic, programmed" responses to questions, and so forth. She gave the assembled officials an ominous warning:

> I am a victim of Guyana, but I am alive and very mindful of my responsibility to try and inform others about the tragedy. I hope this Committee, during the course of its investigation, will also be mindful of perhaps the singularly most important fact of Jonestown: *It can happen again.* (AFF 1979a:24-29; italics ours)

Likewise, Rabbi Maurice Davis baldly stated of the Unification Church:

> You have a prescription for violence, for death, for destruction. It is a formula that fits the Nazi Youth Movement as accurately as it describes the Unification Church...or the People's Temple. (AFF 1979a:77)

And then he asked the Congressmen a rhetorical question replete with some of the most vitriolic imagery ever offered in ACM literature:

> How many Jonestowns must there be before we begin to do something? Gentlemen of the Congress: I am not here to protest against religion, or against religions. I am here to protest against child molesters, for as surely as there are those who lure children with lollypops in order to rape their bodies, so, too, are there those who lure children with candy-coated lies in order to rape their minds. (AFF 1979a:79)

Not surprisingly, there were those who not only predicted violence in this country similar to that in Jonestown but who also claimed to have anticipated the latter massacre. Thus Daphne Greene, an outspoken West Coast ACM activist and mother of a Unification Church member, stated:

> The events of the People's Temple came as no surprise. Indeed, it was highly predictable and was merely a harbinger of what is sure to happen as cults see themselves threatened by actions of an aroused populace. (AFF 1979a:82)

Joe Alexander, Sr., deprogrammer and one-time operator of the Freedom of Thought Foundation rehabilitation ranch in Tucson, Arizona, called for an expanded use of temporary conservatorship laws and pleaded: "Let's not have another Guyana tragedy" (AFF 1979a:56).

Unlike the 1976 hearings, Dole's in 1979 offered equal time to civil-liberties advocates and to spokespersons representing the Unification Church. The allegations we have sampled thus far did not pass unchallenged. In general the rebuttals of the ACM's opponents followed a fairly standard argument firmly grounded in First Amendment rights and assumptions of cultural relativity. Thus Dean Kelley, Director for Civil and Religious Liberty in the National Council of Churches and appearing on behalf of the American Civil Liberties Union, stated:

> We would be suspicious of an attempt to form a legal distinction between so-called "cults," a term that is usually used in a derogatory sense to apply to religions we don't understand and don't like, to distinguish them from what are thought to be more legitimate religions. (AFF 1979a:37)

Likewise, Jeremiah S. Gutman, Director of the American Civil Liberties Union, stated:

> We have resorted and heard today resort to such words as pseudo religion. The first Amendment doesn't permit a distinction between religion and pseudo religion, because to do so would be to say that some religions are truthful and others are pseudo or false. (AFF 1979a:68–69)

And later he lashed out at the legitimacy of the meeting itself as a part of a "witchhunt" employing a "McCarthy-like catalog" of cults. He commented bluntly on law professor Richard Delgado's proposed regulations for "conversionist activities," which included, among other protections for the "religious consumer," mandatory full disclosure of one's affiliation and intent to proselytize, a required "cooling off period" for converts, and government licensing of religious recruiters: "I can't imagine how a lawyer could even suggest that such a procedure could pass muster under a First Amendment test" (AFF 1979a:72). Gutman referred to compulsory psychiatric treatment of cult members, another Delgado suggestion, as "Sovietation medicine."

Others were equally hard on the core themes of ACM ideology that ran through much of the earlier testimony. Rev. Barry Lynn, an ordained United Church of Christ minister and denomination official, criticized allegations of psychological harm resulting from cult involvement:

> To arrive at this conclusion they [the anticultists] engaged in unsystematic chronicling of terrifying anecdotes and quasi-scientific reports which lead them to believe in a theory of "mind control" at least as dubious and incomprehensible as the theologies of the religious groups they attack. (AFF 1979a:97)

A Catholic priest from the New York archdiocese had proclaimed, "A true religious movement will be able to withstand any investigation. It is the ones that are falsely labeled that will fail" (AFF 1979a:97). In response to similar statements, President Neil Salonen of the Unification Church criticized the very holding of such a quasi-official meeting and predicted that it would have a "chilling effect on the free exercise of...beliefs" (AFF 1979a:118).

State Hearings and Investigations The ACM, as we have shown, did not lack for sympathetic public officials and legislators at the national level who were willing to pick up on a promising wedge of attack against cults. This propensity was even more the case at the state level. The regional orientation of the various ACM groups, as well as the opportunities for more frequent contact at the local level, made it natural for them to focus heavily on influencing such state officials as prosecutors and legislators. By the summer of 1979 sympathetic allies in state houses had initiated bills to alter laws covering charitable solicitations, income-tax exemptions, and property taxes (so as to curtail financial expansion by such groups as the Unification Church). Or they called for investigations of new religions in such diverse states as Illinois, Wisconsin, New Jersey, Pennsylvania, Rhode Island, Texas, Minnesota, Connecticut, and Michigan. For example, the Connecticut General Law Committee conducted an informal investigation of only the Unification Church's activities (and not those of other new religions) in that state. In the Illinois House of Representatives, Betty Hoxsey, amid some controversy, sponsored House Resolution No. 121 to create a temporary six-member commission (three of whom were American Civil Liberties Union members) to investigate "illegal activities of religious cults who are coercing our children to join up with them." During the subsequent hearings Hoxsey dismissed First Amendment considerations with her statement: "Any true religion doesn't have to worry about investigations into illegal activities...because they would not commit any illegal acts" ([Springfield] *Illinois Times* 6/21/79). The Minnesota House Judiciary Subcommittee, at the encouragement of Wallace Martin, president of Free Minds, Inc., held similar hearings at which such anticult spokespersons as Richard Delgado (lawyer/professor/deprogramming advocate) testified. In Pennsylvania, House Resolution No. 20 established yet another investigative committee to study groups that employed "improper mind control techniques in their recruitment," techniques that presumably "undermine voluntary consent, employ duress, and interfere with free will." While regional ACM groups could and did continue to press for legislative/investigative action by federal officials (for example, a national petition coordinated by the Maryland chapter of the Individual Freedom Foundation, a widespread ACM group, was distributed nationally within the ACM, its signers urging Congress to continue the investigations begun by the House Subcommittee on International Organizations into possible law violations by the Unification Church), they nevertheless put much energy into swaying state governments toward the ACM ideology (AFF 1979b; IFF 1979b, 1979c).

New York state—where the Unification Church had its national headquarters, seminary, newspaper, printing houses, Moon's private residence, and many of its American members—witnessed perhaps an inordinate share of such anticult activity and illustrates the range of repressive political action that ACM members and/or sympathetic legislators sought to implement and legitimate. The most extreme of these political attempts at social control occurred in late 1977 when Assemblyman Robert Wertz introduced bill AB9566-A to amend New York's penal law with a new section entitled "Promoting a Pseudo-Religious Cult." The bill aimed to make promoting such a cult a felony. Most state legislative proposals did not reach such extremes. It is worth quoting Wertz's proposed addition to the New York penal code in full:

> A person is guilty of promoting a pseudo-religious cult when he knowingly organizes or maintains an organization into which other persons are induced to join or participate in through the use of mind control methods, hypnosis, brainwashing techniques or other systematic forms of indoctrination and in which the members or participants of such organization engage in soliciting funds primarily for the benefit of such organization or its leaders and are not permitted to travel or communicate with anyone outside such organization unless another member or participant of such organization is present.

The bill failed in 1978, in part due to its dubious constitutionality and in part due also to a vigorous countercampaign against it by persons associated with the American Civil Liberties Union and various new religious groups. However, Jonestown suddenly made legislation calling for further social control measures seem more justified. Thus in March 1979 Wertz sponsored a bill to allot $500,000 for forming a committee to study the mental-health aspects of cults and to print and disseminate to adolescents on a state-wide basis booklets containing ACM ideology. The link between the events of Jonestown and Wertz's sponsorship was explicit:

> There is no mistaking the detrimental effects so-called "pseudo-religious cults" have on the youth of this country. In the wake of Guyana...it should be evident that such legislation is sorely needed. (Wertz 1979)

And he added: "There is, of course, a concern that established and conventional religion not be jeopardized by a program to impede the growth of cults." The Unification Church responded to this proposed legislation the following May with demonstrations in Albany led by the Ad Hoc Committee against Nazism, its members dressed in Nazi-style uniforms and composed of students from the Unification Theological Seminary. The bill subsequently was postponed amid the usual concerns over constitutional issues.

However, a more serious legislative inquiry emerged in New York state during the summer of 1979 and forced the Unification Church on the defensive for a time at least. In mid-1979 apostate Christopher Edwards, author of the ACM potboiler *Crazy for God* (1979), made public charges of child abuse in the Unification Church:

> "I never saw proper medical care given to anyone but the top leaders in the Church," said Edwards. He added that during his eight-month membership in the Unification Church in California he saw as many as six children locked into a small trailer "not adequate for adults, let alone children," and that there were similar occurences at the church center in Tarrytown, N.Y. (Stathos 1979)

By midsummer of 1979 the child-abuse allegations against the Unification Church had come to the attention of Howard L. Lasher, a Brooklyn assemblyman chairing the State Assembly's Committee on Child Care. With the incidents of Jonestown still fresh in mind and generalizing from the latter to the Unification Church and to cults in general, Lasher began in July to solicit testimony from both cult and anticult spokespersons on alleged cult child abuse. Typical of his solicitations for information was his letter of July 19 to the Church of Scientology of New York. He wrote:

In my capacity as Chairman of the New York State Assembly Child Care Committee, I have become increasingly concerned with the welfare of children living in communal situations. Although this matter was brought into focus last fall by the tragedy in Jonestown, I do not imply that every group is suspect of the extremes practiced by that one infamous organization....I would like to make certain that groups located in our state offer safe environments for minors who are involved with them and that these children are protected from maltreatment or abuse. (Lasher 1979)

In Lasher's opening statement at the two-day hearings convened on August 10 at the World Trade Center in New York City, he again reiterated the Guyana theme:

In the aftermath of the mass suicides last November in Jonestown where, of the 910 people who died, 260 were children, the existence of and practices of cults has become of deep concern to myself and other members of the assembly. (Stathos 1979)

Of the more than 20 witnesses who appeared during the hearings, the majority were hostile to the Unification Church. The latter persons included Christopher Edwards, Rabbi Maurice Davis, Jean Merritt (a psychiatric social worker and founder of Return to Personal Choice, Inc.), and Galen Kelly, a private investigator turned deprogrammer. Among the witnesses for the Unification Church were Michael Young Warder, publisher of *The News World* (the Church's daily newspaper in New York City), its former president Farley Jones, Professor Warren Lewis of the Church's seminary faculty, and representatives from the Alliance for the Preservation of Religious Liberty (APRL) and the American Civil Liberties Union. The questioning of Unification Church representatives began on the subject of children in the Church. Committee members probed for details of the ages of such children, provisions for their schooling and/or day care, and sanitation and health facilities available to them. Soon, however, the committee became sidetracked on the inevitably sensational questions concerning the larger operation and resources of the Church. Its witnesses such as Michael Young Warder berated the committee for its dubious constitutional appropriateness in investigating cults and not other religious groups, stating: "I feel that there has been too much emphasis on the government's concern with the new religions" (Stathos 1977). Instead, Warder challenged the committee to put funds and "more teeth and a little more punch" into control of heroin and narcotics as well as into criminal justice in general.

The Unification Church did not treat Lasher's hearings lightly, for in spite of popular stereotypes about celibate Moonies the Church in fact had married members, some of whom had young children either being raised in conventional nuclear family settings or in special nurseries while their parents were dispatched elsewhere on assignments important to the movement. Unification Church witnesses reported back to leaders their expectations of further trouble from the hearings. The special theological significance of the family for Unification Church members, however unusual its appearance to outsiders, gave this particular issue extraordinary seriousness. On the final day of the hearings Farley Jones wrote to Church President Neil Salonen:

> From the questions they asked, they had caught wind of the nurseries in Tarrytown. . . . The most dangerous point they are considering is to extend the conservatorship laws of New York to include the children of cult members. If the parents [members of cults] can be proven to be mentally incompetent then the children will be made wards of the state. (Jones 1979)

Likewise, Michael Young Warder, in a memorandum to various Church officials, expressed his uneasiness and cautioned them to anticipate further harassment from Albany:

> I believe it is reasonable to expect that the Tarrytown nursery will be visited by a New York State Agency of some sort in the near future. It may be an agency charged with supervision of "foster care facilities" or perhaps the State Health Department. Evidently, our nursery is in the category of a "foster care facility." I would suppose the nursery staff should check the statutory limitations for foster care facilities as soon as possible. (Warder 1979)

Warder recommended the Unification Church's public-relations office prepare a "basketful of literature" for each committee member, including a demographic profile of Church membership. He also suggested that remarks made by Galen Kelly be preserved for a possible libel suit or other pending litigation. (Kelly, who admitted sometimes using legally questionable tactics, had boasted to the committee that he had gotten into legal trouble only twice out of 130 deprogrammings, neither of which occurrences produced indictments.)

Summary and Conclusions

The 1970s witnessed the emergence of a number of new religious movements amid a more general resurgence of religiosity in the

United States. These new religious movements were quickly met by a countermovement primarily organized and orchestrated by the families of youths who had joined these movements. The ACM throughout its history never resolved basic organizational problems, however, and hence remained a loose coalition of regionally organized groups that cooperated in certain of each other's activities and campaigns and served as a communication network for concerned parents. Despite its organizational problems the ACM was moderately successful in harassing new religions through its dual strategies of direct action and lobbying of institutions with a sanctioning capability. For a variety of reasons the Unification Church became the ACM's principal target and was characterized as the archetypical cult. The Church's development was not thwarted, however, and by the mid-1970s the ACM's attack on it had been substantially blunted.

The tragedy at Jonestown reinvigorated the ACM at a time when its fortunes seemed to be declining. People's Temple had not been treated as a part of the cult problem because of its association with a recognized denomination and Jones's political ties with local community leaders, in spite of the existence of a group of disgruntled relatives of People's Temple members who had formed an ACM-style organization. The events at Jonestown both regalvanized the ACM and rekindled public apprehensions about the dangers of cults.

Although caught unprepared by Jonestown, as were other segments of American society, the ACM quickly seized the opportunity to trumpet its claims of the cult menace. The brainwashing metaphor underpinning its ideology was adopted to explain the deaths at Jonestown; violence, both inner- and outer-directed, was portrayed as a characteristic feature of cults. Numerous apostates came forward and testified to having received suicide training, and once again the Unification Church became the ACM's chief target, this time as the suicide cult.

The political/legal restraints that had impeded ACM attempts to initiate or implement repressive measures against cults continued to frustrate their anticult campaign. However, in the wake of Jonestown the ACM's renewed anticult campaign, coupled with heightened apprehensions about cults among the public and some political leaders, resulted in a symbolic crusade against the Unification Church and other new religious movements. Numerous state and federal hearings were conducted which had the objective of discrediting these movements and clearly locating them outside the category of legitimate religion. There was virtually no possibility that these hearings would eventuate in the passage of law that would pass constitutional

muster. Thus Jonestown had the effect of demarcating the boundaries
of public values by linking cults and violence but did not bring on
formal institutionalized repression.

8
Religious Movements and the Brainwashing Issue
Thomas Robbins and Dick Anthony

The legitimating rationale for what some civil libertarians regard as ominous religious persecution entails the allegation that devotees of cults have been subjected to brainwashing, mind control, or coercive persuasion at the hands of cultists who have enslaved them by using psychological conditioning techniques in a superficially voluntary context. The horror of Jonestown has drastically shifted public attitudes toward cults and has appeared to vindicate brainwashing notions.

The validity of brainwashing as a scientific concept is problematic to say the least. As Thomas Szasz has commented (apropos of the Patricia Hearst case), one cannot really wash a brain any more than one can make someone bleed with a cutting remark (Szasz 1976). Similarly, Dr. Walter Reich has argued, also apropos of the Hearst case, that psychiatry lacks the expertise and clinical experience for making definitive pronouncements on alleged brainwashing; moreover, "Psychiatry endangers itself—debases its coinage—by entering areas in which it lacks expertise" (Reich 1976).

Brainwashing appears to be a mystifying and inherently subjective metaphor, which is now being used as a simplistic explanation for intense sectarian commitments, as well as a way of attacking groups against which charges of explicitly physical coercion cannot be substantiated. Such pseudoscientific metaphors satisfy the hunger for simple mechanistic explanations for complex social phenomena. Persons who wish to persecute unpopular but nonviolent and law-abiding movements can use the brainwashing metaphor as a foundation for disclaiming any violation of the rights of participants when seemingly arbitrary measures (like deprogramming) are imposed. The imputation of brainwashing implicitly defines certain persons as zombies and robots. Such persons are allegedly not responsible social actors and thus may be therapeutically coerced for their own good and to restore them to autonomy. On the other hand, persons who for whatever reason temporarily accepted an unconventional or authoritarian ideology may find it comforting or convenient to deny any responsibility for their prior involvement by accepting a deterministic explanatory mystique that implies their own passive victimization. Either way, a simplistic and misleading notion is being used in an essentially superstitious manner to rationalize certain actions.

Brainwashing is essentially an occult notion similar in some ways to traditional ideas of spirit possession, whereby someone whose behavior is insupportable is viewed as possessed by an alien demonic force that consumes the victim's authentic personality and must be ritually exorcised (Shupe, Spielmann, and Stigall 1977a). After the exorcism/deprogramming all is forgiven the deviant individual because—allegedly—not his authentic self but his alien brainwashed/possessed self was acting or thinking strangely. Notions of spirit possession and exorcism are rampant in popular culture and have invaded psychology via brainwashing and mind-control mystiques.

The concept of coercive persuasion, as developed by Lifton, Schein, and others, is less occult than brainwashing, but it is being used against cults in a misleading reifying manner. Coercive persuasion is a model (or set of models) that has heuristic value in the analysis of indoctrination processes and the dynamics of authoritarian groups. When these models are applied to movements such as Hare Krishna and the Unification Church they sensitize the observer to some (manipulative, constraining) aspects of indoctrination within cults while possibly desensitizing the observer to other elements of the social situation. However, it is imperative to realize that the psychologically coercive aspects of social processes within authoritarian movements vary in intensity. It is unreasonable to simply equate the degree of "milieu control" within Hare Krishna or the Unification Church with the situation within prisoner-of-war camps where armed guards, fences, and barbed wire operate to physically constrain the inmates. As Alan Scheflin and Edward Opton have argued in *The Mind Manipulators*, indoctrination within cults represents a noninstance of true coercive persuasion because, although elements of classic coercive-persuasion syndromes are present in these situations, they are usually significantly attenuated. Isolation is one factor tying "so-called brainwashing to religious cults; it is a central facet of each. But when one looks closely, any apparent similarity dissolves." Isolation in religious movements "is of necessity only partial" (Scheflin and Opton 1968:61). Moonies witnessing on city streets are susceptible to numerous influences the Unification Church cannot really control. Not infrequently the putatively robotized members of a controversial cult are actually living and/or working outside of the movement.

When concepts of brainwashing, mind control, or coercive persuasion are applied to social movements, certain assumptions are often made that are not really intrinsic to scholarly coercive-persuasion models. One such assumption is the notion that mind-controlled converts lack free will and personal autonomy. Free will is not really an empirical concept; it is more a philosophical assumption that we assign to adult human behavior and withhold only in extreme cases (like psychosis or senility). At present, however, the suspicion is spreading that a vast reservoir of persons exists who are not rational, responsible, or autonomous: the so-called insane and mentally ill, the economically disadvantaged who have been brutalized by oppressive life conditions, the victims of brainwashing, the religious cultists, the television addicts, and the like. But as the general assumption of personal autonomy goes down it drags with it the conceptual basis of individual rights, which are generally viewed as presupposing prior rationality and responsibility. One consequence of this development is the practice of legal deprogramming via court-ordered temporary conservatorships, which were frequently granted to parents of cult converts during the period from 1974 through 1977 but have declined in the aftermath of *Katz* vs. *Superior Court* (Lemoult 1978:640). In the wake of the post-Guyana hysteria over cults, this practice could be revived. Or instead, courts and legislators may heed the calls for legally institutionalizing a temporary cooling-off period during which converts to authoritarian sects would be forcibly separated from their religious groups and compelled to seek therapeutic counseling (interview with Professor Richard Delgado, "Federal Intervention in Cults," *US News & World Report* 12/11/78). Such a proposal, which contemplates the forcible confinement of adults who have neither been convicted of a crime nor declared insane, presupposes the essential nonrationality and mental slavery of converts, who can therefore be subjected to physical coercion for therapeutic purposes.

A second assumption that creeps into allegations of mind control practiced by religious groups is the medical-model view of authoritarian religious involvements as induced mental pathologies. Certain religious beliefs are consigned to the realm of involuntary pathological symptoms. Despite growing criticisms of the medical model and its extension to more and more areas of life (such as "caffeinism," "tobacco-use disorder"—Goleman 1978), the importance of the medical model is necessarily enhanced in a society that is in moral flux and in which authorities are hesitant to acknowledge punitive intent; thus they increasingly rely on psychiatrists and psychologists to provide benevolent therapeutic rationales for social control. The scope of the medical model is also increased in a society in which therapy and medical care is increasingly paid for by third parties such as social-security or health-insurance plans. There have already been demands that People's Temple survivors from Guyana receive government-subsidized psychotherapy. This demand may foreshadow the day when persons leaving unorthodox religious movements and cults can routinely receive subsidized treatment from a government or a health plan for the serious medical condition of "destructive cultism," which one medical doctor views as an actual disease syndrome (Shapiro 1977; *National Enquirer* 10/10/77). These trends notwithstanding, there are serious philosophical and epistemological difficulties to be faced in treating shared spiritual commitments as mental pathologies (Needleman and Baker 1978:49-62, 106-152, 201-208).

A final assumption implicit in imputations of brainwashing or mind control involving social movements is that no uncoerced person in his or her right mind could possibly accept a given ideology or lifestyle. This is a rather arbitrary premise. For centuries people have joined authoritarian and totalistic movements and willingly surrendered elements of intellectual freedom and flexibility in exchange for rewards associated with a sense of normative structure, a sense of purpose and meaning in life, or relief from anxiety and anomie. In *Pagan and Christian in an Age of Anxiety*, E. R. Dodds argues that Christianity appealed to persons in the later Roman Empire in part because

> it lifted the burden of freedom from the shoulders of the individual: one choice, one irrevocable choice, and the road to salvation was clear.... In an age of anxiety any "totalist" creed exerts a powerful attraction.... (Dodds 1963:133-134)

What is denounced as coercive mind control in the practice of certain authoritarian communal groups may also be viewed as commendable monastic discipline and austerity, which makes a favorable and vivid contrast to the permissive and hedonistic context of modern American life. Given the increasing moral ambiguity and normative breakdown of American culture, many systems and disciplines that appear deviant to most citizens can find voluntary (but often temporary) converts.

Notions such as brainwashing and coercive persuasion are not necessary to justify investigations and possible prosecutions of groups that are widely alleged to resort to actual physical violence and coercion. Conceivably other aspects of wealthy religious or therapeutic empires such as the Unification Church or Scientology may bear some investigation.

Clear dissimulation in proselytizing (such as running an alleged summer camp without acknowledging religious training on the premises) or deceptive solicitation of funds (as by concealing the identity of one's religious institution) can be attacked directly through statute. What is to be feared is the possibility that such subjective concepts as mind control will be employed as rationales for using tangible physical coercion after straining at the rather dubious gnat of brainwashing.

Conclusion

Various sociologists and other social scientists have linked the present spiritual ferment and upsurge of unconventional movements to structural dislocations in American society or to a sociocultural context of normative flux and value dissent. It is arguable that these sociocultural analyses are not really incompatible with psychologistic brainwashing formulations; the prevailing normative ambiguity and cultural confusion reduce individuals' resistance against cultist mind control. There is some merit to this argument; however, the implicit premise of imputations of brainwashing involving social movements is that no uncoerced person in his or her right mind could possibly accept a given deviant ideology or lifestyle. Harvey Cox has analyzed the "myth of the evil eye" whereby "it is thought that no sane person could possibly belong to a movement 'like this' and therefore the participant must be there involuntarily" (Cox 1978:227). In contrast, analyses of deviant movements as responses to normative breakdown or cultural disorganization imply that a situation is emerging in which individuals can voluntarily opt for seemingly bizarre patterns because either the assumed normal constraints on religio-ideological deviance have become eroded or else needs for meaning and affiliation have emerged that cannot be adequately met by traditional institutions. Perhaps "protean man," as Robert Lifton has termed a prevalent modern identity type, must continually experiment with exotic and sometimes authoritarian and fanatical role identities; or perhaps only a surrender to an overwhelmingly totalitarian demiurge can produce for some persons the sense of autonomy and decisive, authentic decision making that is systematically undermined by an impersonal bureaucratic milieu.[1]

It is conceivable that the context of an oppressive bureaucratic society erodes the sense of personal autonomy and authenticity that is encouraged by traditionally dominant normative orientations. Social movements may provide contexts for putting into operation social identities that are not tied to bureaucratic instrumental roles and to depersonalized mass society settings. The fragmentation of daily life into limited involvements in impersonal bureaucratic institutions of work and study enhances the appeal of commitment to an all-embracing system that will integrate one's life and give meaning to one's existence. Given the structurally volatile and marginal status of overeducated postadolescents in a society with high levels of unemployment and underemployment, an upsurge of youth movements is not a surprising development. Neither is it really shocking that a number of these groups regiment their converts and segregate them from mainstream structures and processes that are not capable of meeting the expressive needs of many young persons or even of providing them with satisfactory employment. Such movements, however, tend to have a rapid turnover and frequently evolve over time in a more adaptive and accommodative direction.

In a culture pervaded by anomie, one cannot really infer coercive manipulation or brainwashing from seemingly irrational patterns of self-renunciation and asceticism. The philosopher William Barrett has made this point eloquently;

> The frenzies of asceticism, which may seem mere aberration and abnormality to our secular minds, are in fact the inevitable means to which the human animal is driven to give meaning to his existence. Rather than be meaningless, we shall find ourselves seeking out devices of our own that are equally extreme. We create by denying ourselves. So long as we drive ourselves in the toils of some discipline we cannot believe that our life is meaningless. In the tensions of the will—the simultaneous striving and surrender—the ghost of nihilism departs. (1976:38)

9

Moral Philosophy and the Absurdity of Jonestown: A Study in the Democratization of Tragedy

Edmund L. Erde

We are probably ripe for a revival of the organic theory of society and the state. And, though this is a topic that must be taken seriously, it is also one that is going to need to be handled with great caution and subtlety, if we are to avoid the crudely conservative emphases of earlier versions of the theory. (Toulmin and Graham 1979)

What a cynical principle of education it is to say in effect: "We shall stand by and watch, as long as all the harm you do is done to yourself." (In other words, about you we really do not care.) "But when you touch an Other, then watch out! We will intercede though the damage for the Other might be rather minor, but we will abstain even if the harm to yourself is beyond repair." Is this not a formulation of the maxim that on the political and social level turns a culture into a butcher's shop? And should not, in the context of education—and not as a high standard, but rather as a minimum—the focus be first and foremost on the individual child so that when an influence is to be exerted it is assessed first in terms of the child's own requirements, and only after that, and often as a last resort, in terms of the protection Others may require. (Bergmann 1977)

There is a very long, very detailed federal report: *The Assassination of Representative Leo J. Ryan and the Jonestown Tragedy* (U.S. Government 1979; see especially Clement Zablocki's Foreword). The title's use of the term "tragedy" in connection with the Jonestown events wants exploration. I will argue that the stark change in meaning from its classic use into today's use—from "a noble story that told the fall and demise of a hero" to "a major sad event"—is not just a corruption of the language[1] but is a consequence of a moral-political worldview that is democratic in an honorific sense. The point is not merely linguistic; instead, it is that what appears to many philosophers the most compelling moral-political theory seems to have implications which are made explicit by a certain kind of event—the deaths at Jonestown or those at the Munich Olympics or the incarceration of Japanese-Americans during World War II. Understanding these explicit implications may provide greater philosophic understanding, and even some philosophic progress.

The Jonestowns[2] are important in a general philosophic sense because, when considered through moral theory, they can illuminate what Camus calls "the absurd." By using this term Camus was trying to characterize the intrinsic conflict between human desires and the impossibility of fulfilling them. This conflict can be observed in many contexts and at many levels. For example, people want Truth with a capital "T", but they get only shifting theories; people want immortality, but they get only assurance of death.[3]

The *concept* of the absurd, Camus tells us, can arise in a person as the reverberation of a *feeling* of the absurd, a feeling such as one gets from watching a television newscaster who seems to be speaking intently while the audio portion of the broadcast is not coming across. We can have this absurd feeling in response to his mute appearance.

Jonestown can occasion in us the feeling of the absurd. This is indicated by the title of some of the literature about it. "Tragedy" as in the title of the federal report and "massacre" as in Charles Krause's *Guyana Massacre* (1978) are words that bristle with feeling—the feeling of the absurd. If the human cravings for knowledge and immortality are ingredients in our understanding of both the feeling (the notion) of the absurd, images of what Jonestown must have been like before, during, and after the deaths can also tie to our feelings of the absurd, through the horror of what must have been the sights and the smells and the numbers, the numbers of dead.

But the question arises: Is it rational to process this feeling of the absurd and its context as a proper thread to tie to the notion of the absurd, and if so, at what level or in what context? I will argue that it is rational to do so, despite some powerful reasons to the contrary. I shall argue that the context or level at which the absurd should be understood vis-à-vis Jonestown is the level of the apparently intrinsic contradiction in our views of what we want from society and what it can supply.

To sharpen this issue about feelings and numbers, of which so much has been made by the press, consider, first, that "massacre" strongly connotes large numbers being killed (in a way that "tragedy" need not). Second, Krause, in his "eyewitness report," complained that he was numbed by seeing the carnage; he was alarmed by his own desensitization about not caring whether 5 or 500 had been killed. Third, there is a technical philosophic argument about numbers and responsibility which, if I may be permitted to translate it into the language of philosophizing about the absurd, concludes that numbers have nothing to do with our taking inventory of the *notion* of the absurd in the moral-political or social contexts. I turn now to that argument.

Two years before Jonestown, John M. Taurek published an essay entitled "Should Numbers Count?" (1977). Taurek was concerned with whether, if one must choose among two or more groups of persons in need of help, one should (could rationally) use a difference in the numbers of persons in the groups as a ground for the choice. He challenged the common-sense view that in most of the obvious kinds of cases one could rationally ground choosing to save the larger group just in its being the larger group. Taurek argued this challenge through several examples such as the following: If the only available batch of medication could be used to treat either only one particular patient or only five other particular patients, we have no compelling ground for choosing the five. (Shortly, I will apply his form of argument to issues about the ages of those who would die.)

Taurek's argument[4] is that each person who dies loses the total remainder of what would otherwise be his or her life (it is this loss or waste of the unused portion that seems to connect with the tragic). Take the perspective of the endangered person. It is not morally condemnable that he or she tries to influence the choice in such a way that we come to save his or her group, even when he or she knows that greater numbers will be lost by that choice. Such moral innocence, Taurek seems to argue, should apply universally. If the small group is innocent in wanting to be favored, their innocence should attach to anyone who agrees with them. Thus, we ought not to appeal to numbers in making our disinterested choices among groups.

Taurek's further conclusion is that it makes no logical sense to talk about instances of suffering being added together. One cannot take the sum of the suffering in a given time and place and logically judge it to be greater or less. It makes no sense, he says, to speak in this way. And if one cannot be adding, it follows that one cannot care about the numbers. One can only care about, empathize with, individuals. In the context into which I am importing this argument, we could put the conclusion: Numbers should not contribute to the rational framing of the notion of the absurd.

Although Taurek's argument has to be imported into the context of the Jonestown episode,[5] the argument speaks to a general philosophical question that is central to the discussion of this essay: What is the relationship between logic and emotion for ethical assessments? Before taking this on at the technical philosophic level, let me take stock of how nonphilosophers seem to view the matter. The subtitle of one of Krause's chapters is "The Babies Went First." This certainly is an emotional appeal at least in the respect that somehow, in some of our moral reflection, the death of an older person feels more acceptable than the death of the young. But Taurek's argument about numbers would seem to have an analogous argument about age that could be brought to focus here. If everyone who dies loses everything, then the old lose as much of the remainder of their lives as do the young. If the old could not be blamed for wanting to live longer, then under the principle that what is not wrong for one judger is not wrong for any, it would follow that it would not be wrong to save the old and forsake the young when a choice must be made. Many of us are more upset when we hear of deaths in large groups or hear of children's deaths than we are when we hear about one killing or about the death of some elderly persons (*not* that we need to be unmoved by the deaths of the elderly). But our feelings seem irrational under Taurek's argument.

Still, we find it intelligible that people become martyrs or that they die for the sake of others. We could find it reasonable that someone cover a grenade with his or her body to protect the larger group of people he or she cares about. To sacrifice oneself for a group of strangers, however, seems less intelligible. At Jonestown, most of those who died seemed to die for Jones, for their patriarch.[6] They were not strangers sacrificing themselves for strangers.

Jones, though, strikes us as mad.[7] He apparently had thought about mass suicides for years before the Jonestown event. He repeatedly considered "revolutionary suicide," and implied that such an event would change important social and political features of American life. Also, in the midst of Congressman Ryan's visit, Jones behaved as though he felt trapped by very hostile forces. He might have felt that his group was a unity whose plight was a sum of what the individuals went through; the summing, though, is unintelligible given Taurek's position. It is certainly unintelligible if the group is considered an aggregate of individuals and not understood as a body politic.

Now Taurek's argument is an explication or articulation of some of the generally unnoticed implications in the moral philosophy that can most aptly be called Kantian, and which I will take a few pages to articulate. Kant holds that autonomy and self-determination (Kant 1797/1964; Erde 1978) have a logical priority over values, are more fundamental than values; and he argues this thesis on the ground that, without autonomy, no moral assessment makes sense. If one is not free to judge or act, then one's opinions or behaviors cannot be praiseworthy or blameworthy, though they may be fortunate or unfortunate. Thus, for Kant, autonomy is the logical sine qua non or the ground of morality; it is the concept that synthesizes the diverse ingredients of moral reasons, and, as such, its injunctions cannot be violated on grounds of value. Autonomy, then, is the logical ground of all valuing in that each person is a bestower of values—no objective value exists independent of rational thoughts. In being the logical ground of values, autonomy is immune to attack from values since it seems impossible for value to be used to defeat its own ground.

The Kantian position tells us to test for whether actions respect the autonomy of others (for whether actions are rationally consistent with autonomy in general) by having us universalize the rules we use when we describe and justify an action. If the result of the universalization is incoherent, the justification of the act fails—that is, the rules that describe and are proposed to justify the action do not respect autonomy. For example, suppose I say what I do not really mean or believe. One way of universalizing this instance renders the rule: No one can ever say what he or she means. This rule yields an incoherent consequence: it uses communication to render communication impossible. Using universalizing as a test, being rational in this sense is part of autonomy.[8]

This is the sense of universalizing upon which Taurek's argument depends. It depends also upon another aspect of Kantian ethics—that each autonomous individual must be respected in and of himself or herself, not according to how he or she may be used by others. Again, the value or the usability of a person is extraneous to respecting his or her autonomy. Each person is an end in and of himself or herself. As an end in one's self, a person is an origin of value judgments about anything that is not autonomous.

In this kingdom of ends, violations of autonomy do not add up. Each violation totally blocks the logic of the moral order. Respecting the boundaries of the kingdom of ends and the members of it—respecting the logic of universalizing—is an all-or-nothing thing; thus, adding in this sphere makes no sense.

This Kantian proposition is the background of Taurek's argument against numbers, for in the kingdom of ends-in-themselves no counting makes sense. This background is also the background of the more accepted kind of contemporary ethical theory.[9] The rival kind of theory is a social ethic best known as "utilitarianism" in which counting and assessing likely outcomes of events (goods and bads, pleasures and pains, happiness and unhappiness) is exactly the mandated thing. This ethic calls for pursuing "the greatest good for the greatest number."[10] Utilitarianism can be understood to be the source of much American political and social thought—including the police powers of the state, the majoritarian principles regarding voting, and even the construction of a federal Constitution in which the separate states could be found to be able to cooperate better than they could under the previous Confederation.

One of the most serious complaints with utilitarianism, though, centers around the use of numbers to justify sacrificing some few for the good of many. The theory, it seems, can justify too much: The Grand Inquisitor (Dostoevsky 1880) burns a few thousand for the security of some millions, Hitler destroys several millions for the sake of the purity of many more. Thus, on the one hand, there are good conceptual reasons and historical examples to support Taurek. On the other hand, Taurek's conclusion seems to run against our moral intuitions in the cases that he attends to, for it is in just such cases that numbers claim moral relevance.[11] How alienating it would be never to be able to take stock of who are the victims and how many there are. The concept of *equality of persons*, which is implicit in the account of a kingdom of ends, precludes adding—while some intuitions seem to mandate it! Is the mandate from our emotional side rather than our rational side? Should we try to understand the ethical dimension as purely emotional? (Is the absurd stalking us, here, too?)

Although "massacre," "tragedy," and "horror" do connote emotional reactions to events such as Jonestown, important arguments in the philosophic literature speak against understanding moral judgments as emotional reactions. There may be, for example, negative emotional reactions to things that are morally neutral or even positive (other variations on the combination of feelings and assessments are obviously also possible). To understand better these concepts that employ expressions of the absurd, I will look briefly at an argument about the nature of moral concepts.

The philosophic insights in favor of understanding moral judgments as conceptual rather than emotional (for interesting contemporary excursions into this orientation, see Jarrett 1979) have been articulated powerfully by Julius Kovasi in his *Moral Notions*. He argues that evaluations (including those built into moral notions) are not added onto factual discernments (descriptions), but rather that the evaluative aspects of a notion are organized as part of the rational activity of concept formation (1967:25). That is, we sometimes devise concepts for (that is, with the point of view of) aiding in the human activities of describing and we sometimes devise concepts for (that is, with the point of view of) aiding in the human activities of assessing interpersonal behaviors and rules about such behaviors. The point is that even our framing of notions that are designed to communicate facts requires our having and being aware of an agenda or orientation or set of endeavors which gives the notions their role. For science or commerce, we want to describe the world of objects. For sanctioning endeavors (ethically or legally), we want to evaluate persons, actions, rules, and judgments about all of them. Descriptive concepts and evaluative concepts are rational in that they are framed as sets of rules used for achieving certain human ends (describing and evaluating, respectively) (1967:70ff.); thus all concepts are devised by humans for human ends. The ends that frame descriptive concepts, Kovasi claims, relate to our enterprises with things (for instance, inanimate objects), whereas the ends that frame our moral notions relate to our tasks aimed at understanding ourselves as rule-following, rational beings (Kovasi 1967:147).

A problem with this analysis which Kovasi points out is that it includes too much; it allows such notions as *cleverness* to be grouped with the moral notions. To home in on morality, after having disposed of descriptive notions, we would have to distinguish prudential notions from moral ones.

The moral point of view frames notions (and shortly we will consider whether *tragedy, massacre*, and *horror* are framed from the moral point of view) which seem to be those that assist in evaluating how people shall relate to others when anyone of a set of people S_1 could be in a position (or role) vis-à-vis anyone else of a set of people S_2 and when all of the facts, motives, actions, and circumstances can be known by all involved. Perhaps merely as a subset of the point of view that could be called "moral," a democratic morality would hold that S_1 and S_2 should, by and large, vaguely be thought of as having the same potential membership. That is, anyone should be able to become a senator—the office is supposed to be open to all[12]—or anyone should have a chance at being a physician. But in nondemocratic societies this kind of equality is not part of the stipulated or primitive orientation.[13]

Our society is supposed to be a democracy in the honorific sense. But only in the sense that its written law (what legal philosophers call "positive law") usually supports equality is it coming close to enacting its ideals. In claiming that our society is well advanced merely with regard to written law, I am alluding to the fact that discrimination is forbidden either by statute or precedent of cases. For example, such positive law would forbid rejecting someone from medical school on grounds of race. But our society still falls short of actualizing other important ideals of democracy, because the equality that is assured promises only opportunity to compete (likely as an adult); it is not possible to presume that all competitors will have equal access to boundless resources, as was presumed in the early years which framed the republic (Commager 1978).

How alienating it must have been to people such as those in Jonestown, and from Jones's point of view—a Catch 22, an absurdity in Camus's sense—to be told that everyone can scramble and succeed in this society. That line of rhetoric is classical Jacksonianism—a pervasive and consistent strand in the value system of Americans (see Hastings Center Studies 1974 for several pertinent essays). This is the political view for people who understand ethics as Kant did. Where sufficient resources for all make coercion or manipulation of others unnecessary, each of us should *leave others alone,* respect the autonomy and self-determination of others as if each of us was an atom of independence and rationality, or as if events in the kingdom of ends were so incommensurable (because they are atomic) that they can never be added together. The classical hero from the Western movie is a stereotype that fulfills many of these requirements.

Adoption of such an attitude is supported by a social Darwinism that purports to be an ethic. Intellectual leaders of the nineteenth century typify these attitudes. William Graham Sumner (see Boller 1969:58–59), for one, saw the poor and underprivileged as victims of their own nature and past; he saw rights as civil rather than natural, and thus he thought that one must win whatever one will have. Oliver Wendell Holmes, Jr., for another, saw the victim of natural selection as the acceptable correlate of historical progress (Boller 1969:152).

Evolution toward greatness, if possible for a vast portion of a society at all, could, it seems, take place in two ways: either by having the nongreats fall out along the way or by bringing the vast number in society along to near greatness. Neither of these seems to have happened in America, yet. The fragmentary equalization that had taken place has been a shortening of the ends of some fictitious normal (bell-shaped) curve and an increase in its height. This distribution may be true for both vicious and noble characters, as well as for the distributions of the qualities of life that each one of us can experience.[14] In short, the heroic disappears as a moral concept and the hero disappears as a moral agent. The equality of persons takes over the vacated conceptual space. The bland middle class takes over the vacated social space.

Such equalizing speaks to changes in the nature of tragedy in a profound way that is important to our ponderings about Jonestown. The federal report, mentioned above, used "tragedy" in its title. Classically, a play could be called a tragedy and a hero could be called tragic; in order for the play to be a tragedy it had to feature a tragic hero. But there has been a general change in idiom; events now can be called tragic. To construe "tragedy" in the title of the federal report in its classic sense, we would have to say that someone was a hero with a tragic flaw. We could see Jones's life or Representative Ryan's life in that way. But the title seems to intend applying "tragedy" to the decline and demise of everyone who suffered—in just the way newspapers can call a car crash a tragedy just because many members of the same family have been killed.

This is a paradoxical consequence. In some ways it is Kantian-Jacksonian while in other ways it is not. It is so in that the decline and fall of anyone might now be taken as the loss of a person of intrinsic worth; so now equality reigns. It is not Kantian-Jacksonian in that declaring something tragic might be taking as tragedy losses of the kind Taurek found to be irrational—a loss of a family or a young person or a large group. This ingredient seems to rely upon a position that is, like our reaction to Jonestown, natural but hard to understand, hard to intellectualize. Why *is* the loss of any group or of any young person tragic, now? The following is my desperate attempt at an answer that must be approached indirectly by way of an excursion through the mind-body problem.

In the seventeenth century, René Descartes crystalized the mind-body problem. After having doubted everything, he began his philosophic reconstruction of things that he could know for certain with his experience of or his perception of himself thinking; and he puts the point as though that perception is not a bodily experience. Later in his argument, he constructs grounds for belief in experiences of his own body and/or encounters with other bodies on the grounds that God (His existence and nature were deduced in the meantime) is not a deceiver. But metaphysical puzzles abound about how such intrinsically different kinds of substances as mind and body could interact and epistemological puzzles abound about how one can be sure that other people have mind and are not just robots reacting.

Two styles of solutions are customarily tried as responses to the mind-body problem: the first (which follows Descartes) argues that on the basis of analogous bodies and behaviors one is entitled to conclude that there are analogous minds inside; the other (which has given rise to behaviorism) argues that mental language really should be understood as or translated into or reduced to behavioral language, that nothing is inside (save biologic matter).

A powerful philosophic response to the mind-body problem and the two reactions has been supplied by Wittgenstein. John Cook provides a systematic account of Wittgenstein's analysis. It is about how the concept of *human beings* fits into our lives and helps solve (really dissolve) the dualism puzzles (it also helps us to understand the democratization of tragedy). Cook opens his essay "Human Beings"[15] with the following quotation from the *Philosophical Investigations*: "Only of a living human being and what resembles (behaves like) a living human being can one say: it has sensations; it sees; is blind; hears; is deaf; is conscious or unconscious" (Wittgenstein 1958:281). Cook argues that Wittgenstein devised a convincing means of rejecting both behavioristic reductionism (where mental predicates have some criterial relationship to behavioral predicates) and Cartesianism (where analogical arguments ground the inference that similar mental events take place within similarly behaving bodies). Wittgenstein's move is to reject the shared presumption that perceiving bodily movements is epistemologically prior to knowledge of the concept *human being*. He attends instead to how we use the concepts *body, human being, bodily movements,* and the like, and he reminds us that mental predicates such as "dreaming" or "thinking" make sense only in connection with human beings and what behaves like them. In other words (which Cook does not use)[16] these predicates arise for use about animated humans who are perceived to be such.

These concepts are *given*; they are not constructed from something thought to be more basic. This stipulation also reminds us that the way the concept *human* and its close relatives (for example, *child*) work—no inference need be supposed to have occurred when a person makes an appropriate response, as to another's suffering. The expression "suffering behavior" has a clear use, for example, in an acting class, but not in a real case of human injury or hurt. As Cook says, "There is not an undercurrent of uneasiness that runs through all my various encounters with other people tempting me to recoil from them in horror or suspicion. I do not, for instance, suffer queer feelings that my children may be altogether unlike me in some essential respect. When one of them comes crying to me with a bumped head or a bleeding foot, I do not gaze wonderingly at the child, thinking: What can be happening here in this thrashing, noisy thing?" (p. 141). Cook quotes Wittgenstein's *Zettel* (1967: sections 540, 541) (and might well have gone on quoting) to the effect that there is a primitive—that is, a prelinguistic—reaction to tend to or treat others who are in pain. This rejects the intelligibility of any question about why human beings seek to assist the afflicted. If the reaction is primitive, then by definition of "primitive" and "explain" it cannot be explained.[17]

Wittgenstein's generalization about humans and his assertion about the primitive may be wrong. The Ik, though a problematic counterexample, do provide a counterexample.[18] Real villains provide others. Wittgenstein's point would be less questionable had this primitive game been what we seemingly want to ingrain in everybody who doesn't play it.

The moves of the game include the primitive, more humane way of responding—mastery of the language games that use "human" and "person." Thus we have, I believe, a very deep answer to the question, "What is so important about being a human being?" The answer contained in Cook's analysis of Wittgenstein is that the concept *human* is the keystone of our moral vocabulary; our language games about experiences such as pain, joy, or sickness and our language games involving praise and blame are grounded in or created for use about human beings and what resembles them.

In being members of a public order through having learned our language from our groups, we are not just Kantian persons. For example, we frame and recast our language in order to democratize it—so that "slave" or "chairman" have to undergo historic changes in the rules of their use in order to accommodate for democratically mandated changes in awareness and practices.

That these appeals, both (1) to the place of the concept *human being* and (2) to the roots of the language, are public, tailored to needs involving interpersonal commerce, should help us understand our reaction to Jonestown. We are unhappy about human death in general because death means a loss from a certain pool of things. We have developed a system of significance and a style of life through our language that are about members of that pool. We are unhappy about Jonestown in particular, in part because those deaths indicate how much a failure (whether inevitable or not) of caring or nurturing or educating still tinges our democracy and the world. I take this to be an answer to the question about how the notion of the absurd should relate to us the survivors of Jonestown. I turn now to how the victims of Jonestown could have been reacting to their experiences and to how and whether the absurd clearly applies to their context.

Before they left the United States, the victims had all the rights of everyone else in the republic, though rights on paper and rights in fact are not the same. In spite of rights, we hear about alienation a great deal. To clarify its nature we should look closely at what kind of people followed Jones and followed him knowing they ran some high risks.

Because the classified version of the federal report is unavailable, a full picture is not available. The unclassified version starts its inventory in the following way:

> Some of the young adults were college graduates out of upper-middle-class backgrounds which provided privilege and even luxury. Their parents were often college-educated professionals or executives. Frequently, their families were active in demonstrations against the Vietnam war, campaigns for racial equality, and other social causes. In some cases, the young People's Temple member had been alienated by the "emptiness" of his family's wealth. (U.S. Government 1979)

The remaining categories include poor young minorities who were typical products of the ghettos, elderly poor and middle-class fundamentalists of all races, younger humanistically oriented people who were drawn to Jones's agnostic-socialist-Marxist espousals.

Many of the people were broken spirits but apparently (given the first description on the list) some were not excluded from the American dream. Their presence indicates a disaffection with the equality of rights and/or superiority of wealth; and if they could claim no right to be tragic heroes in today's America, they (and all of Jonestown) knew that they needed a better sense of identity than Darwinistic success in a Jacksonian world can supply.

What is needed may be indicated by suggesting that there is a common point in our terms "morality" and "moral support." The commonality is indicated by the place of the concept *human being* as described by Wittgenstein. Human beings are the focus of moral language (a common institution) and moral theory (a rare, professional institution). Humans, their concepts, and their actions are sanctioned, instructed, and constructed by other human beings around them. The social roots of identity are intrinsic. The term "moral," whether regarding *assessment* or *support*, refers to the intrinsic social nature and needs of human beings.

The kind of freedom realized in America thus far may be the best we humans can ever get, but the tension between the freedom mandated by the Jacksonian-Kantian model as a precondition for being a moral subject/agent may be overdrawn, as is indicated, say, by Frithjof Bergmann in his *On Being Free*. Bergmann argues that there are pros and cons to freedom and that the language of freedom is too vague, too emotional, and too widely invoked to be of any conceptual help in understanding the moral order. Instead, he argues, we should look to whether people can act in ways that they find compatible with their sense of identity. (Do I identify myself as free when I act on my concept of rationality alone; *or* when I act on rationality together with my other individual feelings and reactions and aspects; *or* when I fly in the face of what seems mandated by rationality or prudence or desire or anything else?) Bergmann argues that different notions of self-identity correlate with different experiences of freedom. But the feeling of freedom in one's actions is the feeling to be fostered: assuming that I am not importantly deceived by others, I am free when I am at home with what I am trying to do.

Obviously, the people who were attracted to Jones (and to other cults and cult leaders) do not have the required sense of identity. This lack may come about because society has not provided enough nurturance of self and self-identity and it may come about because society has not taught people how to filter out from their inclinations (and thus how to filter out from what would become their selves) the negative or destructive tendencies that they have. It may well be that our track record is as good statistically[19] as it can get. Nevertheless, the deaths at Jonestown stand as a gruesome reminder that there are failures and that the failures have touched the lives of people who are supposed to be equal with everyone else—not merely equal under the rules of a rough and tumble game of scramble for material advantage, but equal as members of the kingdom of ends. The victims at Jonestown were not noble, because no one now is noble. They were human beings, though, and as such they were instances of the kind of creature that our moral notions are framed to be concerned with. The suicides stand as an index of how, as a society, we either abandon our fellow humans (who are the source of our moral concepts) or how we ignore their feelings of failure as persons. The suicides also indicate how the victims felt about us.

From a group that symbolizes the source of our own moral concepts, this is a painful, absurdist message. Jonestown, then, is horrible not alone because of the odor we could faintly imagine or the sight we dimly see there. It is horrible because it marks how we all fail one another and how our highest moral posture ironically comes back to haunt us. Thus it goes to the heart of the *concept* of the absurd, and the democratization of tragedy.[20]

10
Self-Sacrifice as Demonic:
A Theological Response to Jonestown
Stanley Hauerwas

When you are without ideals, you live alone and die rejected. (Jim Jones)

The end justifies the means. (Jim Jones)

The Moral and Religious Challenge of Jonestown

When confronted by such horrors as happened in Jonestown we naturally seek to provide explanations that leave our everyday world
intact. For Jonestown is a challenge to some of our most cherished
assumptions. We like to think that we live in a modern age where
people are beyond this kind of behavior. Therefore the fact that more
than 900 relatively normal people could commit mass suicide simply
lies quite beyond our comprehension. It seems to raise questions like
"How could the most advanced society the world has ever produced
develop a political system that resulted in the murder of 6 million
Jews and others it called undesirable."

We assume that being modern involves at least agreement that no
one ought to take religion too seriously, especially if it is going to ask
any real sacrifices from us. Thus advocates of religion, from the more
sophisticated to the craziest, tend to hawk their wares by promising
that religion will provide us with meaning or at least reinforce our
profoundest desires about what a fulfilling life should be. Any idea
that religious convictions might challenge our deepest beliefs about
ourselves or ask us to make extraordinary sacrifices is simply unthink-
able.

Therefore we can look at the pathetic deaths at Jonestown only as
some kind of pathological mistake. How did these people miss the
important lesson that the lowest possible priority for anyone should
be willingness to die in the name of a religious cause? What must be
remembered is that religion is a dangerous thing and that being dangerous it must be properly domesticated before being given any allegiance. Religion, like certain kinds of drugs, should be taken only in
moderate amounts and under carefully controlled conditions.

We thus think ourselves protected from terrible events such as Jonestown by our assumption that religious convictions do not really involve matters of truth or falsity. Rather, religious beliefs are matters best left to the conscience of each person since religious convictions are largely a matter of opinion. And after all, who would be willing to die for an opinion? Like Pilate, we look on the deaths at Jonestown, wash our hands, and ask "What is truth?"

Yet it will be my argument that our attempts to dismiss or explain what happened at Jonestown as a mistake or as pathology—though certainly much that happened there was pathological—are dangerous trivialization. In contrast, I will suggest, we should take seriously what happened there as an act of revolutionary suicide that should initially be morally honored and respected. Not to honor the people's willingness to take their own lives in a cause they believed true and good is to avoid far too easily the challenge of Jonestown for our secular society as well as for our established religions. Yet it is my contention that what happened at Jonestown was not just a mistake but a form of the demonic that must be recognized and condemned. What went wrong at Jonestown is not that people died for what they believed but that they died for false beliefs and a false god. Their willingness to take their own lives demonstrates the demonic character of their beliefs. I contend that the traditional condemnation of suicide, both personal and revolutionary, by Jews and Christians turns out to be an essential test for considering whether religious convictions might stand the test of being truth.

We often forget that Jews and Christians, no less than Jim Jones, held and hold beliefs for which they think it worth dying. The question was not whether they should die for their convictions, but how they should die. Jews and Christians believe that their lives are not theirs to do with as they wish. Rather they belong to an Other who alone has the right to determine when they will live and when they will die, their existence has value only if such a God exists. Therefore they are prohibited from taking their lives but are equally required to be ready to give their lives if their continued existence depends on their renouncing loyalty to the very Being that made their lives worthy in the first place.[1]

Only in the context of such a tension can the moral significance of the category of martyrdom be appreciated. To be a martyr means that one's death can be clearly distinguished from the immorality of suicide[2] and thus honored as a necessary consequence of one's faith. But it is obviously difficult to distinguish clearly between an act of suicide and an act of martyrdom since isolated acts of either may appear similar. There is no final empirical test to be able to separate the one from the other; rather, final determination must rest on the good judgment and wisdom of the witnesses.

However, Christians and Jews have developed some strong checks through which we may be able to clearly distinguish suicide from martyrdom. An essential one is the refusal of Christians and Jews to lay hands on themselves to end their lives.[3] To lay claim to being a martyr requires that the person be put to death. Christians and Jews believe their task is to live, not to die. We do not seek our death and we refuse to be agents of our death. The agent, if any, must be someone else.

It is tempting in our age to think such distinctions at best irrelevant, even positive distortions of reality. Thus we think irrational those who would be willing to stop life-maintaining measures on an irreversibly ill and dying patient but refuse to administer a drug or inject an air bubble that would precipitate the patient's death. Is it our view that if the patient is going to die anyhow it matters little how? That if some people are stupid enough to hold beliefs that might put them in danger it matters little whether they take their own lives or have others do the deed for them?

Yet such objections fail to understand the profound values that such symbolic scruples are seeking to preserve. By making those who seek to destroy us do the actual killing, Jews and Christians make clear their conviction of the goodness of God's creation. It is not their business or their prerogative to determine when they should die—that they leave to God. Their task is learning how to live faithful and true to the God they deem the source of all that is true and good about our existence. Only when we can make this kind of distinction can we simultaneously honor those who died at Jonestown and condemn what they did. However, before developing this point it is necessary to suggest why those who would explain what happened at Jonestown as pathological fail to deal with its moral and religious reality.

The People's Temple Experience: Can There Be an Explanation?

The first thing anyone feels about Jonestown is naturally the sheer horror of what happened there. It is important not to lose too quickly our sense of horror. For horror is a particularly important moral response as it indicates an appropriate reaction to what we simply feel is incomprehensible. What is truly horrible cannot and should not be explicable in terms of our conventional categories. Rather we must be willing to let the horrible remain foreign and frightening if we are to avoid self-deceptive accounts that may only reinforce more deeply our false perceptions.

To let the matter rest there, however, is almost an impossibility for those of us with intellectual pretensions. Our task is to explain and an event such as Jonestown is simply too rich not to have an explanation attempted. Indeed, Jonestown in many ways is a boon because it invites the kind of intellectual speculation that can make a career. At the very least it offers the opportunity to demonstrate whatever theory we may have about what is the nature of our society or what is causing our particular problems. It is of particular interest to anyone who has the high ambition to understand the current phenomenon of cults because it seems to provide crucial material that will help us understand better the causes of the cults and, perhaps, the result of their doings. And I have no doubt that many of the theories concerning what Jonestown tells us about American society and the cult phenomenon have much to commend them.

I cannot pretend to have read widely the many explanations that have been given about Jonestown. As a matter of fact, one of my frustrations in trying to think about and understand the life of those involved with People's Temple is a lack of any trustworthy accounts and information about them.[4] We can hope to have better descriptions in the near future about Jones and the people who trusted him so completely. It may well be, however, that such accounts will come not from those trained in the empirical methods of the social sciences but rather from those with a novelist's eye for ambiguity and pathos.

Yet the news reports and follow-up articles about Jonestown have reflected theories and explanations that have some plausibility. It is particularly important to note that these theories and explanations are deeply informed by many of the assumptions enshrined and promulgated by social scientists and others who represent the intellectual orthodoxies associated with the contemporary university. Reporters for *Time, Newsweek*, the *Washington Post*, and the *New York Times*[5] may not be scientists, but they often write as people deeply informed by the social-scientific view of society. Thus their perception, as well as the ways they inform our perception of Jonestown, come theory-laden with the explanatory power and assumed wisdom of our science.

The explanation they provide us of Jonestown, I think, looks something like this: Jonestown was possible only because Jim Jones preyed on the dispossessed and poor in our society. The people that made up People's Temple, with a few notable exceptions, were poor black and whites whom Jones was able to supply with a new sense of status and purpose. For these people are the losers in our society and no fate is worse than theirs in a society that makes money success the primary determinant for one's own and others' regard. Jones was able to make these people feel like winners, like somebody, because he gave them a coherent community and an explanation for why they had felt oppressed, the causal economic and societal forces that they now knew how to name as well as how to oppose. Like all significant religious leaders, Jones offered them a plan of salvation at once religious and political.

Thus People's Temple thrived on the rootlessness that many people seem to feel in our culture. Its members were people simply unable to exist without some belief, some cause, that would supply them meaning and purpose. Jim Jones offered such a cause and he showed he was serious exactly because he demanded extreme sacrifices from them. His demand that they turn over all their financial resources to the church was not itself an indication he was a scoundrel; in fact, by demanding sacrifices he indicated the substantial nature of the community.[6] Nor did his wish to be called "Dad" appear absurd; rather it was a profound indication that they had become part of a new family—and this time a family that would not betray them.

At a more profound level the willingness of the community to place trust in Jim Jones can be and has been interpreted as the inability of people to stand freedom. This explanation is meant to cut deeper than the mere claim that rootless people are tragically open to the kind of manipulation in which Jones was so adept. For rootlessness seems to indicate that we have a cultural problem that we need to rectify; but "inability to stand freedom" speaks more directly to the human condition. We assume we ought to be able to stand freedom, and if those who so uncritically followed Jim Jones could not stand it then the burden of proof rests on them rather then on our culture.

The fact that Jones fed on the economically and culturally deprived of our society is not sufficient to account for the ways he was able to convince some of them to kill and many to die. For that accounting we need theories of mass hysteria coupled with the isolation of Jonestown. It is no doubt true that Jones could never have persuaded so many to die if they had still been in San Francisco. Certainly the air of unreality created at Jonestown, as well as a sense of sharing the sacrifices and the deprivation necessary for survival there, created the possibility of a mass suicide that otherwise would have been impossible.

But such explanations, while no doubt containing some truth, are secondary to the undeniable reality of Jim Jones's personal power. I think there can be little question that in the last years of his life he was certifiably crazy. But there is also little doubt that he was an extremely powerful person with considerable insight and organizational skill. He was certainly charismatic, but it is also true that much of his power was based on the fact that he often spoke the truth. That is not to say that any intellectual sense can be made of his peculiar blend of Marxism and Christianity, but the intellectual incoherence of his views makes little difference. He obviously was a man who had not much use for theories. Rather, he simply used whatever seemed handy to articulate, for those that followed him, truthful claims about their existence and the injustice of our society.

Jones was right after all that we do live in a society of fear and hate; that is not news for anyone who had recently read the New Testament. The early Christians seem also to have thought that we always live in a world ruled by the powers of fear and hate. Yet Jones, unlike pastors in more established forms of Christianity, was able to present this view clearly and effectively to a group of people who had the experience to know it was true. Moreover, Jones held out a strategy designed to help them live in such a world—he offered an alternative community where love, not hate, would rule. Thus he claimed, "This is why we're here. It's for these children. It's all for them. We have to work, and work, and work, and we have to stay together for these babies! So that they can have a world full of love. A world where there is no hate! A world where there is social equality! A world with racial equality! A world with economic equality!" (Kerns and Wead 1979:41).

To be sure, this kind of idealism appears strikingly naive to those of us who think we have learned better. But Jones cannot so easily be dismissed. He did not just hold it up as an outcome to be realized in the future. He made it a present reality for many of those who followed him. People's Temple did become a place where blacks and whites discovered they could be brothers once they had both discovered who was their real enemy. People's Temple did provide people with their first experience of being responsible for someone else's life. People's Temple did offer the opportunity to experience the exhilaration of learning that you are capable of being loved and thus of loving.

Moreover, such love and community was not to be limited to those who participated in People's Temple as Jones was able to translate that experience into a program. He gave his people a cause, an adventure, a sense of being chosen. Because they had been blessed they now had the peculiar responsibility to witness and to transform the wider society into one of love and equality. Jones offered people something more profound than just meaning and status; he offered a mission.[7]

The sacrifices they must make along the way were intelligible only in the light of such a mission—even the ultimate sacrifice that he required from them.

It seems easy after the event for us to think that the followers should have been able to spot Jones's paranoia and, perhaps, charlatanism. But I think that opinion is a failure to appreciate the genuine complexity of a figure like Jones. To be sure, he did use some of the tricks of any religious huckster; but they were incidental to his power over his people. Or it may seem that his increasingly bizarre sexual practices and demands should have caused many to have second thoughts; but again his demands did have a kind of rationality from within the world he had created. Even his use of blackmail and physical threat made sense to a people who were convinced that they were dealing with someone who had his hand on the pulse of the very power of the universe.

Moreover, all attempts to dismiss Jones as a charlatan, someone who was seeking his own interest in a narrow sense, simply fail to fit the facts. Jones, no doubt, was cynical about much he was doing and about many of his followers. But he was a true believer. There is no sign that he had any doubt about the ultimate righteousness of his cause or of himself.[8] Indeed, if he had been blessed with some disbelief it might have been enough to save 900-odd lives. But he did believe that his message was true and that he was crucial to its truth—so crucial that he could ask these hundreds of people to die rather than continue living without him.

Yet the very recognition of Jones's power as the primary explanation for what happened at Jonestown only increases our difficulty with any attempt to explain what happened there. Even if Jones was the figure that made possible their revolutionary suicide, then how do we explain such power? It seems to be a power correlative to our horror of the suicides—that is, we know of no ready way to explain either. Both seem inexplicable given our everyday assumptions about how the world works, or at least should work.

I believe that we can account for the peculiar power Jones held over his people only if we will recognize that he was making an essentially religious appeal that did offer a way, such as every significant religion offers, to deal with distressing aspects of our existence. Of course, since the mass suicide the more established forms of religion in our society perhaps have tried as much as possible to show that their genuine religion is not like that offered by Jones. But in fact what is embarrassing about Jones, in spite of some clear differences, is how close much of what he had to say parallels normative Christianity.

Like the early Christians, Jones thought in global terms about the struggle in which he was engaged. It was a struggle between light and darkness, between good and evil. Any people who would be worthy of such a struggle must be converted entirely from their former way of life. They must be willing to sacrifice everything—wealth, security, family, life itself—if their life was to be transformed. And like the early Christians they understood that such a task was fundamentally political. As one of Jones's followers rightly claimed, "Jones has always wanted to build a multiracial, peaceful, egalitarian society. Here we have the opportunity to create human institutions from cradle to grave, literally. Social change is really our focus. We don't see that religion and politics are separate" (Krause 1978:69).

Moreover, we must remember that early Christianity was no less disruptive of family life than was Jones's Christianity. You must leave father, mother, wife, and husband, for now the Christian community is your true family. Even more radical was the early Christian assumption that some should be freed from all familial ties for service to the Kingdom. It is no wonder that many decent pagans saw Christianity as a threat to everything they held dear. For their sons and daughters to convert to such a religion was bound to ruin promising careers. Even though there is no question that Jones used the sexual ethic he developed for his own personal pleasure and also used intimidation for maintaining his church, it is also true that much of what he had to say about the family had precedent in Christian history.

It is not my purpose to try to show that Jones was an orthodox Christian; he certainly was not. Indeed, his very success is a judgment on the church and on our society for giving people so little religious substance that they could not recognize heresy when they saw and experienced it. Jones was successful because he was able to co-opt the general religiosity of people, legitimated by vague reference to Christian symbols, and to turn that religiosity into a powerful force by putting pieces together in a perverted manner. What is tragic is that no one was well-enough schooled in a normative tradition to challenge Jones's understanding of God or Jesus. A people who have lost any sense of how religious traditions are capable of truth and falsity can easily fall prey to the worst religious claims, having lost the religious moorings that might provide them with discriminating power. No one challenged Jones when he threw the Bible away, saying that it got in the way of his followers' perception of him.

The discrimination to make such a challenge was perhaps too much to ask of those who followed Jones, but it is not too much to ask of those who stood religiously outside People's Temple. But alas, we live at a time when the more orthodox forms of Christianity refuse to pass judgment on any religious phenomenon on theological grounds for fear that such judgments might violate the norm of tolerance. Like all good secularists, Christians today do not condemn the beliefs of cults but rather criticize them only for practices that seem to violate people's autonomy.[9] After all, beliefs are a matter of personal choice, not subject to claims of truth or falsity. Only actions can be condemned and those only on a basis that is shared by our general culture.

So we lacked and continue to lack the resources to explain as well as condemn what was happening in People's Temple. For any explanation of People's Temple necessarily requires religious claims, since Jones's power and the ultimate sacrifice of those at Jonestown had a religious nature. Sociological and psychological factors may help explain some of what went on there, but the fact that hundreds of people committed revolutionary suicide cannot be explained so easily. They killed themselves because they thought they should die for what they believed the truth. No doubt some were murdered, but many willingly and bravely died because they thought such a death was consistent with the truth they had learned and experienced through the ministry of Jim Jones.

From our perspective we think their deaths foolish because they did not have to die. After all, the murder of Congressman Ryan and the reporters did not mean the end of Jonestown or of People's Temple. Rather, it meant the arrest of Jim Jones and those who had perpetrated the act. But from the perspective of those who thought their very existence depended on Jim Jones, such jailing meant nothing less than the dissolution of the community that they now identified as their very life. To lose the community was equivalent to losing their life. So, like the martyrs, they chose spiritual life rather than spiritual death. Better to be dead in body than face the living death that would come with the destruction of People's Temple.

Suicide, Martyrdom, and Truth

Some may object that I have given a far too favorable interpretation to what happened at Jonestown. Jones, after all, was a seriously sick man who had successfully convinced his 900-odd people to go along with his madness. That is the long and short of it and nothing further needs to be said. To take their deaths seriously as revolutionary suicide makes it sound like those poor ignorant people might have known what they were doing and thus should be treated as worthy moral agents.[10] Better to explain their deaths psychologically than to open up the possibility that their deaths had any meaning.

Yet I have tried to assume the point of view of the people of Jonestown, tried to show that psychological and sociological explanations fail to do justice to the reality of their deaths. They rightly died for what they believed. They rightly described their act as revolutionary suicide, for their deaths were meant to protest a world that would not allow the existence of the kind of community they were trying to build. The kind of society they envisioned was revolutionary, at least in principle, for it would require of wider society a transformation that would be nothing less than revolutionary. The pathos of their death can be felt when we reflect on how distant from the vision that Jones had originally burned into their imaginations was the community they experienced at Jonestown under his leadership. But even the distance between fiction and reality cannot undo the reality of a group of people who thought their beliefs true and so were willing to die for them.

That fact is just the problem. For the beliefs for which the Jones followers died were in fact false. The people were not wrong to worship God, but the god they worshiped was false. Yet even false gods have their power and such power cannot be countered simply by denying their existence. Rather, false gods like false worship can be countered only by the true God and true worship.

The faith generated by Jim Jones was demonic because it was a faith not in God but finally in man. No surer sign of the demonic character of that faith was the followers' willingness to take their own lives. For the willingness to take their lives, and the lives of others,[11] manifests the assumption that they must insure their own existence. The Jewish and Christian prohibition against suicide is not based on the inherent sacredness of life but rather on God's sovereignty over all life. Our life is not for us to do with as we please, but rather we must learn to look on our life as a gift that is not ours to dispose.

Nor do Christians and Jews think this prohibition a mere prejudice or opinion peculiar to them. Rather they think that the prohibition against suicide is a true statement about the way life should be lived in the presence of God. The prohibition against suicide is thus not just a normative recommendation but indeed a statement about the very nature of human existence as bounded by the power of God. Those, therefore, who would contemplate and indeed even practice suicide as did those at Jonestown must be judged worshipers of a false god.

That judgment does not mean they are not martyrs, but that they are not martyrs to the true God. Rather they are martyrs of a society which no longer believes that issues of truth and falsity pertain in matters religious. They, like many, thought it better to believe something rather than nothing. Their mistake was to take such belief seriously, not realizing that religious devotion is in the society's outlook primarily a personal matter. In a more profound sense, however, they cannot even be martyrs. They were merely passive victims. They were victimized not just by Jim Jones, but by a society and by religious institutions that supply no means to discern the demonic, much less bestow the power to deal with it.

Our society often piously applauds those who seem to be self-sacrificial. Those at Jonestown were such to a degree that few of us would approve. But their mistake was not that they were willing to give their lives for what they believed but that what they believed was so wrong. In the absence of substantial beliefs their sacrifice became an end in itself, legitimating all the smaller but very demanding sacrifices that made them part of People's Temple in the first place. Their sacrifice, unlike that of Jewish and Christian martyrs, was demonic because it served not the true God of life but powers that we think we avoid by denying their existence.

Jim Jones was right that without ideals we live alone and die rejected. He offered ideals that promised community, something worth sacrificing for, and death among friends. But the means he used to form such a community should have been a sure sign that what People's Temple served was not the truth. Our tragedy is that there was no one internal or external to that community able to challenge the false presuppositions of Jones's false ideals. Our continuing tragedy is that our reactions to and our interpretation of the deaths at Jonestown reveal accurately how we lack the convictions to counter the powers that reigned there.

Part Four
Report of a Former Member of People's Temple

The chapter in the final section of this volume strikes an entirely different tone from the rest. This conversational and unstructured account was written not by a scholar but by a former cult member. It offers a phenomenological view of what it is like to be a member of a violent cult. Chapter 11 brings us back to People's Temple and to the ability of members to progressively rationalize the most inhumane forms of discipline until they found themselves trapped at Jonestown with only fear, hunger, and the Truth According to Jim Jones.

11
Jonestown Masada
Jeannie Mills

Little Tommy Kice was acting spoiled. He wouldn't eat all the food they put in front of him. Jim said he had to eat it because everyone had to eat all the food on their plates. He made Tommy eat it but then he vomited it up into his plate. Then Jim took a spoon and made him eat the vomit. Tommy threw it up again and Jim made him eat it again. Tommy was screaming and yelling but Jim made him eat it anyway. (Mills 1979:162)

If I had said to Jim Jones or to anybody else that I think it was really terrible what he did to Tommy Kice, then I would be saying that Jim Jones was making a very serious mistake. And you just didn't do that. Now, because I couldn't complain to anybody, I couldn't really formulate the thoughts clearly in my own mind. Suppose, for example, you're a radio broadcaster and you do a program that you know is really awful. You haven't prepared it, and as you're doing it you think, "My God, this is the worst program I've ever done." But then you come out, and the stage people say, "That was great." The audience says, "That was fantastic." And you get all these letters, and everybody says, "You helped me understand the situation, your program was the highlight of my life." And you go home and your family says, "Honey, you really did a fantastic program." That's very much like what was happening to us. We knew it was atrocious when Jim did things like he did to Tommy, but everyone was saying it was so wonderful. Plus the fact that afterwards, after the Tommy Kice incident, all of our children started cleaning up everything in their plates; they were much more mature and adult than they had been. So I felt, "It works." Therefore, "Father" has once again shown his tremendous intelligence, his concern for people.

Jim had just begun...I have seen by divine revelation the total annihilation of this country and many other parts of the world. San

Editor's Note: Jeannie Mills is the author of *Six Years with God*, about her experience as a member of People's Temple from 1969 to 1975. She had recently interviewed most of the survivors of the Jonestown event when she wrote this.

> Francisco will be flattened. The only survivors will be those people
> who are hidden in the cave that I have been shown in a vision.
> Those who go into this cave with me will be saved from the poison-
> ous radioactive fallout that will follow the nuclear bomb attack.
> (Mills 1979:122)

We were going to come out of the cave and repopulate the earth. In
fact, his repopulate-the-earth theory was so funny. He was telling all
of the old people that they'd be having babies. Edith Cloydell, a little
seventy-year-old grandmother, was told that everyday she should lu-
bricate her vagina because after the atomic bomb, she'd be having
babies; that's how dumb some of the things were, and yet people
didn't laugh at that, not a bit.

I think my religious upbringing had made me gullible. Once you
think of it, Heaven, Jesus, the miracles are all really as mystical and
as ridiculous. Jesus is going to come, and the trumpets are going to
sound, and we're all going to be pushed up to a place where there's
pearly gates. Any person who could believe that could be just as likely
to believe a human being who says, "Look, here I am; by some supernatural means, I have found out the day the bombs will go off; there
is a place where we can go, and we can protect ourselves." What's the
difference between that and a bomb shelter? I felt he did have some
prophetic gift. And I thought, "If I can't believe in Jim Jones, then I
wouldn't have believed in Jesus Christ. What kind of a skeptic am I?"

I was extremely naive. I went to a Seventh Day Adventist school, I
went to church, I was a Campfire leader, I was a youth representative—
that's my background. Tim Stoen—his background is almost the
same as mine: leader in his church, top student, very, very sheltered.
His mother was very strict, and he'd never got out into the world.
Naivety is a great factor. The kids coming from the other cults are
similar. The one that joins the cult is the best kid in your family, the
one that always got straight As, the one that was the cheerleader, the
one that was doing so well in college, because they just don't know.
They're so pure and noble, and so when somebody comes up to them
and says, "I'll take you out to dinner," they say, "Well, of course.
How sweet. How wonderful you are." We'd never been told that
there's no such thing as a free lunch. So, when somebody comes along
and says, "I'll give you a free lunch," you say, "Oh, thank you very
much."

> From time to time, Al and I would ask one another, "What did we
> do with our lives before we joined this group?" And we would

answer that life hadn't seemed worthwhile until Jim instilled a sense of purpose in us and gave us a reason to live. We wanted to please him, because we believed that he loved us. We were certain that as long as we stayed in his group, our lives would continue to be blissful. (Mills 1979:131)

It's just like having a family. You work every month to pay the bills; you save a little; that gives you a sense of purpose. Our purpose was making our group grow from day to day, making it more powerful.

For example, every time we made a political ally, that made us more powerful. When we wrote thousands of letters to the Senate to get Judge Carswell defeated in his bid to gain a seat on the Supreme Court—the power that we felt! Suddenly, as a group we were invincible. We could actually make major changes in the United States government.

This was going to be our family forever. In society, you move, you change jobs, you go to different schools, you get a divorce, and you have this feeling of impermanence. But in People's Temple, even if you get divorced or change jobs, or *whatever* change you may make in your personal life, this family structure was permanent. We had the feeling, we will *always* be together. And it felt good. It felt comfortable.

We felt that none of this would be possible without the leadership of Jim Jones. And he continually told us, the only way that any group can be cohesive is if the leader has all power and everybody trusts his judgment. Jim Jones said, "I am the cause. You don't even understand what the cause is. You just relate to me. I am the cause."

I don't think that Jones was such a fantastic human being; it's just the tremendous reverence that we gave him. We surrounded him with this aura of power. He used to laugh about it. He says, "I could be five-by-five and the ugliest thing in the world, but as long as I have power, I will always be respected, and I will always be feared. Women will always want me."

He began to hint broadly that he was none other than "God Almighty." In a secret meeting he told us that he knew his previous incarnations..."I lived thousands of years ago as Buddha. Then I spent a short incarnation as the Bab, the person who founded the Bahai faith. I have lived on earth as Jesus the Christ, and my last incarnation was in Russia as Vladimir Lenin." (Mills 1979:181)

By this time we had been thoroughly schooled in reincarnation. Reincarnation is really a precious belief for me because by my former beliefs, I was condemned to hell. I was sure I was going to hell because in marrying my second husband, I was an adulteress. I had been thrown out of my church, and therefore unless I left my husband whom I loved very much, I would go to hell. So, when Jones introduced reincarnation, suddenly a lot of things made sense: like the retarded baby, the extremely rich, the crippled. Why they all had only one chance at heaven never made sense to me. So, reincarnation was important to me.

Jones started telling some of us who we had been in previous lifetimes. And our beliefs are really a funny thing: my husband and I were going through a Russian book, and we found a man that my husband thought was him. The man had died three days before my husband had been born. So, we didn't have any reason not to believe in Jones working miracles. We watched these Lenin movies and the facial structure of Lenin and Jones looked very much alike. And signs would happen, like Jones had picked up a cat that was walking around and was holding the cat in his hand, and Al took a Polaroid picture. He came back in and laid the picture down on my lap. The cover of the book I was reading showed a picture of Lenin holding a cat, the exact same pose! Here were two pictures by sheer coincidence sitting on my lap, and they looked alike. Jones's face looked exactly like Lenin's face in the book. These kinds of things happening made me think, "Well, it might be true. Why not?"

We had really stopped any logical thought. We were living more reactively than anything. I remember during this time, I was working until four in the morning. I began at eight—a lot of times not getting any sleep at all. I never dreamed while I was in People's Temple. When I lay down, I was out like a light.

During the first suicide rehearsals in California, if there had been real poison in the drink that he passed out, I would have taken it for several reasons: one is that life was so hard; it would have been an easy way out. I can remember when I endured those long meetings. They'd talk about people maybe going to prison someday. I prayed, "Please let it be me!" It would be such an easy out, such a rest. No more meetings, no more sermons. I mean literally this is where my head was at, because we were so *tired*. These meetings would last until three or four in the morning, and we *had* to stay awake. We'd be watching the movies of the Nazi concentration camps, of the Chilean concentration camps, tortures, the electrodes being strapped to the genitals of people and them going through the agonies—that's what we were being fed with in a very sleepy state, and our minds weren't thinking rationally. That's why it's so hard for researchers to understand. You say, "But you sound so logical. How could you have done this?" Those are irrelevant questions. We were so tired, we were so weary, we weren't thinking.

> The attorneys wrote a release form which each person had to sign before being beaten... Now that Jim felt legally safe, there was no stopping his cruel beatings. He decided that the belt didn't hurt enough, so he had the guards bring in long elm switches. They kept breaking under the force of the hard whacks, though, and Jim realized that he would have to use something much sturdier. (Mills 1979:260)

When the beatings started, it changed a lot. It changed from love to fear. By this time we were totally in there because we were afraid to leave. And the fear was many-faceted: we were afraid of losing our church families, we were afraid of not playing our part in this ultimate cause, we were afraid that we would miss out on the promised land (Jonestown, that is), which was when all of the beatings and everything would supposedly stop, we were afraid that we would be separated from our children, we were also under the fear that we would be beaten. I mean, there was continuous fear. Anything you did, you thought, "Oh, my God, what if somebody turns me in and Jones doesn't like this?" And fear was just as complete a master as love had been earlier. Everybody we've talked to has had almost exactly the same experience.

Now, an interesting thing is that nobody really recognizes that change (from love to fear) until they get out and get deprogrammed in one way or another. But there is a changeover, a "snapping" thing that goes on in your mind when all of a sudden you step outside of the experience and look back at it, and you become logical. Okay, there are still people today who claim, "There were never beatings in People's Temple. Jim Jones was a loving, wonderful person." I was just on a radio station in Berkeley and a lady called in and she says, "I was a member for fourteen years and Jim Jones was the most wonderful person I ever knew and I would never speak against him, even though I lost a sister down in Jonestown." People like her haven't had that opportunity to step away from the experience and look at it logically. While I was in People's Temple, I didn't know that I was being ruled by fear. I thought I was still in there because I wanted to be in there. If you would have come to me a week before we left and said, "I want to help you out," I'd have said, "You're crazy." There

was this daily sensation of "Oh, my God, I might get beaten," but not
the sensation of "I'm only here because I'm afraid," you know, "no
cause exists, nothing exists, I'm just here because I'm terrified." That
thought never occurred to me.

> One afternoon we received an emergency message. "Come to
> Church immediately for a special meeting." ... When we arrived, it
> was obvious that Jim was very upset. He began, "Eight people left
> the Church last night. They cut the telephone wires so Tom couldn't
> call to warn us ... These eight people might cause our Church to go
> down. They could say things that would discredit our group. This
> might be the time for all of us to make our translation together."
> (Mills 1979:231)

This was the first time he said we're going to kill ourselves together
(and then be "translated" to another galaxy). Before that we just
thought it could happen—somehow we'd die and it would come out
looking like such a noble thing. "History will judge us and know
that we did the right thing." Jones was always afraid of being discredited in history; that was his greatest fear. Isn't that interesting?

He thought that they would find him dead with the hundreds of
dead followers around him. I think that he probably had the Masada
incident in mind. He never mentioned it, but I think that probably
was in the back of his mind: how marvelous the event would be!
Then also, he talked about Leningrad a lot, like a fortress holding
out. And see if we had done that, then these defectors, these ex-
members of the Church, who were going around telling lies, these
people would be made to look like fools, because of the tremendous
impact of all the dead followers being so loyal to Jones that they
would die for him.

> ... Oh, God. I tell you I don't care how many screams you hear. I
> don't care how many anguished cries, death is a million times pref-
> erable to ten more days of this life. Will you quit telling them they're
> dying. If you adults would stop some of this nonsense. Adults ...
> adults ... adults ... I call on you to stop this nonsense ... I call on
> you to quit exciting your children when all they're doing is taking a
> quiet rest, when all they're doing is taking a drink that makes them
> go to sleep. That's what death is, sleep. [*Shrieking sounds in the
> background.*] Take the life from us, sleep. We're laying down. We're
> tired. When you commit suicide, it's an act of revolutionary suicide
> to protest against the conditions of an inhumane world. [Exerpt

from a tape recording of Jim Jones's final speech to his congregation during the administration of the cyanide drink.]

Once they got into the Jonestown camp, members of People's Temple were no longer under the illusion that this was paradise. For example, Burt Godfrey went down to Jonestown thinking it was paradise, and then he discovered that they served rice three times a day. After the third meal of rice, he says, "Hey, what's all this rice shit?" So they said Burt Godfrey's a troublemaker, and he was put on a work crew, where they make you work twice as hard and twice as fast as anybody else for the first two weeks. Up in San Francisco, they were being told that it was fruits and vegetables and no work and lots and lots of sex and everything that paradise is supposed to imply. But the minute they got down there, they were stuck in the fields for fourteen hours a day. There wasn't enough food. There was rice and beans and tea and gravy, and that's just about it. When Congressman Ryan came down, it was the first good meal they'd had in years. So they were no longer under any illusions. But there were still people who were so mind-controlled that they'd come back and still say that Jonestown was a beautiful place.

All the survivors from the Jonestown massacre said that they really felt that it was just another ritual—a loyalty test—until they saw the babies foaming at the mouth. I think that it took five minutes from the time the first baby got poisoned to the time he started foaming at the mouth. When the yelling and the foaming started, that's when they realized what was happening, and that's when they got themselves hidden from the rest of the crowd. This is how some of the survivors managed to escape.

I think that the translation—the idea that everyone would be translated to another galaxy after we killed ourselves—is maybe one percent of the motive that people had for killing themselves. It's something mystical. It's like when you're dying, you can say, "Well, I'm going to go to Heaven." The same way with this translation thing. I mean, you hope that there's something better outside than what you're leaving. But I don't think that anybody really counted on that, any more than just a hope.

Also, there's another factor here. The people were still operating under a very mind-controlled state. They weren't thinking of what they were doing. They were reacting to orders.

Another factor is that the only news they got was from Jim Jones. They were told and believed that the Ku Klux Klan was running wild in the streets of San Francisco, that blacks were being killed, that for example, all the Safeway stores were being closed down. Every piece of news Jones got, he exaggerated. Remember when the Safeway stores went on strike? He said they had all closed down. Remember when that earthquake or flooding or something happened in Los Angeles? He said that the whole city of Los Angeles had been devastated. Okay, their picture of the United States was one of total chaos. And Mark Lane, the one human being outside of Jim Jones that they trusted, he said, if any of you escape, the CIA will torture you. So, they felt that there was no alternative. They felt that they couldn't go back to America, that they'd cut off all their ties with their families, that the government was going to get them if they got out. So, really, they felt that there was no choice. Tim Stoen, when he came out, he thought he was going to be arrested, he was scared to death to come to California; he called me twice from Europe. He said, "I don't dare come to California. The government has got all these papers on me (false confessions that Jones had made the members sign). They'll arrest me." Jones had told everybody, "Never go back. You'll be put in jail for the rest of your life."

I'd say about 90 percent of the people killed themselves because they were coerced to do so. You have to remember that they had guns pointed at them. In order to put it into perspective, you have to realize that the people at Georgetown (the capital of Guyana) and the people at San Francisco were sent a message that this is the time to kill yourself, okay, and the only person who did it was Linda Amos.

I talked to Mr. Gurvich, that investigator who went down to try to find his daughter's body, and he's the only person that I know who went through every body. He says cyanide apparently makes your body go rigid in the position you're in. It's very lifelike. And these people were fending off attacks, he said. There were a whole bunch of big men who had blows to the skull, blows to the back, where they apparently had to be subdued to take the drink. Many of them fell down in the position holding their arms up so that somebody wouldn't hit them. You get a totally different idea of what had happened than you got in the press, where the main thing that you saw was Jack Beam, Ravina Beam, and their daughters. To see these other bodies, you had to go past many, many smelly bodies, and it was very hard to get there. And oh, the faces, the bloated faces were so awful. The black faces looked like the Darth Vader mask.

The people nowadays who say that Jonestown was an aberration, something totally different than other sects or cults, are people who are followers of some guru or baba or followers of some leader of their own, and it's threatening to them. But I can tell you, People's Temple was *not* the biggest and the baddest. The end was the worst that ever happened historically, but there are groups that are far more mind-controlling than People's Temple. There are groups where they ritually talk about suicide, where the members carry things to kill themselves. Worse than that, there are groups where instead of talking about internalizing violence, they talk about externalizing violence. If we go down the list, like the SLA and Manson, both of these were far more violent in the end result than People's Temple

I definitely think that something like Jonestown could happen again, especially now that Scientology just lost a $2 million law suit; Children of God just lost a $1 million law suit. These organizations are so very wealthy that they're not going to take this lying down. They realize this could be the end of their organization. If one person could win a law suit, there are another 150 out there who are equally swindled and who are just going to come right in and say, "I want some of the pie, too." So, I think some serious problems could potentially happen.

Most of the groups that we hear of in the news haven't been backed into a corner yet. Other sects have left the country, several groups because the pressure was getting intense. There's a cult all over the United States—whenever there's troublemakers, they're shipped over to India. If we hadn't cared about the people down in Jonestown, what would have happened is: Guyana was getting sick and tired of them; they would have been shipped out of there, gone over to Russia, and probably would have ended up in a Russian labor camp. Nobody would have heard a word more. That's where Jones went wrong. He was a tiger backed into a corner, and nobody would let him out.

Conclusion:
Religion and Violence
Ken Levi

What *really* happened at Jonestown? Even now, accounts differ. But Jonestown is a fact. It is a tragedy; it is, as Erde tells us, an absurdity. It violates autonomy insofar as values were used to defeat their own grounds. It signals a failure in our democracy. It confounds our concept of human nature. It demands our understanding.

The contributors to this book have attempted to explain Jonestown as a cult phenomenon. But what kind of a cult phenomenon? Different groups, ranging from the ACM (anticult movement) to the news media to various scholarly professions, each present us with different conceptual frameworks in which to view religious violence. To put it simply, if an anticultist, a reporter, a psychiatrist, a sociologist, a theologian, a philosopher, and a cultist were all present during the same episode of religious violence, each would come out with a different version of what had happened.

The anticultists would see mindless zombies with glassy stares, acting under the cynical guidance of a master manipulator, the hypnotic cult leader ruthlessly exploiting them for his own personal profit. Some former cult members may also share this view, inasmuch as it enables them to see themselves as passive victims not really responsible for their own prior actions. According to Anthony and Robbins, psychological notions of mind control present a more sophisticated but similar view of violent cultists as brainwashed automatons.

Sociologists (including myself) tend to view cult violence as a symptom of fervent commitment, similar in form to the kind of commitment that one might encounter in a business corporation or political party. The "spiritually arrogant" cultist is self-willed (to the extent anyone can be) because his actions are meaningful to him, in the same sense that the patriotic soldier fights for a cause that is meaningful to him.

The experience reported in Chapter 11 of this book presents a somewhat different, more complicated image. Fear plays an important part. Members of People's Temple are portrayed as personally disorganized, anxious, and guilty. Coerced and prodded and exhorted, even at the moment of ultimate sacrifice in Jonestown, they seem less moved by religious fervor than by a blend of all too mundane human emotions, ranging from the cocky irritability of the rifle-toting guards to the brittle officiousness of the nurses at the cyanide-drink tubs to the bovine acquiescence of people shuffling forward in their line.

Conceptualizations about *what actually happened* necessarily underlie explanations for Jonestown in particular, or for any episode of sectarian violence. In this case, since the images of what happened are so various, it is unlikely that we will be able to agree on a single, general explanation. Perhaps the best we can do at this point is to return to Chapter 1 and, using the three theoretical approaches in that chapter as an outline, summarize the major points of agreement among the different authors in this book.

Societal Context

Chapter 1 suggests that extremist cults arise in times of rapid change involving extensive structural differentiation, pluralism, and secularization. Psychic and economic deprivations are aggravated by these changes, which undermine social cohesion and make society less attractive to its members.

By themselves, these changes would not be sufficient to produce the cult phenomenon. But, as Zurcher, Redlinger, Armour, and Hauerwas remind us, our society is also conducive to extremist religious movements. The First Amendment protecting freedom of speech and assembly, the tradition of religious pluralism and relativism, the separation of church and state, all encouraged a long history of new religions in this country and provided a precedent for others to follow. People who already accept religious, psychic, or transcendental phenomenologies would be especially receptive to these kinds of groups.

Within this societal context, favorable to the emergence of new religious groups, something occurred to make these groups especially popular at the beginning of the 1970s. In a negative sense, one factor certainly was the failure of political protest groups of the 1960s to channel people's grievances. On the other hand, most of the contributors to this volume agree that the grievances themselves arose from rapid social change. Moreover, this change did not take the form of a reaffirmation of traditional values and structures. On the contrary, the shock that occurred in the 1960s resulted in "empirical, this-worldly, secular, humanistic, pragmatic, utilitarian, epicurean, or hedonistic culture" (Zurcher, p. 62 of this book, quoting Kahn and Weiner). The effect was to loosen the grip of traditional bonds and traditional standards—or any standards.

Rapid social disorganization had the general effect of creating psychic confusion and frustration. But can we specify the effect more

precisely? Zurcher focuses on self-concept and the need for "a worka-
ble anchorage for social interaction." Rapid change thrusts the individual into an uncomfortably "reflective self-concept" (who am I?
what is my purpose in life? and the like). Society no longer sustains
earlier roles. Nor does it provide any new roles, but rather requires
that one organize one's life around transience.

The "solid and simplified" self-concepts offered by cults can be
viewed as one among a wide range of antidotes to the shock of social
change. As Zurcher notes, we witnessed a proliferation of hucksters
selling everything from insight to status to physical beauty in an
attempt to provide us with some kind of anchor for the self. The
1970s, in addition to religious cults, also brought assembly-line plastic surgery, health clubs, crisis hot lines, the attack on the Equal
Rights Amendment, Anita Bryant, Richard Nixon, and a general
return to traditional values. Jim Jones was merely one of many "helping people be somebody."

This panacea is especially poignant for the nobodies of our society.
Richardson reminds us that the members of People's Temple were 80
to 90 percent poor urban blacks. This poverty distinguishes it from
groups such as the Divine Light Mission or the Unification Church
or Hare Krishna, where most of the members were middle-class
whites. Violent cults, as opposed to cults in general, seem to contain
the extreme outcasts of our society. The Church of the Lamb of God,
Manson's Family, Synanon, and People's Temple include people who
are not just "psychically deprived," but *economically and socially
deprived as well.*

For the extreme outcasts of our society, as Erde notes, being told
that anyone can make a success of himself *on his own* must seem
particularly absurd. The Jacksonian-Kantian vision of every man as
an atom of independence conjures up a sense of identity unattainable
for most of them. The fatally autonomous groups that they set up to
care for themselves may indeed signal a tragic failure of caring and
nurturing in our society as a whole. As Hauerwas notes, "Jones told
them the truth about their condition in society and offered them
something meaningful and substantial in return."

Society always has its rootless people. But the context of the 1970s
created a fatal blending of two kinds: (1) extreme outcast elements of
society, with their usual—if somewhat exaggerated—complement of
woes; and (2) those members of the college-educated middle class with
organizing ability and wherewithal, who had become psychically disenchanted with the values that society had to offer.

Sectarian Context

According to Chapter 1, religious violence is most likely to occur in sects that enforce a single version of the truth by exercising total control and demanding total loyalty. Enforcement mechanisms are the more effective the more isolated the group is from society as a whole.

The single version of the truth that sect members adopt is not just thrust upon them. As various contributors note, violent cultists come from cultures that already accept violence, to some degree, and that already accept religious or mystical phenomenologies. Furthermore, as Zurcher notes, the novice may readily adopt a single, categorical, and rigid set of standards in order to achieve the consistent social self-image that he or she requires.

Adherence to the cult's ideology is also reinforced by a system of total control. Both violent and nonviolent cults employ many of the same enforcement mechanisms. However, violent cults appear to stand out in three particular ways.

First, they are more centralized and less bureaucratic. A single charismatic leader, such as a Charles Manson or a Jim Jones or an Ervil LeBaron, exercises authority directly, in much the way a father controls his family. The exercise of such control is consistent with groups that are fairly small and localized. The *absence of bureaucratic structures*, in the form of elaborate rules or administrative officials, enhances the personal authority of the leader and creates ambiguity and disorganization among the members, which in turn may contribute to the pervasive atmosphere of fear and anxiety. In contrast, bureaucratic structures help to prevent spontaneous, impulsive reaction to emergency. Otherwise, a high-school basketball team might occasionally lapse into a violent mob.

A second control mechanism, linked to violence because of the ambiguity, anxiety, and fear that it creates and because of the unchecked power that it confers, is the cult leader's sway over *psychic forces*. An overinquisitive novice can be put off with a facile, "Well, you're nothing but a human. How could you ask questions like that?" or "It's your spirit entities talking, not you." Finally, cult leaders exercise ultimate psychic power over salvation or damnation in the spiritual realm—the individual member must always wonder: will I be saved?

A third distinction between the violent and nonviolent cults has to do with the *intensity* of their controls. As Richardson (in Chapter 2) and Anthony and Robbins (in Chapter 8) point out, there is a difference between love bombing and physical coercion, between group chanting and torture. Some cults even murder deviant members to quiet dissent and instill general terror.

The violent cultist is not just controlled, of course; he is also *committed*. As Hauerwas notes, demands for self-sacrifice are characteristic of established as well as new religious groups. But in the extremist cult, membership is an all-or-nothing proposition. A death spiral enters in when the more the member gives, the more the leader demands. Those who hold back risk being labeled traitors, apostates, or heretics. For people who have sacrificed so much psychologically, it would not be a big step, according to Zurcher, to sacrifice physically as well.

In accounting for religious violence, all contributors to this book emphasize, above all, the importance of one particular factor: *isolation*. Margaret Mead has written that the cause of universal peace would be advanced by the development of multiple cross-cutting networks that dilute rigid group boundaries. The opposite of this utopian vision is the isolated group, the structural isomorph of fanaticism.

When Jim Jones went to Guyana, it was as if the suicide process had already begun. People's Temple, in isolating itself from society, progressively cut itself off from the human enterprise (that "pool of things" that Erde talks about). Ervil LeBaron emerged at the outermost reaches of Protestantism as the head of a sect (Church of the Lamb) of a sect (Church of the Firstborn) of a sect (as Mormonism once was). The isolation is "a physical isolation that bespeaks genuine social isolation" (Galanter 1980). It is maintained either through remote seclusion, in walled camps or jungle settlements, or through the kind of nomadic lifestyle pursued by the Bo Peep Movement or the Church of the Lamb, whose members kept their anonymity by staying constantly on the move.

The function of such extreme isolation is not only to aid in the resocialization process (Redlinger and Armour), but also to enhance the total control of the cult leader over all aspects—religious, political, legal, economic, social—of his members' lives. The cult becomes autonomous in a way that its members never were. Violent cult leaders claim religious authority and civil authority as well. They become a law unto themselves. In the absence of the general society's ability to police their activities, they keep their own store of weapons and exercise the right of any sovereign state to use ultimate force.

Isolation cuts people off from temporizing reference groups, allowing them to become fixated on one interest or fear to the exclusion of all others. And isolation cuts people off from wider, more peaceful means of redressing their grievances. By the time Congressman Ryan flew down to Guyana, Jim Jones was indeed cornered, and his followers were too.

Sectarian Beliefs

Chapter 1 hypothesizes that cults will not practice violent behavior (no matter how authoritarian they are) unless they also have a set of beliefs that express hostility to outsiders, that literally encourage homicide or suicide, and that (in the case of suicide) portray a positive afterlife.

More specifically, the afterlife is seen in apocalyptic-millenarian terms. Not only will true believers be saved but moreover nonbelievers will be damned. The world plunges into darkness while selected cultists rise on a beam of light to nirvana. This dichotomy of damned and saved mirrors the absolutist, worldly division between them and us. As Zurcher writes, a categorical membership needs a categorical belief system to sustain it.

Another bulwark of spiritual arrogance is the denigration of outsiders, especially heretics, apostates, defectors, traitors, and false prophets. These people are the boogie men whom sect children are raised to fear. They are a threat to the cult and they deserve to die and be damned. Hatred of the apostate serves what sociologists call a boundary-maintaining function, which is reinforced psychologically by projecting onto kindred others what we fear in ourselves (Galanter 1980, personal interview).

A second class of hateful outsider is the political opponent. Richardson traces Jim Jones's hostility toward the CIA and the Ku Klux Klan to the paranoia that someone who is not only a civil-rights activist but a socialist as well might be expected to feel in American society. But People's Temple was not the only cult with reason to be paranoid. Shupe and Bromley document the very real threat that the anticult movement posed and continues to pose to new religious groups. The ACM's attempt to outlaw cults, to pass temporary-conservatorship laws, to take away licenses for child-care clinics, or to remove tax privileges could seriously hurt these groups. Opposition from the ACM accounts, somewhat, for deviance amplification on the part of the cult.

But if most cults in the United States had political enemies, they also had political friends. They enjoyed First Amendment privileges and were able to employ batteries of lawyers to defend themselves. The very system that allowed religious sects to proliferate in the first place also provided for their maintenance. Those cults that became violent, however (and thus seriously criminal), seem to be the ones that lacked political support. Ervil LeBaron, for example, saw the Mexican government favoring the side of Joel, his rival at Los Molinos (Levi 1980). Other cult leaders either lacked political support from the outset, owing to their own criminal records or records of mental illness, or else lost their political support later in consequence of bad publicity (and the inability to counteract it). Sectarian groups are likely to adopt a categorical stance toward outsiders, the more categorically they themselves are opposed by the system that contains them.

Finally, in addition to beliefs regarding the afterlife and outsiders, there is some question about violent beliefs, per se, and whether they are necessary to produce violent behavior. Will a highly committed cultist do *whatever* the group tells him to do, including violence? Or does he also need to believe that the violence he is being urged to commit is good?

Beliefs seem to play an important part. To begin with, violent cults often issue out of such violent subcultures as the prison subculture or the inner-city ghetto. Ervil LeBaron emerged from a tradition of Mormon Dannites, Mexican Ejiditarios, and Old Testament prophets such as Elijah—who slew the 450 false priests of Baal (Levi 1980). Cults also create their own violent norms. Richardson notes how Jim Jones cleverly tied his suicide rehearsals into the communion rite. Finally, violent cultists are given explicit guidance, well in advance, on why, how, and when to kill. Followers of Ervil LeBaron were, by report, consistently being drilled in the use of weapons against their enemies. In the Bo Peep cult, members were allegedly being instructed that murder not only paid off for the murderers but that it could mean salvation for the victims as well. More peaceable cults, such as the Divine Light Mission or the Unification Church, may make oblique references to defectors meeting with horrible deaths in freak airplane accidents or losing their immortal souls in the afterlife, for example. But they do not specify or teach killing to the extent that the violent cults do.

Discussion

We have reviewed the way various chapters in this book expand and clarify those distinctive features of violent cults delineated in Chapter 1.

Regarding the breakdown in societal cohesion, the contributors place special emphasis on the *scope* of breakdown, leading to social and economic as well as psychic deprivation. The effect is to cause people to turn elsewhere not only for their material needs but for their sense of esteem and sense of identity as well. A fortuitous mixture of people results—society's traditional outcasts joining with the newly alienated middle class who bring to the group the organizing ability and resources necessary for it to become self-sufficient.

Regarding sect cohesion, the *total isolation* of the group—physical, social, and psychic—enables it to set up its own law, administered by a volatile and unstable centralized system of control, without the stabilizing, rationalizing, routinizing influence of a bureaucratic structure. This effect provides a plausibility structure (Redlinger and Armour) for the implausible, and enables the death spiral of commitments between leader and follower to go unchecked.

Regarding cult beliefs, *categorical distinctions* between humans and nonhumans, saved and damned, good and evil, provide a constant source of justification for the total exclusion of certain groups of people.

The contributors to this volume have generally described the violent cult as a *categorical system*. This is a tentative description, which remains to be widely tested, further specified, and more closely examined for what it implies about nonsectarian violence and nonviolent sects.

Concerning nonsectarian violence, many features of the violent cult could also appear in boys' gangs or basketball teams or business corporations or political terrorist bands. But when violence does occur in one of these secular groups, we often attribute the violence to a *particular religious feature* of the group, such as its charismatic leadership or ideological fervor.

Concerning nonviolent sects, even they may have a potential for religious violence. According to Durkheim (1912), religion deals with the sacred as opposed to the profane, with the metaphysical underlying the physical. In that case, religion is particularly compatible with the categorical system of the violent cult. Other systems—political, economic, legal—hearken back to religion for their groundings. Religion provides its own certainties, and is therefore uniquely equipped to establish total independence from its societal matrix, to become totally isolated from the human pool, to make categorical distinctions between people and nonpeople. The emphasis on faith in such a metaphysical system requires individual commitment, undermines bureaucratic order, can make revelations of the cultic leader unassailable, and adds up to a sacrament that, contrary to Marx, is not always an opiate. It could be cyanide.

Notes

Chapter 2

1. Because United States officials did not order immediate autopsies on those who died in Guyana, we will probably never really know how many died by suicide and how many were murdered. Some reports indicate that a number of gunshots—perhaps 80 or 90—were heard at the time of the mass deaths; these might indicate that several were shot. Mark Lane, who was at Jonestown at the time of the mass deaths, had been quoted as saying that they were more like My Lai than mass suicide. Dr. C. Leslie Mootoo, Chief Medical Examiner for the Guyana government and the first medically trained person to arrive at Jonestown, told reporters, "I do not believe there were ever more than 200 persons who died voluntarily." He said this after autopsies had been performed on some victims and after an inspection of other bodies and of the scene of the deaths. This question has been most fully discussed in a series of articles by Deirdre Griswold in *Worker's World* (November and December 1978), a series that also poses some profound questions about possible CIA involvement in the Jonestown tragedy. Griswold, who accuses the United States government of deliberately destroying evidence by not performing autopsies, points out a number of intriguing ties between People's Temple and the CIA. She suggests that some of the white leaders in Jonestown may have been CIA agents, and that Jonestown may have been a tragic pawn in political struggles involving the United States, Cuba, and Guyana. The fact that the United States government did not order immediate autopsies is nearly inexplicable, and the government has been severely criticized for its actions in the matter. (See Griswold's December 22 *Worker's World* piece for information on this debate, along with the *New York Times* of December 19, 1978.) This chapter assumes that a sizable number of people did indeed commit suicide, and tries to help understand that strange event.

2. This writer was interviewed by a number of major newspapers and news magazines immediately after the Jonestown tragedy, but experienced difficulty getting most to adopt anything but a simplistic psychiatric view that used concepts like "brainwashing," "mind control," and other such terms to explain the event.

3. The fact that People's Temple members chose to take their lives—if indeed they chose; see note 1—in an act of collective suicide and also to murder their small children is extremely upsetting, and we have trouble understanding such an event. The difficulty is compounded by a usual failure to understand suicide on an individual level. Most people assume that anyone who has committed suicide must have been insane; they have difficulty accepting the idea that someone could, on the basis of information available, make a rational decision to terminate his or her life. However, most suicides are acts done by someone who is not technically insane.

4. For a good example of this tendency, see *Newsweek* (12/4/79), "The World of the Cults," which discusses the four groups mentioned.

5. There is much debate over whether the First Amendment is under duress because of the efforts of the deprogrammers. For the largest collection of papers on this issue, see the edited volume by this author entitled *The Brainwashing-Deprogramming Controversy* (Richardson, forthcoming).

6. I do not include Synanon in this grouping of "other new religious groups," as has been done by some commentators. See Robbins et al. (1978) for a good summary of research and writing on new religions.

7. There are probably understandable reasons for this misperception about the group's class and racial composition. For one thing, most of the new religions had a different class makeup, and people may have simply made a wrong inference that People's Temple was similar. Also, one would expect that the people in People's Temple who had the most education and the longest list of viable alternatives by which they could live would be the most prone to defect. And they did. But the preponderance of members was black, and poor black at that.

8. Especially in light of the mass murder/suicide in Guyana it is difficult to assess the purity of Jones's motives in developing a group that relied mostly on poor blacks for its membership and for much of its financial resources. Some accuse him of blatantly exploiting his target population and doing so with little real concern for their plight in racist America. Thus Jones is thought by some to have been a shyster and a crook. Others defend his earlier efforts to develop a racially integrated and egalitarian church, the while admitting that in the later years Jones changed dramatically and for the worse.

9. This argument does not intend to impugn the motives and efforts of famous black leaders like Father Divine or Daddy Grace by suggesting that People's Temple was exactly like earlier black sects and cults; it obviously was not. Jones was not black, a crucial difference. Whereas he led his flock of black followers into mass murder and suicide, some of the black religious movements of urban America have accomplished much to relieve the material and psychological suffering of blacks.

10. Some of the newer religious groups have been forced to defend themselves from attacks by detractors, but the usual approach used has been through the courts and in other generally acceptable methods. A few of the newer groups have been accused of forcibly incarcerating members, but such charges do not seem substantial. Certainly nothing like the concentration-camp atmosphere of Jonestown has been found in any of the newer religious groups.

11. One very intriguing fictional account of suicide for a cause (which I wonder if Jim Jones read) is Gore Vidal's *Messiah,* a novel about a new religion that developed in this country and swept around the world. This plausible-sounding religion was built around the idea that suicide is good instead of bad. In the intriguing novel people were encouraged by an extremely charismatic leader to die voluntarily, and die they did, by suicide.

Chapter 3

In addition to the references cited here, this article is based on personal interviews by the author conducted in Georgetown, Guyana, and in California during the summer of 1979.

1. It is questionable whether the term *cult* has any sociological utility. Harold Fallding (1974:27) has observed that it is a value-laden term often used by members of one religion to describe a heretical or competing religion of which they disapprove. Fallding does not want to "plunge into relativism" so he tries to retrieve the term *cultism* for sociological use by defining it as ascribing "sacred status to anything in the profane, actualized world." But this definition just displaces the problem of allegedly false religion onto the definition of *profane* which itself can be defined only within a religious

perspective! Even if this definition were granted, it is not self-evident that People's Temple would qualify as a cult; the classification of cult for other new religious groups such as the Unification Church or the Krishna Society is an equally dubious proposition. They are all better construed simply as deviant religious sects.

2. Even the constitutional guarantee is under attack. Prior to the Jonestown events, the Justice Department (texts in Krause 1978:171–185) had carefully examined the legal issues involved in investigating religious sects, and determined against such action. But since Jonestown there have been suggestions, for example by William Randolph Hearst (*San Francisco Examiner* 12/10/78:2B) and by a law professor, Richard Delgado (*New York Times* 12/27/78:A23), that totalitarianism in the name of religion should not qualify for Constitutional protection. Also, the *Washington Post* (12/16/78:3) reports that main-line churches have been reexamining their stands on freedom of religion in light of the Jonestown events.

3. The list of these religious swindlers, if it is kept by God's angels someplace, must be a long one indeed! Some would want to suggest that even in the end, Jones plotted to make off with the loot. One theory holds that he planned to escape with his personal nurse at the conclusion of the cyanide poisonings. But this theory seems far-fetched to the *New York Times* (12/25/78:A15) reporter who attended the Guyanese coroner's inquest where it was proposed: it did not account either for the bequeathing of Temple assets to the Communist Party of the Soviet Union or for the suicidal "lost hope" Jones expressed in the taped portion of the mass murder/suicide episode.

4. Only one contemporary explicitly interracial communal group immediately comes to mind—Koinonia Farm in Georgia, a Christian group founded in the 1940s.

5. Kilduff and Javers cite the imminent appearance of negative news articles as a cause of Jones's departure.

6. People's Temple had already begun to undergo the first of Lifton's limitations— the "law of diminishing conversions"—before the move from San Francisco to Guyana.

7. On the trip into Jonestown with Ryan, People's Temple lawyer Mark Lane told reporter Charles Krause (1978:37) that perhaps 10 percent of Jonestown residents would leave if given a chance, but "90 percent...will fight to the death to remain." The State Department has suppressed the tape recording of the mass murder/suicide, but I have heard a pirated copy of it, and the event clearly involved a freewheeling discussion of alternatives, with vocal support as well as pointed resistance voiced for the proposed "taking of the potion" (cf. *New York Times* 12/10/78:A28; 12/25/78:A16).

Chapter 5

1. Published news reports include portions of *New York Times* and *Washington Post* news services, the Associated Press, and a few other sources. News analyses were gleaned from the *Los Angeles Times* and from writers Ron Javers, Marshall Kilduff, Charles Krause, Laurence Stern, and Richard Harwood. More scholarly sources include other chapters in this volume, as well as Hall (1979), Melton (1979), and Johnson (1980).

Chapter 6

1. One need only think of the Hare Krishna cult members wearing "straight" clothes and wigs in airports to understand what we refer to.

2. We discuss the full implications of social and geographical isolation in a following section of the chapter. At this point, it is sufficient to note that isolation is often a crucial mechanism of social control.

3. These are two related points. First, we are indicating that main members when not in the presence of neophytes may (must) play out different characterizations of their selves as they interact with a different set of actors. Care must be taken to isolate such interaction from neophytes since contradictions, plans, or the like might be revealed. This is the second point, namely, the internal organizational planning of events, their sequencing, and so on, must not become known to the neophyte but are revealed through interaction. This not to say that all cults, sects, and such groups, have explicit timetables, but to point out that ideally they should. "Institutionalized" religious groups as well as elite military units do have such timetables for learning as do, of course, schools (Goffman 1959 and 1961).

4. The mission and message that arise in a sect or cult cannot be understood apart from the sociohistorical context of the period which for success must harbor the vision and visionary and followers receptive to the vision.

5. Weber (1920-1921:166ff) draws the crucial analytic distinction here between the forms of asceticism: world-rejecting and inner-worldly. That these two forms of asceticism are clearly seen in the leaders and the followers of latter-day cults and religious movements attests to Weber's keen insight into the character of these charismatic movements: on the one hand, they can take the stance that involvement in the things of this world results in an alienation from God; on the other hand, the obligation of the charismatic leader and his followers is the transformation of the world according to the prescriptions of the set of mystical, ascetic ideals. A charismatic leader and a religious movement can exhibit both of the traits in its history: The Jones People's Temple went through periods of retreats from the world and times of active social and political involvement prior to the mass ritual suicide in the Guyana jungle.

6. Stace (1960) discusses the internally generated or introverted and the externally generated or extroverted mystical experiences. Brim (1968) uses the notion of self-initiated socialization to conceptualize the process whereby adults redirect and ultimately transform their lives by themselves. Brim says: "We emphasize here that self-initiated socialization need not involve in significant changes in personality than those which result from the outside world. Large changes in personality have been demonstrated to come from within (Brim 1968:191)." Brim goes on to note that less spectacular but no less significant incremental personality changes may result from what he terms "personality drift" (Brim 1968:191ff.).

7. In another context, the evidence provided by Erikson's (1976) study of the Buffalo Creek disaster suggests how a single event (the flood) can result in the radical restructuring and reinterpretation of people's lives. The reports of flood survivors are filled with accounts of their meaningless lives, of their view of the universe as unpredictable, and of their utter unconcern with things of this world.

Chapter 7

1. The reasons both for this revival of religiosity among some more traditional denominations and for the sudden growth spurt manifested by some new movements have been fairly extensively studied by social scientists. For an analysis of the selective growth of the more fundamentalist Protestant denominations, see Bibby (1978) and Kelley (1972; 1978a); for reviews of the background sociocultural conditions of the new religious movements cited in this chapter see Foss and Larkin (1979), Bromley and Shupe (1979:57-95), and Bellah (1976).

2. That the ACM continually fell short of its goal to arouse anger and alarm over cults in the public at large is in no small measure a consequence of its failure to define unambiguously and consistently just what a cult is. Definitions ran the gamut of per-

sonal preference and idiosyncratic prejudice, ignoring theological and organizational differences and producing hodgepodge lists that included not only new groups such as Scientology, the Unification Church, and the Children of God but also more familiar ones such as Jehovah's Witnesses, the Old Catholic Church, and the Armstrong World-wide Church of God. Since there was broad disagreement within the ACM as to what groups composed any cult list once one moved beyond a few of the major groups such as "the Moonies," "the Krishnas," and "the premies" (the Divine Light Mission), we shall not render the term cult any more precise (on this definitional labeling problem in the ACM, see Shupe and Bromley 1980).

3. Exaggeration of membership size, deliberate or inadvertent, is a common feature of religious statistics. Aspiring minority religious groups can be expected to overesti-mate membership for public-relations purposes; countermovements also have a vested interest in inflating figures in the course of seeking to persuade the general public and officials of a pervasive, imminent threat. For example, at the 1979 Dole hearings in Washington, D.C., ACM spokespersons offered various cult membership estimates ranging from 2 million "victims" and 4 million affected parents (AFF 1979a:79) to 10 million "victims" (AFF 1979a:25). Elsewhere the deprogrammer Ted Patrick freely esti-mated 20 million Americans involved in cults (Siegelman and Conway 1979:56). The Unification Church alone was reputed among journalists to have a membership num-bering in the tens of thousands (among others: Rice 1976; Rasmussen 1976). For a correction to these exaggerations, see Bromley and Shupe (1979:133).

4. J. Gordon Melton of the Institute for the Study of American Religion apparently was collecting data on the group in the early 1970s as part of a larger survey of all American religious bodies but not because the group had been defined as a new reli-gious movement.

5. It was easy for opponents of the Unification Church to cull Moon's speeches for Armageddon rhetoric and heady last-days imagery that spoke of confrontations with Satanic Communism and hinted at possible casualties among Church members. Such references to altruistic death hardly resembled detailed suicide instructions, however, as the following excerpt from the *120-Day Training Manual* (Sudo 1975:43), now out of use, illustrates: "If the Parents [the Moons] are alive, at the price of my own life all mankind can be born anew. But if I am alive and the Parents' life [sic] is lost, no mankind can be saved. Then the Parents' life must be more precious than the life of the children...a prayer: 'Father, I can give my life. In the case of emergency please take my life first. If only you and Mother and Father's family can be saved, I am willing to die.'"

Chapter 8

1. See the account of Mark Rasmussen, who researched a Moonist workshop as a participant observer. He comments: "The desire to abandon reason for emotion had to be present before the person came to the workshop...and the new identity that emerged from the workshop experience was an assertion of self that came from submis-sion...It was a willful submission" (Rasmussen 1977:14).

Chapter 9

1. Herman Hesse (1973) implies that this kind of change is a misfortune.

2. That the name of a place can enter into the public idiom as the name of a kind of event is important and interesting in itself. Commenting on the expression "a Munich" in his book *Moral Notions*, Kovasi (1967) points out that it is because of the general

features of a certain moral kind that a place name becomes a kind of event name. Hence we really have to know the relevant features and history to know how to use the term as a general moral term.

3. The absurd has a special bearing on Jonestown because People's Temple was a religious organization and the absurd is a declaration of atheistic living. Under absurdist principles as Camus develops them, a hero is one who lives an absurd life, favoring his/her senses over devotion to abstractions. And siding with history rather than eternity, an absurd hero could become a conqueror; his/her mission is to revolt against the paradoxes of human life while never losing sight of the paradoxes. This outlook makes both desperate suicide and belief in an external source of meaning a logical blunder, but it seems to allow the conqueror to murder or to commit something like revolutionary suicide. Later, in *The Rebel* (1956), Camus tries to rule out such murder, but whether he is consistent with the earlier work is a difficult question.

4. Taurek's argument seems to miss in some sense the question about number that could be asked about Jonestown; that is: Does the quantity 9, 90, or 900 victims make a rational difference in our assessment of the event?

5. Taurek's argument seems to be off center in part because no one had to choose which group to save. But in an article about Mark Lane, the magazine *Mother Jones* (August 1979) attributes to Lane remarks to the effect that the State Department foresaw that the group might accept suicide in preference to defections.

6. Jones thought of the rehearsals of mass suicides as tests of the loyalty of members of People's Temple to him (rather than of their loyalty to People's Temple or to any ideology) (Krause 1978:60-61).

7. Mad, though in this day and age we know how shaky it is to attribute madness, how much relative to points of view disagreements are. Jones could have thought *we* had the world wrong. This difference heightens our sense of the absurd. Hauerwas's essay in this volume is interesting in sorting out relative assessments.

8. Thus, young children are not autonomous—they must be reared rather than left to their own devices, and they may be thought of as valuable rather than as value givers (autonomous). Thus, our moral concern with them is not immediate. It is mediated by what they can become. Our feelings about children and some notions of moral concern thus do not square well with one another. For Kantian ethics, children are less important than our natural intuitions and reactions would suggest.

9. Stuart Hampshire (1978) claims that we are breaking away from utilitarianism. That we are doing so is evidenced by the numbers of moral philosophers who are Kantian. Hampshire also claims that the utilitarians placed *human* desire at the center of moral concern. His characterization of this placement makes it seem akin to the Kantian position that persons are the origins or bestowers of all value. Hampshire finds the utilitarian position (and by my inference the Kantian position) archaic and hubristic.

10. For the early history of this slogan and an account of classical utilitarianism, see MacIntyre (1966).

11. There have been reactions to Taurek's position. Cf. Parfit (1978) and the exchange between Parfit and Charles Fried (Parfit 1979). Parfit's particular moves are not of relevance here (they are very difficult to follow, anyway). What is relevant is the *form* of his moves, to wit: the *premises* and *intuitions* that we would find unacceptable presuppositions within Taurek's position. Thus, our moral intuitions are the data for framing the moral theory. Thus, if something is counterintuitive there are important strikes against it.

12. I am alluding to John Rawls's second principle; see Rawls (1971:60).

13. I say "stipulated" or "primitive" because reductionistic equality is not adequate to democratic society. See Flathman's critique (in Pennock and Chapman 1967:38-68). I am opposing Flathman's position.

14. The implications of this for aesthetics (as "aesthetics" applies to art and as it refers to experience) are drawn by Susan Sontag (1973:27-48). They may illuminate our field, too, for Walt Whitman's ideology of generalizing beauty, Sontag argues, really abolishes beauty in obliterating it, eroding it, or parodying it; as a consequence of this equality there are no heroes—the power to discriminate is gone—for it is a violation of equality to dignify one person by making him a photographic subject while not dignifying all. Even the photographs are or have to be thought of as moral equivalents. (The reshaping of the bell-shaped curve is a metaphor I am borrowing from Bergmann 1977.)

15. Cook 1969. Raziel Abelson reads Strawson's well-known "Persons" as I read Cook's "Human Beings" (in his *Persons*, 1979: ch. 6). Abelson does not mention Cook but admits of his interpretation that Strawson might not recognize his own thought (p. 58). In connection with an interpretation of Wittgenstein's use of form of life, see Erde (1973:208-217).

16. It should be noted in passing that Cook does not endorse my reading of his paper—as he has seen me put it to use in this way.

17. Clearly this is inadequate. Some kinds of explanations can be given of what may be called primitive. Even if colors are primitive, much about them can still be explained in terms of physics. Thus, I should say that the primitive cannot be explained by reduction to some more basic rule. I owe this point to Richard Hull, responding to some of these pages written first for use in another context.

18. Turnbull 1972. This is a problematic counterexample, because the Ik rapidly became the horror that they were through abrupt intrusions into their traditional form of life.

19. Speaking statistically, there is an argument about numbers (regarding Jonestown and regarding Taurek's essay) that numbers do not make a difference. The average number of deaths daily in the world during 1977 was 150,000. Any usual level of confidence would find the 940 deaths at Jonestown (on one November day in 1978) statistically insignificant. For that reason, Jonestown must be probed for its moral significance.

20. I wish to acknowledge significant help from James B. Speer on an earlier draft of this chapter.

Chapter 10

1. For a fuller working out of these themes see my *Story Shaped Society: Toward a Constructive Christian Social Ethic* (forthcoming, 1980).

2. For an attempt to argue why Christians have rightly thought suicide to be immoral see my *Truthfulness and Tragedy: Further Investigation in Christian Ethics* (1977:101-115). This essay was written with Richard Bondi. For the most complete historical account of martyrdom, see Frend (1967). Frend quite rightly identified the issue of martyrdom as fundamentally political. Thus he says: "The problem which the Christian posed to the Empire was fundamentally the same as that posed by Judaism, namely the reconciliation of the claims of a theocracy with those of a world empire. In the West, the problem continued to dominate history in one way or another for fifteen hundred years, until obscured by the new ecclesiology of the Reformers. Lyons (one of the first mass Christian martyrdoms), however, set the stage, for there the claims of the state and the pressure of popular opinion confronted in the starkest term the claims of

Christian confession and witness." Thus the claim of revolutionary suicide, at least in principle, is not unlike Christian and Jewish martyrdom insofar as each involves profound political conflicts.

3. The deaths at Masada are often mentioned as a counterexample to this prohibition, but it is by no means clear that the undeniable heroism of the defenders of Masada is justification for their final act. Indeed, most orthodox Jewish thinkers continue to condemn this act as suicide.

4. Besides the newspaper and weekly news-magazine accounts of Jonestown I have had to rely almost entirely on Krause (1978) and on Kerns and Wead (1979). None of these sources provide the kind of information one would like to have about the actual people who made up People's Temple, how the Temple was organized and run, what were the primary beliefs of the people, and the like.

5. The primary reports on Jonestown are in *Time* and *Newsweek*. In addition there is Winfrey (1979:39-50). Also of interest is Novak (1978).

6. There is no doubt that Jones acquired great wealth through the Temple, but there is no indication that he was interested in using that wealth for his own personal enhancement. Jones did not desire money, but power. And the power he wanted was not the everyday kind we are familiar with but the power to determine the meaning of other people's lives.

7. Novak perhaps rightly suggests that the clue to what was wrong with People's Temple lay in its utopian optimism. In contrast, he argues that Christianity, while sharing many of the ideals of utopians, is not utopian. Instead, "the God of Christianity and Judaism permits his people to wander in history in a wilderness. The sufferings, loneliness, anguish, and misery he permits them to share are fathomless. The Jewish-Christian God is no *deus ex machina*, no Pollyanna, no goody-two-shoes. He obliges each individual, in the darkness, to exert his or her own inner liberty and choice. He is the God of liberty. He exacts enormous and wearying responsibilities. The God we turn to on Christmas is not a God made in our measure, nor is he a function of our needs, personal or social. He does not rescue us from our responsibilities, mistakes, or betrayals. He offers no escape from the toils of history, chance, and contingency. He transcends our purposes and needs. Many cults today, political and pious, offer an easier messianism, a happier salvation, a more utopian political and social hope. The God of Jews and Christians obliges us to struggle and to suffer, even when there is no hope. There is no valid escape from freedom, even in despair; such is the anti-messianic messianism of Christmas" (1978:6). While Novak is right in his contrast it is not clear that People's Temple is easily or rightly described as utopian. The people seem to have understood that they were in a struggle that would not be over soon.

8. I think we simply do not know enough about Jones at this point to speculate about his understanding of himself. He obviously believed in his ideals, at least at one time. The influence of Father Divine on him in many ways seems to have been decisive, but that does not mean that he ever doubted the truth of what he was saying. He may have been a man who, recognizing he held no substantial beliefs of his own, asked greater and greater sacrifices of his people in hopes that they would not notice the thinness of the religious claims at the basis of his church. And in an even more ironic twist, the more people he convinced of the righteousness of his cause, the more he convinced himself.

9. One of the ironies of our contemporary situation is that many of the charges against the cults as practicing brainwashing, made by Christians, is exactly the kind of charge that could be and was made against Christian conversion. Even so, some cults

may well be engaging in practices that are coercive. But the issue is finally not whether the means of converting are coercive, but whether what they are asked to believe and do is true. The form of conversion that should be characteristic of Christians cannot in principle be coercive since Christians believe the only thing that should convince another of the truth is truth itself.

10. One of the most disturbing aspects of reactions to Jonestown is the inherent racism and class prejudice implied. The assumption is that if these people had just been better educated and well off they would not have fallen for this kind of cheap and trashy religion. There is no empirical or moral basis, however, for such an assumption.

11. One of the most overlooked aspects of Jonestown has been the failure to understand the connection between the murders and the suicide. For the murder of Ryan and the others was a sign of the community's insecurity in their beliefs. Indeed it is my conviction that anytime a religion must resort to violence to secure its beliefs that is a sure sign that something has gone wrong with its claim to worship the God of truth and peace. Unfortunately Christianity provided Jones with many past precedents for the violence he used to protect his community. The use of violence is a sure sign that the community trusts not God, but themselves.

References

ABC-TV
    1979   "Good Morning America." Interview with former Unification Church member, Jan Kaplan, January 19.

Abelson, Raziel
    1977   *Persons.* New York: St. Martin's Press.

Ahlstrom, Sydney E.
    1978   "National Trauma and Changing Religious Values." *Daedalus* 107:1.

American Family Foundation (AFF)
    1979a   "Information Meeting on the Cult Phenomenon in the United States." Transcript of proceedings. Lexington, Mass.: American Family Foundation, Inc.
    1979b   "The Advisor." *Journal of the American Family Foundation*, August.

Arney, William R., and William H. Trescher
    1976   "Trends in Attitudes toward Abortion, 1972-1975." *Family Planning Perspectives* 8:117-124.

Babbie, Earl R.
    1973   "The Third Civilization: An Examination of the Sokagakkai." In Charles Y. Glock, ed., *Religion in Sociological Perspective*, pp. 235-260. Belmont, California: Wadsworth.

Back, Kurt
    1971   *Beyond Words—The Story of Sensitivity Training and the Encounter Movement.* New York: Russell Sage Foundation.

Bandura, Albert
    1973   *Aggression: A Social Learning Analysis.* Englewood Cliffs, N.J.: Prentice-Hall.

Barnard, Chester
    1971   *The Functions of the Executive.* 30th Anniversary Edition. Cambridge: Harvard University Press.

Barnartt, Sharon, and Richard J. Harris
    1980   "Recent Changes in Predictors of Abortion Attitudes." Paper presented at Population Association of America, Denver, April.

Barnes, Douglas F.
    1978   "Charisma and Religious Leadership: An Historical Analysis." *Journal for the Scientific Study of Religion* 17:1.

Barrett, William
    1976   "On Returning to Religion." *Commentary* 62 (November).

Becker, H. S.
    1960   "Notes on the Concept of Commitment." *American Journal of Sociology* 66.

Becker, H. S., et. al.
    1961   *Boys in White: Student Culture in Medical School.* Chicago: University of Chicago Press.

Beckford, James A.
    1976   "New Wine in Old Bottles: A Departure from Church-Sect Conceptual Tradition." *Social Compass* 23:1.

Bellah, Robert N.
   1976   "New Religious Consciousness and the Crisis in Modernity." In C.
          Glock and R. N. Bellah, eds., *The New Religious Consciousness*. Berke-
          ley: University of California Press.
Benedict, Saint
   1975   *The Rule of Saint Benedict*. New York: Doubleday Image Books.
Berger, Peter
   1963   *Invitation to Sociology*. Woodstock, N.Y.: Overlook Press.
Berger, P., and T. Luckman
   1967   *The Social Construction of Reality*. Garden City, N.Y.: Doubleday
          Anchor Books.
Bergmann, Frithjof
   1977   *On Being Free*. Notre Dame, Ind.: University of Notre Dame Press.
Bibby, Reginald W.
   1978   "Why Conservative Churches Really Are Growing: Kelley Revisited."
          Journal for the Scientific Study of Religion 17.
Blake, Herman J.
   1972   "Is the Black Panther Party Suicidal?" *Politics and Society* 2:3.
Blumer, Herbert
   1969   *Symbolic Interactionism: Perspective and Method*. Englewood Cliffs,
          N.J.: Prentice-Hall.
Boller, Paul F., Jr.
   1969   *American Thought in Transition: The Impact of Evolutionary Natural-
          ism, 1865-1900*. Chicago: Rand McNally.
Brim, Orville G., Jr.
   1968   "Adult Socialization." In John A. Clausen, ed., *Socialization and Society*.
          Boston: Little, Brown.
Bromley, David G., and Anson D. Shupe, Jr.
   1979   *"Moonies" In America: Cult, Church and Crusade*. Beverly Hills, Cali-
          fornia: Sage.
Bromley, David, Anson Shupe, Jr., and J. C. Ventimiglia
   1979   "Atrocity Tales, the Unification Church, and the Social Construction of
          Evil." *Journal of Communication* 29 (Summer):42-53.
Brown, Roger
   1965   *Social Psychology*. New York: Free Press.
Burnham, Kenneth E.
   1979   *God Comes to America: Father Divine and the Peace Mission Move-
          ment*. Boston: Lambeth Press.
Cameron, Norman
   1963   *Personality Development and Psycho Pathology: A Dynamic Approach*.
          Boston: Houghton Mifflin Co.
Camus, Albert
   1955   *The Myth of Sisyphus*. New York: Vintage Books.
   1956   *The Rebel*. New York: Vintage Books.
Carden, M. L.
   1969   *Oneida: Utopian Community to Modern Corporation*. Baltimore: Johns
          Hopkins University Press.
Carroll, J., and B. Bauer
   1979   "Suicide Training in the Moon Cult." *New West*, January 29.
Castaneda, Carlos
   1968   *The Teachings of Don Juan: A Yaqui Way of Knowledge*. New York:
          Ballantine Books.

1972a   *A Separate Reality.* New York: Simon and Schuster.
1972b   *Journey to Ixtlan.* New York: Simon and Schuster.
Citizens Engaged in Reuniting Families (CERF)
1976   "Memorandum." January 30. Scarsdale, N.Y.
Citizens Freedom Foundation (CFF)
1978   "News." December 15. Redondo Beach, California: Los Angeles Volunteer Parents Chapter.
Clark, Elmer T.
1949   *The Small Sects in America.* Rev. ed. New York: Abingdon-Cokesbury.
Cohn, Norman
1970   *Pursuit of the Millennium.* New York: Oxford University Press.
(1957)
Commager, Henry Steele
1978   *The Empire of Reason.* Garden City, N.Y.: Doubleday.
Committee Engaged in Freeing Minds (CEFM)
1976   *The Unification Church: Its Activities and Priorities.* Parts I and II. Arlington, Texas: National Ad Hoc Committee.
Conway, Flo, and Jim Siegelman
1978   *Snapping.* New York: Lippincott.
Cook, John
1969   "Human Beings." In Peter Winch, ed., *Studies in the Philosophy of Wittgenstein.* New York: Humanities Press.
Coser, Rose Laub
1975   "Complexity of Roles as a Seedbed of Individual Autonomy." In Lewis A. Coser, ed., *The Idea of Social Structure.* New York: Harcourt Brace Jovanovich.
Cox, Harvey
1977   *Turning East.* New York: Simon and Schuster.
1978   "Deep Structures in New Religions." In Jacob Needleman and George Baker, eds., *Understanding the New Religions.* New York: Seabury Press.
Davis, Fred
1968   "Professional Socialization as Subjective Experience: The Process of Doctrinal Conversation among Student Nurses." In Howard S. Becker et al., eds., *Institutions and the Person: Essays Presented to Everett C. Hughes.* Chicago: Aldine Publishing.
Davis, Rex, and J. T. Richardson
1976   "The Organization and Functioning of the Children of God." *Sociological Analysis* 37(4):321–340.
Dodds, E. R.
1963   *Pagan and Christian in an Age of Anxiety.* New York: Norton.
Dostoevsky, Fyodor
1880   *The Brothers Karamazov.* "The Grand Inquisitor." Part II, Book V, Chapter 5.
Douglas, Jack D.
1976   *The Social Meanings of Suicide.* Princeton: Princeton University Press.
Durkheim, Emile
1951   *Suicide.* New York: Free Press.
(1897)
Easthope, Gary
1976   "Religious War in Northern Ireland." *Sociology* 10(3):427–450.

Edwards, C.
    1979   *Crazy For God.* Englewood Cliffs, N.J.: Prentice-Hall.
Eisenstadt, S. N.
    1968   "Charisma and Institution Building." In S. N. Eisenstadt, ed., *Max Weber on Charisma and Institution Building.* Chicago: University of Chicago Press.
Ellwood, Robert
    1973   *Religious and Spiritual Groups in America.* Englewood Cliffs, N.J.: Prentice-Hall.
Engels, Frederick
    1964a   "The Peasant War in Germany." In Reinhold Niebuhr, ed., *Karl Marx*
    (1850) *and Frederick Engels on Religion.* New York: Schocken.
    1964b   "The Book of Revelation." In Reinhold Niebuhr, ed., *Karl Marx and*
    (1883) *Frederick Engels on Religion.* New York: Schocken.
Enroth, Ronald M., E. E. Ericson, Jr., and C. B. Peters
    1972   *The Jesus People.* Grand Rapids: Eerdmans.
Erde, Edmund
    1973   *Philosophy and Psycholinguistics.* The Hague: Mouton.
    1978   "Free Will and Determinism." In Warren T. Reich, ed., *Encyclopedia of Bioethics.* Glencoe, Ill.: Free Press.
Erikson, Erik H.
    1968   *Identity, Youth and Crisis.* New York: Norton.
Erikson, Kai T.
    1976   *Everything in Its Path: The Destruction of Community in the Buffalo Creek Flood.* New York: Simon and Schuster.
Fallding, Harold
    1974   *The Sociology of Religion.* Toronto: McGraw-Hill Ryerson.
Fauset, Arthur Huff
    1944   *Black Gods of the Metropolis: Negro Religious Cults in the Urban North.* Philadelphia: University of Pennsylvania Press.
Felton, David, ed.
    1972   *MindFuckers: A Source Book on the Rise of Acid Fascism in America.* San Francisco: Straight Arrow Books.
Festinger, Leon
    1957   *A Theory of Cognitive Dissonance.* Evanston, Ill.: Row, Peterson.
Festinger, Leon, H. Riecken, and S. Schacter
    1956   *When Prophecy Fails.* Minneapolis: University of Minnesota Press.
Finney, John M.
    1978   "A Theory of Religious Commitment." *Sociological Analysis* 39 (1): 19-35.
Flathman, Richard
    1967   "Equality and Generalization: A Formal Analysis." In J. Ronald Pennock and John W. Chapman, eds., *Equality: Nomos IX*, pp. 38–68. New York: Atherton Press.
Foss, Daniel A., and Ralph W. Larkin
    1978   "Worshiping the Absurd: The Negation of Social Causality among the Followers of Guru Maharaj Ji." *Sociological Analysis* 39(2):165–174.
    1979   "The Roar of the Lemming: Youth, Postmovement Groups, and the Life Construction Crisis." In Harry M. Johnson, ed., *Religious Change and Continuity.* San Francisco: Jossey-Bass.

Frend, W. H.
1967   *Martyrdom and Persecution in the Early Church.* New York: New York
        University Press.
Galanter, Mark
1978   "Why Cults Turn to Violence." *US News & World Report,* 12/4/78:23-29.
Glenn, Norval D., and Erin Gotard
1977   "The Religion of Blacks in the United States: Some Recent Trends and
        Current Characteristics." *American Journal of Sociology* 83 (2, Sep-
        tember):443-451.
Glock, Charles Y.
1964   "The Role of Deprivation in the Origin and Evolution of Religious
        Groups." In R. Lee and M. E. Marty, eds., *Religion and Social Conflict.*
        New York: Oxford University Press.
Glock, Charles Y., and Robert N. Bellah
1976   *The New Religious Consciousness.* Berkeley: University of California
        Press.
Goffman, E.
1959   *The Presentation of Self in Everyday Life.* Garden City, N.Y.: Double-
        day Anchor Books.
1961   *Asylums: Essays on the Social Situations of Mental Patients and Other
        Inmates.* Garden City, N.Y.: Doubleday Anchor Books.
1963   *Stigma.* Englewood Cliffs, N.J.: Prentice-Hall.
Goleman, Daniel
1978   "Who Is Mentally Ill?" *Psychology Today* 11.
Gordon, Chad
1968   "Self-Conceptions: Configurations of Content." In Chad Gordon and
        Kenneth J. Gergen, eds., *The Self in Social Interaction.* New York:
        Wiley.
Gouldner, Alvin
1959   "Reciprocity and Autonomy in Functional Theory." In Llewellyn Gross,
        ed., *Symposium on Sociological Theory.* New York: Harper and Row.
Greenfield, Meg
1978   "Heart of Darkness." *Newsweek,* 12/4/78:132.
Griswold, Deirdre
1978a   "Questions on the Mass Deaths in Guyana." *Worker's World,* 11/24/78:
        3-5.
1978b   "Jonestown: Motives for the Murders." *Worker's World,* 12/15/78:5.
1978c   "The Sanitizing of Jonestown." *Worker's World,* 12/22/78:4-8.
Gunn, John
1973   *Violence.* New York: Praeger.
Gusfield, Joseph
1963   *Symbolic Crusade: Status Politics and the American Temperance Move-
        ment.* Urbana, Ill.: University of Illinois Press.
Hall, John R.
1978   *The Ways Out: Utopian Communal Groups in an Age of Babylon.* Lon-
        don: Routledge and Kegan Paul.
1979   "The Apocalypse at Jonestown." *Society* 16:6.
Hampshire, Stuart
1978   "Morality and Pessimism." In Stuart Hampshire, ed., *Public and Pri-
        vate Morality.* Cambridge: Cambridge University Press.

Hargrove, Barbara
    1979   "Informing the Public: Social Scientists and Reactions to Jonestown."
           Unpublished manuscript.
Hartley, W. S.
    1977   Personal communication. Kansas City, Kansas: Department of Human
           Ecology, University of Kansas Medical Center.
Hashimoto, Hideo, and William McPherson
    1976   "Rise and Decline of Sokagakkai: Japan and the United States." *Review*
           of Religious Research 17(2).
Hastings Center Studies
    1974   Vol. 2, No. 3 (September).
Hauerwas, Stanley
    1977   *Truthfulness and Tragedy: Further Investigation in Christian Ethics.*
           Notre Dame, Ind.: University of Notre Dame Press.
    Forth-   *Story Shaped Society: Toward a Constructive Christian Social Ethic.*
    coming South Bend., Ind.: University of Notre Dame Press.
Henry, Andrew F., and James F. Short
    1954   *Suicide and Homicide.* Glencoe, Ill.: Free Press.
Hesse, Hermann
    1973   "Tragic." Theodore Ziolkowski, ed., *Stories From Five Decades.* New
           York: Farrar, Straus and Giroux.
Hillery, George A., Jr., and Paul C. Morrow
    1976   "The Monastery as a Commune." *International Review of Modern Soci-*
           ology, 6(1, Spring):139–154.
Hirschman, Albert
    1970   *Exit, Voice, and Loyalty.* Cambridge: Harvard University Press.
Holzner, B.
    1972   *Reality Construction in Society* (revised edition). Cambridge, Mass.:
           Schenkman/GLP.
Horney, Karen
    1937   *The Neurotic Personality of Our Time.* New York. Norton.
Horowitz, Irving Louis
    1979   "Religion and the Rise of the Rev. Moon." *Nation*, April 7.
Hughes, Everett C.
    1958   *Men and Their Work.* New York: Free Press.
Individual Freedom Foundation (IFF)
    1979a   Newsletter, January. Trenton, Michigan.
    1979b   Newsletter, April. Trenton, Michigan.
    1979c   Newsletter, July. Trenton, Michigan.
Jarrett, James L.
    1979   "Toward Elitist Schools." *Kappan*, May.
Johnson, Benton
    1972   "On Church and Sect." In J. E. Faulkner, ed., *Religion's Influence in*
           Contemporary Society. Columbus, Ohio: Charles E. Merrill.
Johnson, C. Lincoln, and Andrew J. Weigert
    1978   "An Emerging Faithstyle: A Research Note on the Catholic Charismatic
           Renewal." *Sociological Analysis* 39(2):165–174.
Johnson, Doyle Paul
    1980   "Dilemmas of Charismatic Leadership: The Case of People's Temple."
           Sociological Analysis 40 (Winter):315–323.

Johnson, Gregory
    1976   "The Hare Krishna in San Francisco." In Charles Y. Glock and Robert
            Bellah, eds., *The New Religious Consciousness*. Berkeley: University of
            California Press.
Jones, Farley
    1979   "Hearings on Cults Held at the World Trade Center." Memorandum to
            Mr. Salaven, August 10, New York.
Jones, Jim
    1978   "Perspectives from Guyana." *Peoples Forum*, January. Reprinted in
            Krause (1978:205–210).
Kahn, H., and A. J. Weiner
    1967   "The Next Thirty-Three Years: A Framework for Speculation." *Daedalus* 96 (Summer).
Kant, Immanuel
    1964   *Groundwork of the Metaphysic of Morals*. H. J. Paton, trans. New
            York: Harper and Row.
Kanter, Rosabeth
    1972   *Commitment and Community*. Cambridge: Harvard University Press.
Kelley, Dean M.
    1972   *Why Conservative Churches Are Growing*. New York: Harper and Row.
    1978a   "Why Conservative Churches Are Growing." *Journal for the Scientific
            Study of Religion* 17.
    1978b   "Beware 'Open Season' on Cults." *Christian Science Monitor*, December
            18.
Keniston, Kenneth
    1960   *The Uncommitted: Alienated Youth in American Society*. New York:
            Harcourt.
Kerns, Phil, and Dough Wead
    1979   *People's Temple, People's Tomb*. Plainfield: Logos International.
Kilduff, Marshall, and Ron Javers
    1978   *The Suicide Cult: The Inside Story of the People's Temple Sect and the
            Massacre in Guyana*. New York: Bantam Books.
Kilduff, Marshall, and Phil Tracy
    1977   "Inside People's Temple." *New West*, August 1.
Kovasi, Julius
    1967   *Moral Notions*. London: Routledge and Kegan Paul.
Krause, Charles A.
    1978   *Guyana Massacre*. New York: Berkeley Publishing Corp.
Krause, Charles, Lawrence M. Stern, and Richard Harwood
    1978   *Guyana Massacre: The Eyewitness Account*. New York: Berkeley Books.
Kuhn, M. H., and McPartland, T. S.
    1954   "An Empirical Investigation of Self-Attitudes." *American Sociological
            Review* 19 (February):68–76.
Lasher, H. L.
    1979   "Letter to the Church of Scientology of New York," July 19, Albany,
            New York.
Lemoult, John
    1978   "Deprogramming Members of Religious Sects." *Fordham Law Review*,
            March.
Levi, Ken
    1980   "Homicide as Conflict Resolution." *Deviant Behavior* 1:281–307.

Levine, Saul V., and Nancy E. Salter
    1976   "Youth and Contemporary Religious Movements: Psychosocial Find-
            ings." *Canadian Psychiatric Association Journal* 21 (6, October):411-
            420.
Lewin, Kurt
    1936   *Principles of Topological Psychology.* New York: McGraw-Hill.
Lewis, Robert A.
    1975   "A Contemporary Religious Enigma: Churches and War." *Journal of
            Political and Military Sociology* 3 (1, Spring):57-70.
Lewy, Gunther
    1974   *Religion and Revolution.* New York: Oxford University Press.
Lifton, Robert Jay
    1968   *Revolutionary Immortality: Mao Tse-tung and the Chinese Cultural
            Revolution.* New York: Vintage Books.
Lofland, John
    1966   *Doomsday Cult.* Englewood Cliffs, N.J.: Prentice-Hall.
    1977   *Doomsday Cult: A Study of Conversion, Proselytization, and Mainte-
            nance of Faith.* Enlarged edition. New York: Irvington Publishers.
Lynd, Robert S.
    1940   *Knowledge for What?* Princeton: Princeton University Press.
MacIntyre, Alasdair
    1966   *A Short History of Ethics.* New York: Macmillan.
McPartland, T. S.
    1965   *Manual for the Twenty Statements Problem.* Kansas City, Missouri: The
            Greater Kansas City Mental Health Foundation, Department of Research.
            The manual was revised in 1970 by Wynona Hartley (Kansas City, Kan-
            sas: University of Kansas Medical School, Department of Community
            Health).
McPartland, T. S., J. H. Cumming, and W. Garretson (Hartley)
    1971   "Self Conception and Ward Behavior in Two Psychiatric Hospitals."
            Sociometry (December):111-124.
Marty, M. E.
    1977   "The Land and the City in American Religious Conflict." *Review of
            Religious Research* 18 (Spring):211-232.
Marx, Karl, and Frederick Engels
    1959   "Manifesto of the Communist Party." In Lewis S. Feuer, ed., *Marx and
    (1848) Engels: Basic Writings on Politics and Philosophy.* Garden City, N.Y.:
            Doubleday Anchor Books.
Matza, David
    1969   *Becoming Deviant.* Englewood Cliffs, N.J.: Prentice-Hall.
Mead, G. H.
    1934   *Mind, Self and Society.* Chicago: University of Chicago Press.
Melton, J. Gordon
    1979   "Jim Jones, Charles Manson, and the Process of Religious Group
            Disintegration." Paper offered to Society for the Scientific Study of
            Religion, in San Antonio, Texas.
Meltzer, Bernard N., John W. Petras, and Larry T. Reynolds
    1975   *Symbolic Interactionism: Genesis, Varieties and Criticism.* London:
            Routledge and Kegan Paul.
Merton, Robert K.
    1976   *Sociological Ambivalence and Other Essays.* New York: Free Press.

Mills, Jeannie
  1979   *Six Years with God.* New York: A & W Publishers.
Moberg, David
  1978a "Revolutionary Suicide, 1978." *These Times,* 12/6-12:3, 1a.
  1978b "Prison Camp of the Mind." *These Times,* 12/13-19:11-14.
Needleman, Jacob
  1970   *The New Religions.* Garden City, N.Y.: Doubleday.
Needleman, Jacob, and George Baker
  1978   *Understanding the New Religions.* New York: Seabury.
Nelson, Anne
  1979   "God, Man, and The Rev. Moon." *Nation,* 3/31:325-328.
Novak, Michael
  1978   "Jonestown: Socialism at Work." *Washington Star,* December 18.
  1979   "Jonestown: Five Columns." Washington, D.C.: American Enterprise
          Institute Reprint 94. March.
Parfit, Derek
  1978   "Innumerate Ethics." *Philosophy and Public Affairs* 7, No. 4.
  1979   "Correspondence." *Philosophy and Public Affairs* 8, No. 4.
Parsons, Talcott, and Edward A. Shils, eds.
  1951   *Toward a General Theory of Action.* Cambridge: Harvard University
          Press.
Perrow, Charles
  1979   *Complex Organizations.* Glenview, Ill.: Scott-Foresman.
Pritchard, Linda K.
  1976   "Religious Change in Nineteenth-Century America." In C. Y. Glock
          and R. N. Bellah, eds., *The New Religious Consciousness.* Berkeley:
          University of California Press.
Rasmussen, Mark
  1976   "How Sun Myung Moon Lures America's Children." *McCalls,* Sep-
          tember.
  1977   "Promising People the Moon: A View from the Inside." *State and Mind,*
          November/December.
Rawls, John
  1971   *A Theory of Justice.* Cambridge, Mass.: Belknap Press.
Reich, Walter
  1976   "Brainwashing, Psychiatry, and the Law." *Psychiatry* 39.
Rice, Berkeley
  1976   "Honor Thy Father Moon." *Psychology Today,* January.
Richardson, James T.
  1974   "The Jesus Movement: An Assessment." *Listening: Journal of Religion
          and Culture* 9(3):20-42.
  1977   (ed.) *Conversion Careers: In and Out of the New Religions.* Beverly
          Hills, Calif.: Sage Publications.
  1980   "People's Temple and Jonestown: A Corrective Comparison and Cri-
          tique." *Journal for the Scientific Study of Religion* 19:3 (September).
  Forth- (ed.) *The Brainwashing-Deprogramming Controversy.* Transaction
  coming Books.
Richardson, J. T., Mary Stewart, and R. B. Simmonds
  1979   *Organized Miracles: A Study of a Contemporary Youth, Communal,
          Fundamentalist Organization.* New Brunswick, N.J.: Transaction Books.

Robbins, Thomas, Dick Anthony, Madeline Doucas, and Thomas Curtis
    1976   "The Last Civil Religion: Reverend Moon and the Unification Church."
                Sociological Analysis 37(2, Summer):111-126.
Robbins, Thomas, Dick Anthony, and James T. Richardson
    1978   "Theory and Research on Today's 'New Religions'." *Sociological Analysis* 39(2):95-122.
Roof, Wade Clark, and Christopher Kirk Hadaway
    1977   "Review of the Polls: Religious Preference—The Mid Seventies." *Journal for the Scientific Study of Religion* 16 (4, December):409-412.
Rosen, R. D.
    1978   *Psychobabble*. New York: Atheneum.
Scheflin, Alan, and Edward Opton
    1978   *The Mind Manipulators*. New York: Paddington.
Schur, E.
    1976   *The Awareness Trap*. New York: McGraw-Hill.
Selznick, Philip
    1957   *Leadership in Administration*. New York: Harper and Row.
Shapiro, E.
    1977   "Destructive Cultism." *American Family Physician* 15(2):80-83.
Shils, Edward
    1965   "Charisma Order, and Status." *American Sociological Review* 30.
Shupe, Anson D., Jr., and David G. Bromley
    1979   "The Moonies and the Anti-Cultists: Movement and Countermovement in Conflict." Paper presented at the annual meeting of the Association for the Sociology of Religion, Boston.
    1980   *The New Vigilantes: Deprogrammers, Anticultists and the New Religions*. Beverly Hills, Calif.: Sage.
Shupe, Anson D., Jr., Roger Spielmann, and Sam Stigall
    1977a   "Deprogramming: The New Exorcism." *American Behavioral Scientist* 20.
    1977b   "Deprogramming and the Emerging American Anti-Cult Movement." Paper presented at the annual meeting of the Society for the Scientific Study of Religion, Chicago.
Siegelman, J., and F. Conway
    1979   "Playboy Interview: Ted Patrick." *Playboy*, March.
Singer, Margaret Thaler
    1979   "Coming out of the Cults." *Psychology Today* (January):72-82.
Slade, Margot
    1979   "New Religious Groups: Membership and Legal Battles." *Psychology Today* (January):81.
Smelser, Neil
    1963   *Theory of Collective Behavior*. New York: Free Press.
Smith, John E.
    1979   "Into the Secular Void." *Commonweal* (March 16):139.
Snow, David
    1977   "Social Networks and Social Movements: Toward a Microstructural Theory of Differential Recruitment." Unpublished manuscript, Department of Sociology, University of Texas, Austin.
Solomon, Ted J.
    1977   "The Response of Three New Religions to the Crisis in the Japanese

Value System." *Journal for the Scientific Study of Religion* 16 (1, March):1-14.

Sontag, Susan
    1973   *On Photography.* New York: Farrar, Straus, and Giroux.
Spilka, Bernard, Larry Stout, Barbara Minton, and Douglas Sizemore
    1977   "Death and Personal Faith: A Psychometric Investigation." *Journal for the Scientific Study of Religion* 16(2):169-178.
Spitzer, S. P., and J. Parker
    1976   "Perceived Validity and Assessment of the Self: A Decade Later." *Sociological Quarterly* 17 (Spring):236-246.
Stace, W. T.
    1960   *Mysticism and Philosophy.* Philadelphia: Lippincott.
Stark, Rodney, and William S. Bainbridge
    1979   "Of Churches, Sects, and Cults: Preliminary Concepts for a Theory of Religious Movements." *Journal for the Scientific Study of Religion* 18 (June):117-131.
Stathos, Harry
    1979   "Unification Church Stresses Family in 'Cults' Child Hearings." *News World*, April 11.
Stone, Donald
    1978   "New Religious Consciousness and Personal Religious Experience." *Sociological Analysis*, 39 (2, Summer):123-134.
Stoner, Carroll, and Jo Anne Parke
    1977   *All God's Children: The Cult Experience—Salvation or Slavery?* Radnor, Pa.: Chilton.
Sudo, Ken
    1975   *The 120-Day Training Manual.* Belvedere, N.Y.: Holy Spirit Association for the Unification of World Christianity.
Szasz, Thomas
    1976   "Some Call It Brainwashing." *New Republic*, March.
Taurek, John M.
    1977   "Should Numbers Count?" *Philosophy and Public Affairs* 6 (4).
Theilmann, Bonnie
    1979   *The Broken God.* Elgin, Ill.: David C. Cook.
Toffler, Alvin
    1970   *Future Shock.* New York: Random House.
Toulmin, Stephen, and Loren R. Graham
    1979   "The Connections Between Science and Ethics." *Hasting Center Report* 9.
Tracy, Phil
    1979   "More on People's Temple: The Strange Suicides." *New West*, 8/15:18-19.
Train, John
    1979   "The Cult Game." *Forbes*, 3/39:93.
Turnbull, Colin M.
    1972   *The Mountain People.* New York: Simon and Schuster.
Turner, R. H.
    1968   "Self-Conception in Social Interaction." In Chad Gordon and Kenneth J. Gergen, eds., *The Self in Social Interaction*, pp. 93-106. New York: Wiley.

1976   "The Real Self: From Institution to Impulse." *American Journal of Sociology* 81 (March):989-1016.

United States Government
1978   *Investigation of Korean-American Relations.* Washington, D.C.: U.S. Government Printing Office.
1979   *The Assassination of Representative Leo J. Ryan and the Jonestown, Guyana, Tragedy.* Washington, D.C.: U.S. Government Printing Office.

Wallace, A. F. C.
1966   *Religion: An Anthropological View.* New York: Random House.

Warder, Michael Young
1979   "Memorandum to Col. Pak, *et al.*" New York, August 13.

Washington, Joseph R., Jr.
1973   *Black Sects and Cults.* Garden City, N.Y.: Doubleday.

Weber, Max
1947   *The Theory of Social and Economic Organization.* Translated by A.M.
(1925) Henderson and Talcott Parsons. New York: Free Press.
1964   *The Sociology of Religion.* Translated by Ephraim Fischoff. Boston:
(1920) Beacon Press.
1977   *Economy and Society.* G. Roth and Claus Wittich, eds. Berkeley: Univer-
(1922) sity of California Press.

Weincek, David
1979   "A Demographic Profile of Jonestown." Paper presented at the annual meeting of the Association for the Sociology of Religion, Boston.

Wertz, R.
1979   "Memorandum in Support of Legislation—#6085." New York State Assembly, Albany, N.Y.

Wheeler, S.
1966   "The Structure of Formally Organized Socialization Settings." In O. Brim and S. Wheeler, eds., *Socialization after Childhood.* New York: Wiley.

White, Mel
1979   *Deceived.* Old Tappan, N.J.: Revell.

Whyte, William H., Jr.
1956   *The Organization Man.* Garden City, N.Y.: Doubleday Anchor Books.

Wilson, Bryan
1977   "Aspects of Kinship and the Rise of Jehovah's Witnesses in Japan." *Social Compass* 24 (1):97-120.

Winfrey, Carey
1979   "Why 900 Died in Guyana." *New York Times Magazine*, February.

Wittgenstein, L.
1958   *Philosophical Investigations.* New York: Macmillan.
1967   *Zettel.* G. E. M. Anscombe and G. H. von Wright, eds. Oxford: Basil Blackwell.

Wuthnow, Robert.
1976   *The Consciousness Reformation.* Berkeley: University of California Press.

Zablocki, Benjamin
1971   *The Joyful Community.* Baltimore: Penguin Books.

Zerubavel, Eviatar
 1978 "The Benedictine Ethic and the Spirit of Scheduling." Paper presented at the meetings of the International Society for the Comparative Study of Civilizations, Milwaukee, Wisconsin, April.
Zurcher, Louis A.
 1977 *The Mutable Self: A Self-Concept for Social Change.* Beverly Hills and London: Sage.

Index